Praise for *The Sound of Gravel*

"A haunting harrowing testament to survival."   —*People* magazine

"Wrenching and moving . . . Wariner is a survivor, but more important, she's a fantastic writer."   —*Entertainment Weekly*

"An addictive chronicle of a polygamist community."
                                                —*New York* magazine

"Engrossingly readable from start to finish . . . An unsentimental yet wholly moving memoir."   —*Kirkus Reviews*

"This well-written book is hard to put down and hard to forget."
                                                —*Publishers Weekly* (starred review)

"Haunting. Rather than delving into the particulars of the community's beliefs, Wariner reveals them as they arise. This gives great depth to the portrayal of her situation. With power and insight, Wariner's tale shows a road to escape from the most confining circumstances."
                                                —*Booklist*

"*The Sound of Gravel* is a portrait of real courage in a sea of pretenders. Ruth Wariner, you have my respect as a writer and a survivor."
                —Kelly Corrigan, *New York Times* bestselling
                                        author of *The Middle Place*

"*The Sound of Gravel* will haunt you, and Ruth Wariner will inspire with her direct, unsentimental prose. I lost sleep reading this memoir and felt nothing but awe and respect. That Ruth survived to tell this story simply boggles my mind."
                —Jennifer Lauck, *New York Times* bestselling author of
                Blackbird, Still Waters, Show Me The Way, and *Found*

"*The Sound of Gravel* is a riveting portrayal of what it's really like to grow up in a polygamist community. Ruth Wariner's simple writing, her enduring love for her mother and siblings, and her dramatic escape make this an engrossing, deeply moving memoir."

—Claire Bidwell Smith, author of
The Rules of Inheritance and *After This*

"What chance does a girl have in a world where men believe that they (and they alone) are destined to be gods? This is the question Ruth Wariner bravely asks as she brings us into the hardscrabble Mormon polygamous communities of remote northern Mexico. Like a Dorothy Allison of the American West, Wariner shows us the humanity and tenacity in the people she comes from while making no apology for wanting something better for herself. Ruth Wariner has given us an unforgettable portrait of an enduring and deeply misunderstood segment of American society and a deeply moving account of her own determined pathway out."

—Joanna Brooks, author of *The Book of Mormon Girl:
A Memoir of an American Faith*

"A beautifully narrated story that manages to be both heartbreaking and heartwarming at the same time. Told with generosity and without self-pity, I turned each page with admiration of Ruth's resilience and strength of spirit. Powerless as she watches her misguided mother endure a life of servility to her stepfather, Ruth's love for her siblings and determination to break destructive family patterns will fill your heart with hope and triumph. I will not be forgetting this incredible memoir anytime soon."   —Cea Sunrise Person, author of *North of Normal: A Memoir of My Wilderness Childhood, My Unusual Family, and How I Survived Both*

"I can't remember a book that's had a greater impact on me. Beautifully written, Ruth Wariner's powerful, raw memoir will touch your heart like nothing you've read before. Told with unflinching honesty and a childlike innocence, Wariner takes us places—emotional and physical—few will ever experience, or even fathom. Ultimately this book is a testament to the human spirit, a tale of hope. Its stories of tragedy, abuse, trust, and dreams betrayed are more than offset by Wariner's pure goodness: her courage, determination, wits, resilience, and ultimately, in her quest to save her beloved siblings, triumph. Jon Krakauer's *Under the Banner of Heaven* is a very good book. Ruth Wariner's *The Sound of Gravel* is a *great* book, one that will haunt and inspire you for the rest of your life. In her exquisite and powerful telling, Wariner takes us to the darkest recesses of extreme polygamist Mormonism—on a painfully real and personal level—and brings us back to the light."

—April Christofferson, author of *Trapped*

"*The Sound of Gravel* takes us into the complex relationships of families with intransigent beliefs, religious convictions so dogmatic that harrowing consequences are forced upon their children. Ruth Wariner, this child of an isolated polygamist community, not only survives the oppression, but writes this unaffected tale of compassion and haunting sadness."

—Sonya Lea, author of *Wondering Who You Are: A Memoir*

"*The Sound of Gravel* is a powerful indictment against religious fundamentalism and the way zealots control and harm generations of women and children. This is an important, and ultimately triumphant, story."

—Julia Scheeres, *New York Times* bestselling
author of *Jesus Land* and *A Thousand Lives*

The Sound *of* Gravel

The
Sound *of* Gravel

——— *a memoir* ———

Ruth Wariner

FLATIRON
BOOKS
NEW YORK

www.flatironbooks.com

The Library of Congress has cataloged the hardcover edition as follows:

Names: Wariner, Ruth.
Title: The sound of gravel : a memoir / Ruth Wariner.
Description: First [edition]. | New York : Flatiron Books, 2016.
Identifiers: LCCN 2015037663| ISBN 9781250077691 (hardcover) |
    ISBN 9781250077714 (e-book)
Subjects: LCSH: Wariner, Ruth. | Mormons—Mexico—Biography. | Polygamy—Religious
    aspects—Church of the Firstborn of the Fulness of Times. | Mormons—United States—
    Biography.
Classification: LCC BX8680.L48 W37 2016 | DDC 289.3092—dc23
LC record available at http://lccn.loc.gov/2015037663

ISBN 978-1-250-07770-7 (trade paperback)

Our books may be purchased in bulk for promotional, educational, or business use. Please contact your local bookseller or the Macmillan Corporate and Premium Sales Department at 1-800-221-7945, extension 5442, or by e-mail at MacmillanSpecialMarkets@macmillan.com.

First Flatiron Books Paperback Edition: April 2017

10 9 8 7 6 5 4 3 2 1

For Kathy and her kids

CONTENTS

Prologue
1

Part I: The Promised Land
3

Part II: Babylon
79

Part III: Alone
153

Part IV: Breaking
223

Epilogue
331

Acknowledgments
339

Prologue

The room feels crowded, the attention overwhelming. A swirl of women in chocolate-and-sage dresses surrounds me. They fasten the satin-covered buttons on my gown, adjust the ivory flower in my hair. When they've finished their fussing, I stare at my reflection in the mirror, centering my veil at the crown of my head. Over my shoulder, I see my sisters perched on the edge of the bed behind me.

"Are you ready?" I ask.

"Ready." The three look up at me; stand up tall and straighten the hems of their dresses at their knees.

They might be ready, I think, *but I'm not sure I am.* I grew up dreaming of this day. I fantasized about the handsome prince who would carry me off on his white horse, whisking me away into the sunset. And now here I am, convincingly regal in my lace gown and shiny ivory-and-silver slippers. There is a flowering-pink dogwood tree right outside the window of my dressing room, just as there should be, and birds are actually singing in it. I hear their song as I give myself a final once-over.

It is a wedding day just like every bride dreams of, at least until I climb the steps leading to the next room, where my large, loud family waits for me impatiently.

I feel my heart racing in my chest, the blood pulsing in my neck. My face turns warm, and I become flushed. It must be nerves, I tell myself. But I know it's more than that. I know what I will see when I turn that knob and walk through the doorway.

PART I

THE
PROMISED LAND

— 1 —

I am my mother's fourth child and my father's thirty-ninth. I grew up in Colonia LeBaron, a small town in the Mexican countryside 200 miles south of El Paso, Texas. The colony, as we called it, was founded by my father's father, Alma Dayer LeBaron, after God sent him a vision. In that vision, my grandfather was walking in the desert when he heard a voice that foretold of a place that would one day be populated with trees dripping with fruit, wonderful schools, beautiful churches, bountiful farms, and happy, faithful people. My grandfather had grown up in a fundamentalist Mormon family, and he always believed in the polygamist teachings of Joseph Smith. When the vision came to him, he knew he needed to move to Mexico and establish a community that would be a beacon of hope, an example of what comes from living righteously.

My grandfather and grandmother LeBaron established the colony in 1944, and other polygamist families soon followed. Before long, the dry Mexican earth was cleared of mesquite and planted with orchards, pecan trees, and gardens. Cattle were brought in to be raised, and the town grew and flourished. My grandfather boldly predicted that some-day people from all over the world would make pilgrimages to the town, and that the work being done there would be of the utmost importance to the realization of God's kingdom on earth.

My grandfather died before I was born, but I entered childhood in the community that was his legacy. I took my first steps on the dirt roads that ran through the small farming community, tiny rocks and dry dirt getting stuck between my toes and piercing the soft soles of my feet. The trees my grandfather planted offered the shade that first cooled and protected my pale, freckled skin from the harsh desert sunlight. I ran through the peach orchards with my siblings, drank fresh milk from the cows on our dairy farm, and ate vegetables from the gardens my grandfather had first seen in the vision God sent him. My family and I always tried our best to be the happy, faithful people God had promised would come to populate the colony.

"RUTHIE," MOM YELLED to me from the hallway, "Get up quick. We'll be late for church." I rubbed my eyes and pulled myself out of the small bed I shared with my sister Audrey. Even though she was five years older than me, she wore a cloth diaper that often leaked during the night. I took a towel and dried my damp legs as Mom told me to hurry and get dressed. "There's not enough time to get Audrey and your brothers ready," she hollered. "Matt'll stay here and watch the kids and you'll come to church with me."

At five years old and with four siblings, having Mom's undivided attention was a rare privilege. I threw my pink cotton dress over my head and tried to run my fingers through my tangled hair. Mom put my baby brother Aaron in his playpen and called to my older brother Matt, asking him to keep an eye on things. Then she grabbed my hand and pulled me along behind her. I scurried to keep up, taking three steps for every one of Mom's long strides, happy to have been the one chosen to accompany her. The cool morning air was pungent with the scents of the freshly irrigated alfalfa fields, the dairy cows behind our house, and Mexican sage brush.

Every place in LeBaron was within walking distance of every other, and each unmarked, unnamed dirt road led to the church at the center of the colony. As Mom and I made our way to the simple, single-level adobe structure, pickup trucks sped past us, stirring up clouds of dust in their wake. As we got closer, we heard the strains of a piano and singing voices flowing through the two black wooden doors. "We're already late, Ruthie," Mom said, looking down at me through the plastic frames of her glasses. I was used to hurrying at her side; we were always late to everything.

Mom and I rushed past the few saddled horses tied to the crooked, wooden posts that held up the barbed-wire fence surrounding the churchyard. The singing voices grew louder as we entered the church and Mom searched the large, white-walled room for empty seats. The black wooden benches were full of congregants—women in Sunday dresses, nude nylons, and high heels, men in cowboy boots and Western shirts tucked into tight jeans under leather belts with big, silver belt buckles.

We crowded into open seats as Mom pulled out a hymn book from a wooden pocket on the back of the bench in front of us, cocked her neck forward, and squinted to peek over someone's shoulder to find the right page. I loved standing next to her in church. I was mesmerized by her eyelashes, which were usually so blond that I couldn't see them, but on Sundays she wore light brown Maybelline mascara and pearl-pink lipstick that she dabbed over her lips and onto her cheeks.

After playing three hymns, the pianist retired to a pew as a man stepped forward to utter a prayer, which a second man translated into Spanish for the Mexican parishioners on the opposite side of the building.

"Make sure no one can see your underpants, Sis," Mom whispered, straightening the hem of my dress over my knees as the elder called for someone to come up and offer a testimony.

Lisa, my stepfather Lane's sister, walked slowly, her head held high, the wooden heels of her strappy sandals tapping hard against the floor. She stood tall and spoke with confidence. She told us how thankful she was for all the blessings that our Heavenly Father had given her. She talked proudly about her devotion to the cause. She said that even though it was hard to share her husband with her sister wives, even though she sometimes felt jealous, she knew in her heart that she was obeying God's will by living polygamy. Lisa said she loved being a mother and that she was grateful to be the caretaker of the beautiful spirits the Lord had sent her. Then she thanked Him for giving her a good, righteous man to father her children. "After all," she said, "it is better to have ten percent of one good man than to have one hundred percent of a bad one." The women of LeBaron were always saying that, and Mom always nodded her head in agreement.

As Lisa spoke, I gazed at the three large, black-and-white photographs that hung behind the red-carpeted pulpit. The middle photo, bigger than the other two, was of a man with a round, shiny forehead and a square jaw. His dark hair was combed straight back, a few thin strands stretched flat over a bald spot. He wore a crisp white shirt buttoned to the top with a dark tie and matching jacket. His full lips were closed, and he didn't smile, but he had kind and happy eyes that stared out with confidence and authority.

This was my father. He had been the prophet of our church. He died when I was three months old, and no matter how many times I begged Mom to tell me about him, I could sense that there was a lot about my dad that I'd never know. Did he like playing board games and hiking in the Mexican hills like me? Did he like chocolate ice cream or did he prefer my favorite, old-fashioned vanilla? Everyone always said my dad was the kindest, most faithful, God-fearing man they knew. I wished I could remember what life had been like when he was alive.

After the service ended, Mom and I walked back to the farm slowly, relishing the warm sun on our shoulders and stopping to say hello to our friends and neighbors along the way. Very few of the homes in LeBaron had telephones and Sundays were a good chance for everyone to catch up. Mom stopped to talk to Lisa, who was not only my step-dad's sister, but she had also been one of my dad's wives. Even though she was much older than Mom, they were still good friends.

"I loved your testimony this morning," Mom told Lisa. "It really inspired me."

"Thank you, Kathy. Why don't you bring the kids over next Saturday and we can have dinner at my house?" Lisa smiled, her skin wrinkling around her eyes.

"That sounds great," Mom said. "I'll bring dessert."

Mom and Lisa said their good-byes and Mom grabbed my hand, pulling me toward home. "We'd better get back to Audrey and your brothers," she said. The streets were quiet as we walked past adobe homes with spacious yards and gardens surrounded by barbed wire fences.

The farther we got from the center of town, the more spread out the neighborhood became. Eventually we walked past our neighbor's farm and reached the tall earthen banks of the reservoir. Five hundred feet long and fifty feet wide, the reservoir brought water to our irrigation ditches and those of the neighboring farms. Young willow trees lined its perimeter, and we could usually hear families of frogs croaking from its banks. It had been built as a community water supply, but it served as the colony swimming pool too. Adults and children came from all over to frolic and swim in the open-air tank, diving into it from a giant pipe that pumped freshwater from a deep well.

Our house was on the other side of the reservoir, at the end of a long gravel driveway. A tall barbed-wire fence surrounded my step-father's property. Unlike some of the houses closer to town, ours didn't have any flowerbeds or a lawn. Mom was never able to get anything to grow. Except for her Volkswagen Microbus, which was usually broken and parked beside the kitchen door in the side yard, the house sat stark and solitary against the dry Mexican landscape.

An irrigation ditch of steadily flowing water ran along the front of our property. My stepfather had dug out the ditch at the beginning of our driveway so that it was wide and shallow enough for cars to drive through without wetting a car's engine. But when we weren't in a car, we had to leap across the ditch's narrow edge to get to our house.

Mom held my hand and we jumped across. As we landed on the opposite edge, clumps of wet earth crumbled underneath our feet and splashed into the running water.

When we got inside, Mom went to nurse my baby brother, Aaron. I pulled out my Disney coloring book and stubby crayons and made myself comfortable on the living room floor. Matt and Luke went out to play, while my older sister, Audrey, sat on the couch pulling at the cotton threads in her shirt, staring off into the distance, a quiet moaning sound coming from the back of her throat.

"Hush, Sis," Mom said, patting Audrey on the shoulder as she passed back through the living room. "Ruthie, come help me with these beans." I jumped up from the floor and hurried to Mom's side. She pulled a large gunnysack of pinto beans from the corner of our small, square kitchen. "It's important for you to learn how to cook. You'll need to know what to do when you're married and have your own kids." She spilled a pile of the speckled, brown beans onto the kitchen table. "When I married your dad, I didn't know how to make beans or anything else because my mom never showed me." I climbed up onto a chair and began imitating Mom's movements, carefully taking a small handful of pintos and spreading them out in front of me.

"How old were you when you and Dad got married?" I didn't much care for boys, but I knew that I would get married one day. Celebrations were an important part of life in LeBaron. We had lots of rodeos, horseback rides, campouts, bridal showers, baby showers, birthday

parties, and Friday-night square-dance lessons at the church. But weddings were the most important.

"I was seventeen." Mom scanned the pile of beans from behind her
thick glasses, shooing away the flies that had infested our kitchen.
My siblings and I loved hearing the story about how, on one of my
dad's mission trips to Utah, he climbed to the top of a mountain where
he was visited by several resurrected prophets, including Jesus, Moses,
and Joseph Smith. They told my father that he had been selected to lead
a congregation with Colonia LeBaron as its Zion. Out of this visitation,
Dad's church, the Church of the Firstborn of the Fulness of Times
was born.

My father believed that polygamy was one of the most holy and
important principles God ever gave His people. He preached that for
a man to reach the Celestial Kingdom—the highest level of heaven—
he had to have at least two wives. If a man lived this principle, he would
become a god himself and inherit an earth of his own, one just like
our earth. Women who married polygamists, loved their sister wives,
and had as many children as they could would become goddesses,
which meant that they were their husband's heavenly servants. Sal-
vation came from freeing oneself and others from the moral turpitude
of Babylon. My dad had visions in which God foretold the destruction of the United States, which my dad believed was a modern Babylon. That's why he ended up doing much of his missionary work in
the Babylon among Babylons: Las Vegas. That was was where he first
noticed my mom.

"When we were living in Las Vegas, your dad asked Grandpa if he
could court me."

"Court you? What's that?"

"It means that he wanted to get to know me so that he could marry
me." Mom slid more beans across the tabletop. They sounded like plastic pieces moving over a checkerboard. "I was fourteen years old when
I first heard about your dad. We were living in Utah, and your dad

and his brother Ervil were on a mission trip there. One day, they put a pamphlet on Grandpa's windshield. Grandpa saw the pamphlet, took it out from under the windshield wiper, and brought it home." Mom paused to take another handful of beans from the sack. She spread them out on the table and picked out the rocks and dried weeds before sliding the beans into a pot on her lap.

"That pamphlet changed my life. Not long after Grandpa read that paper, he started asking questions at church, questions about Joseph Smith's original teachings and why polygamy was no longer a part of the Mormon way of life. Not long after Grandpa started asking those questions, he was excommunicated from the Church. That's when we moved to LeBaron.

"When the bishop made your grandpa leave the Church, Grandpa took it as a sign from God that your dad was right, that the LDS Church had lost its way. He bought property in LeBaron and moved us down here."

"Did you like moving to LeBaron?" I asked, trying to imagine a time before my mom lived on the colony.

"Well, Sis, it was a real shock for me. I really missed my friends in Utah. I had always been shy, so it was hard for me to move to a new place." Mom looked down at her pile of beans with a somber expression. "But our time here didn't last long. It was too hard for Grandpa to support us in Mexico, just like it is hard here for a lot of people even now. So Grandma and Grandpa eventually moved us to Vegas. A lot of your dad's followers were livin' and workin' as builders and painters in Vegas. Grandpa and Grandma bought a diner there and called it the Supersonic Drive-In. I worked there as a waitress—a waitress on roller skates."

"And that's where you met my dad?"

"Well, I knew about your dad before he first saw me at the diner. Grandpa had been going to your dad's church for about four years by then. I had a dream about marrying your dad and I told your grandpa about it, so he said yes when your dad asked to court me. Our wedding was just a few months later. I became your dad's fifth wife in a small ceremony right here in a living room in LeBaron."

In our dark, bare-walled kitchen far from the lights of Las Vegas, I watched Mom's lightly freckled arm slide another clean pile of beans off the edge of the table into the pot and thought about how different her life was now. Mom had five kids—my older sister, Audrey, my older brothers, Matt and Luke, and the baby, Aaron. Mom always seemed worried and exhausted. I liked imagining her skating around a diner, serving hamburgers to my dad.

"But, Mom, didn't you like Las Vegas? Why did you want to leave?"

The sound of the hard beans hitting the metal pan echoed through the kitchen. "Of course I loved parts of our life in Vegas, Ruthie. I made lots of friends there and I loved music and dancing, but I felt like I wanted more. That's when I started to like your dad. I was only seventeen, but he inspired me to live a life for our Heavenly Father's purpose. I wanted to be a part of his big family and help with his work in the church."

Mom stopped cleaning the beans for a moment, sat back in her chair, and rested her thick brown hair against its back. She always cut her hair herself, and always just above her shoulders, in short, feathered layers. She smiled as a faint whiff of fresh cow's milk drifted through the kitchen window. It mingled with the scent of the green alfalfa fields outside and the cheese curds we kept in a pan on the stove. Except for when it rained, when all we smelled was wet dirt from the adobe bricks and stucco that made up our small, five-room house, the kitchen always smelled like the little mice that scampered along the walls, the cows in the fields outside, and the Mexican sagebrush on the nearby mountains.

"You know, Ruthie, your dad was the most humble man I'd ever met. He always practiced what he preached, and he never turned away anyone when they came to him for help." Mom thought for a moment. "When he asked me to marry him, it was the happiest day of my life.

We were sittin' alone in a car at night. He kissed me and it felt right. Even though he was twenty-five years older than me and already had four wives, I knew I was makin' the right choice. I had never wanted to marry any other man till then."

Mom swept the last pile of pintos toward her with swollen, stubby fingers; she chewed her nails down to the quick, her cuticles red and raw. "Your dad and I hadn't been married for very long when it was my turn to have him spend the night. You know, I only got to see him once a week, and then only if I was lucky. With five wives, his mission trips, and his work, there just wasn't time. Anyway, when it was my turn to have him over, all we had to eat were pinto beans. So I put some water in a pot and then I filled it all the way up to the top with beans. To the top. I didn't know that beans swell up!" She paused and laughed at the memory. "The beans started boilin' and swellin' up and overflowin' out of the pot. I had to pour half of them into other pots. By the time I was done, we had three full pots of beans, and I had to throw half of them out because they soured before we could eat 'em!" She laughed again and flashed her hazel eyes at me, which dazzled with speckles of green when she was happy and turned the color of mud when she wasn't. "Bein' a housewife was all new to me. 'Cause nobody ever taught me how, Ruthie. That's why it's important that you start learnin' now."

Mom pulled herself out of her chair to pour herself a glass of water from the pitcher on the counter. I couldn't imagine a time when she didn't know how to cook. I couldn't imagine a time when she didn't have kids. "But, Mom, if Grandpa gave my dad permission to court you, why aren't he and Grandma still a part of our church?"

"Well, Sis, everything changed after your dad died." Mom took in a deep breath and shook her head. "It was just such a mess. After your dad died, so many people turned their backs on him and left the church. Grandpa and Grandma lost faith and so did Aunt Carolyn and Aunt Judy. They all sold their property in LeBaron, moved to the States, and didn't come back."

"Is that when we went to live in San Diego?"

"That's right. I took you and Audrey and Matt and Luke to go live with Grandma and Grandpa for a while. But I knew I wanted to come back to LeBaron. This is where you kids belong."

I focused on my little pile of beans, continuing to separate them from the dirt and rocks that were in the bag. I didn't remember living with Grandma and Grandpa, but there was a part of me that wished we were still there. I knew we were doing the right thing living God's purpose in the colony, but I envied my cousins in California. They lived in nice houses with bathrooms and they always had new clothes and toys. Sometimes I'd lie awake at night thinking about what it would be like if Mom had never married my stepfather and had never brought us back to LeBaron.

Mom met Lane when I was three and she became his second wife a few months later. My grandparents and aunts were invited to the wedding, but they didn't believe in polygamy anymore so they didn't go.

Mom said Lane was handsome. He had sandy-blond hair, olive skin, and light blue eyes. He wore his hair slicked back behind his ears with long, perfectly trimmed sideburns. He had been an apostle in my dad's church, which is what my mom said she loved most about him. The people of the colony called him Brother Lane.

After they married, Mom moved us onto Lane's eleven-acre farm. Our little house had two bedrooms and one unfinished bathroom that Lane was always promising he'd fix. Until he did, we used a wooden outhouse in the backyard. Lane's first wife lived in another adobe house a quarter of a mile from ours, at the opposite edge of the farm. Mom's house was separated from her sister wife's by a barbed-wire fence, several acres of alfalfa, and a small peach orchard. We didn't have electricity—we were too far out of town, and power hadn't yet reached that far into the countryside—but Lane said it was coming.

Lane was the only father figure I'd ever known, but I never liked him. Whenever he was at church or with other churchgoers, he was happy and friendly, always offering to help them fix their cars or their broken appliances. But when he was at home, he was always cross, threatening to spank me if I cried for Mom's attention. Mom never spanked or hit us, and Lane's temper scared me.

Two years after Mom and Lane were married, she gave birth to my brother Aaron, who I adored instantly. Having a baby around was like having a new pet. Right after Mom came home from the hospital, she told me I could be her little helper, and I was thrilled. Matt and Luke went to the Mexican public school across the highway from LeBaron, leaving me at home on the farm with Audrey, Mom, and baby Aaron. Even though she was the oldest, Audrey didn't go to school. Mom said Audrey was too much for the teachers to handle. I hated being stuck at home with my sister, but I loved helping Mom take care of my baby brother.

Her beans all clean, Mom stood up and scooped my little pile of pintos into her pot. She knelt down underneath the wood-framed window and filled the pot with water from a spigot that sprouted right out of the cement floor. Mom put the pot on the propane stove and lit the burner with a match. The stovetop hissed and the air smelled like sulfur. Mom stirred the beans a couple of times, then went to go check on Audrey, telling me to watch to make sure the pot didn't boil over.

I sat in the kitchen thinking about how different my life would be if my dad hadn't died. If he were still alive, Mom would be happy and would stop worrying all the time about how much it cost to feed all of us and how Audrey seemed so troubled. If my dad hadn't died, maybe my grandparents would still live in the colony with us. I just couldn't understand why my dad had been killed. I knew my uncle Ervil had him shot. Everyone in the colony knew that. Ervil and his followers sent lots of letters to our church elders threatening to kill more people and bomb the town. Mom said that Uncle Ervil was wanted by the FBI and that they had people looking all over Mexico and the United States for him. Each time we got a new threat, Mom would tell us to keep the doors locked. "And if I'm not home and you hear gunshots and explosions," she always said, "take your baby brother and run to the peach trees, cover him, and lie down in the dirt so no one can see you." Uncle Ervil was like a ghost haunting us. Knowing that he and his followers were still out there terrified me. Would Ervil come back for me? And what would happen if he murdered my mom the way he had murdered my dad?

— 2 —

One constant in my family's life was traveling. We had to go back and forth from Mexico to the United States every month to collect food stamps, Medicaid, and cash assistance. Mom would bring us along with her on rickety, old Mexican buses while Lane stayed and worked on the farm. Mom was a US citizen, after all, and in the eyes of the government, she was a single parent. Because Mom was Lane's second wife, their marriage wasn't recognized outside the colony. Lane had a friend who let Mom use his address in El Paso to qualify for welfare.

Everyone in the colony was always saying how Lane had a strong work ethic. He spent every day milking cows, planting and baling hay, fixing tractors, trucks, and other equipment—all of which broke down regularly. But in spite of all his hard work, he never made enough money to provide for his eleven kids and stepchildren. So Mom said we had to help out by going to El Paso every month. Although First-borners, as members of our church were called, believed firmly that the modern-day Babylon to the north would soon crumble under the weight of its people's wickedness, Lane said it was just fine to take advantage of Babylon's beneficence.

Lots of women like my mom—the American wives of polygamists raising their kids in Mexico—would travel north and collect government assistance checks. Many of the men in our colony did construction work in border states such as California, Arizona, New Mexico, and Texas, which provided plenty of addresses for the women to use when it came time to pick up welfare checks, and lots of places to stay too. Mom said that we had to learn to live modestly; that we might be poor, but we were rich in spirit. Being faithful sometimes meant doing without. And we were doing the Lord's work, so why *shouldn't* US taxpayers fund our efforts? Which is how we found ourselves waiting for a bus back to LeBaron from Juárez on a cold, rainy morning in late December.

We huddled together for warmth in front of the Juárez bus station. Above us, a huge Mexican flag flapped furiously in the wind. Juárez was a border town of cars with broken mufflers and loud horns coming from every direction, men on rusty bicycles dodging potholes as the rain poured down, and dilapidated, old trucks that expelled smoke so thick they turned the sky from indigo to black.

Skinny Mexican children, their parents nowhere in sight, huddled on street corners in muddy and torn shoes, each waiting for the chance to sell treats and knickknacks to passersby. They peddled Chiclets, candy, brightly colored ceramic piggy banks, cookie jars, and more. Black-haired boys shoved each other aside for the chance to converge on cars that lined up outside the bus station. They held their hands out to us as we walked by. The chaos frightened me, but Mom seemed completely at ease, numb to it all. She fished a coin purse from her tattered, navy-blue bag and pressed a few coins into the hand of a child selling *banderas,* coconut candies that looked like miniature Mexican flags. We would have preferred gum, but Mom always said no, reminding us of all the times she'd had to cut it out of our hair. Plus, Audrey would put enormous wads of gum in her mouth and swallow them whole.

Inside the station, chaos reigned. A Spanish announcement barked at us from a speaker in one corner, and a radio blared from another. In her left arm, Mom held nine-month-old Aaron and a large, black garbage bag full of Christmas presents she'd bought for us at garage sales and in thrift shops. Her right hand kept a tight grip on Audrey. My sister's skin was a fair as mine, but she had Mom's brown hair cut into a square bob.

Mom said she had never seen a child like Audrey before. One day Audrey would do something harmless, like grabbing my pigtail, but the next she'd yank on it so hard my neck would jerk to one side and I'd fall to the ground. All at once she'd bite my shoulders and pinch my forearms for no reason. But other times she kept to herself and sat quietly on a chair or the living-room couch rocking forward and backward for hours, staring straight ahead off into the distance. Behind Audrey, my brother Matt, a rambunctious eight-year-old with strawberry-blond hair parted down the middle, dragged our one hard-shelled suitcase across the muddy floor. Luke and I carried our clothes in plastic bags. Even at seven, Luke looked like my father, with a strong, square jaw, perfectly straight teeth, and a wide smile. Mom said Luke was developmentally delayed, but unlike Audrey, he was quiet and predictable, full of smiles and softness.

Families with cinnamon-colored skin gave us quizzical looks as we shuffled by, especially the mothers, who tittered to each other in Spanish, their thick, black hair pulled tightly into ponytails. I couldn't help but stare right back, at their bright red lipstick, thick, black eyeliner, stockings, and high heels, and at the men in white straw cowboy hats, their silver belt buckles cinching tight jeans that always led down to fancy boots.

"Hang on tight, Sis," Mom said as I gripped the waistband of her polyester pants. She looked down and smiled, her glasses inched down her nose so far she had to crinkle it to keep them from falling off altogether. "I see an open seat where we can all sit down." She led us to a nondescript bank of green plastic chairs. "You kids stay put," she commanded, and handed Aaron off to Matt. "I've got to call Maudy's store before we leave."

Maudy's was LeBaron's general store. Maudy sold snack foods, *paletas,* and soft drinks out of a room built off the front of her house. Maudy's also served as the post office in a town where none of the homes had addresses, and it housed the only public telephone in a town with almost no private ones. You could call Maudy's from anywhere and leave a message for anyone in town. I listened as Mom called and left the same message she had the day before: to tell Lane that the six of us needed a ride home from the bus stop in LeBaron.

"Cero-uno-uno-cinco-dos-seis-tres-seis. . . . Sí, por favor. Gracias," Mom said in her thick American accent as she winked and smiled at us. Mom never learned to speak Spanish well. I sometimes thought she was only pretending that she didn't speak Spanish so that she wouldn't have to talk to Alejandra, Lane's first wife, who was Mexican and barely spoke English.

Mom left her a message and rushed back to tell us that we needed to head outside to get in line for the bus. Mom had been running from the moment we'd arrived in El Paso, the five of us kids struggling to keep us as she collected our food stamps and waited in long lines at the bank to cash the government-assistance checks. But as soon as we stepped out into the wet December weather, Mom stopped us, transfixed by a refrigerator-size cardboard box on the sidewalk, open at both ends. *What does she need that box for?* I wondered.

"Is someone sleeping inside there?" Mom called out to no one in particular. She stopped and squinted through her glasses to get a better look. She let go of Audrey's hand and tiptoed closer to the open flaps. Sure enough, there was a boy inside. He looked about ten years old— barefoot, no coat, no blankets, no pillow, nothing.

We must have woken him. He bolted out from the box's other end. His T-shirt looked three sizes too small and was full of holes, and the cold had turned his lips dark purple. In Spanish, Mom asked the boy his name. He just stared at her motionless with fear, the way an animal might, the way Audrey sometimes did.

Matt took off his jean jacket and asked Mom if he could give it to the boy.

"Are you sure you want to give your jacket away?" Mom asked. "It's the only one you have, and you might get cold on the bus."

Matt nodded and Mom said okay. My brother walked up to the boy and wrapped it around his shoulders. The boy slipped his arms inside the sleeves and zipped it up quickly. I was impressed by Matt's generosity, even as I said a silent prayer of thanks that my coat was too small for the boy. Mom unzipped our suitcase, pulled out one of my brother's sweaters and a pair of socks. "Here, give these to him too." Matt did as he was told. The boy gave the barest hint of a smile and then crawled back into the box. Matt shrugged his shoulders in his wool sweater, shivered, and stuffed his hands in his jean pockets.

We got on the bus, and Mom handed Audrey a tattered deck of red cards. Card shuffling was one of my sister's favorite pastimes, and one of the few things that Mom could depend on to keep her from pulling at the threads in her clothes. I took off my coat so I could use it as a pillow and thought about the refrigerator-box boy and the children begging and selling candies on the streets of Juárez.

I was jealous of my cousins in the States. They used to live in Mexico too, but after my dad died, Mom's sisters moved to California, not too far from where my grandparents lived. When her Microbus was working, Mom would take us to visit my grandparents at Christmas. Then we'd drive a couple of hours south to where my aunts lived to celebrate the New Year with all of my cousins. Mom's sisters were like her best friends when they were together. My cousins lived in warm homes that were already completely constructed; they had electricity, soft carpets, warm water that came right out of the faucet, washing machines, telephones, televisions, and they even had video games that we took turns playing on their TV. Whenever we left my cousins' house and went back to LeBaron, I'd feel embarrassed about how we lived. Our little house didn't have electricity or even a bathroom that worked, let alone a television with video games. I was so sad that this year we wouldn't be spending Christmas with my grandparents, aunts, and cousins. Mom's Microbus was broken again and she said there was no way for us to get to California. But leaving Juárez, I realized things could be much, much worse. I could be living in a box, wearing torn-up shoes, and selling candy to strangers. I felt sorry for the Mexican children of Juárez, and for a while I forgot I was poor.

The bus drove through miles of mesquite, cacti, and tumbleweeds, and eventually the Sierra Madres came into view. We called them the Blue Mountains because of the way they looked in the afternoon sunlight. Along the road, I saw rain-soaked farms and cattle ranches ringed with barbed wire; one- or two-room adobe buildings that served as homes; small adobe restaurants; and adobe garages for mechanics. But my favorite view from the bus was of the little adobe structures that looked like tall doghouses but had faded statues of the Virgin Mary or Christ on the cross tacked to their roofs. Candles burned on small wooden tables inside the entryways. Mom explained that they were shrines where Catholics went to pray for safe travels during road trips. I was so used to sharing our small, five-room house with my mom and my four siblings that I liked to imagine playing house in one of those warm, cozy little shrines.

As the dark day turned to an even darker evening, the bus came to a stop in the middle of Casas Grandes. Thirty-five miles north of LeBaron, Casas was the closest town to the colony, home to grocery stores, the hospital I'd been born in, as well as our favorite *tortillería*. There, we often found ourselves in long lines as we waited for a dozen hot corn tortillas wrapped in newspaper-thin packages. Back home in LeBaron, Mom would smother the tortillas in homemade butter and roll them up into little butter burritos. There was nothing better.

For some reason, the *tortillería* didn't have a line that afternoon, so Mom had time to pick up a dozen during the few minutes it took Casas passengers to get on and off the bus. Steam rose from the paper as she doled out our one-tortilla allotments. I gobbled mine down as the bus inched away from the city center and back toward the highway. Then I fell into a deep sleep, not waking up until we began our steep descent into the valley of LeBaron. I was never able to sleep through the stomach-dropping sensation of that part of the trip.

I yawned, sat up, and stared out at a slate sky. The clouds looked as if they'd all been made from a single piece of cotton that had been stretched by the wind until holes appeared. To my right, over Luke's sleeping head, LeBaron spread out for a mile on the west side of the highway. During the spring and hot summer months, the colony looked like a quilt stitched out of large patches of dark green, yellow, and orange fabric. But now, in the winter, the patches were nothing but different shades of brown.

As we descended farther, prickly barbed-wire fences that separated farms and neighbors came into focus—the quilt's silver and brown-threaded seams. I lifted myself up by the arms of my seat and looked over at Matt, who was rubbing his eyes. Outside the window behind him, adobe houses with flat, tar roofs nestled against rocky, golden-yellow hillsides—homes of the local Mexicans we often hired as farm and ranch hands.

Then, as we rounded a corner, the *L* came into view. High above LeBaron's humblest homes, on the tallest of the hillsides along the east side of the highway, jagged rocks and round stones had been assembled to create a giant letter *L*. Painted white, it was always visible, but never more so than at dusk, when it seemed to glow. Mom always told me that my father himself had painted the rocks of the *L*.

The road began to flatten out just as we reached the colony. LeBaron was too small to have its own bus station, so residents disembarked at a stop on the highway. As soon as my feet touched the gravel, the cold stung my face like a slap. By this point, the gloomy sky had given way to a starry night. Rainfall from earlier in the day made the air smell like moist dirt. A stiff breeze hit the back of my neck. I shivered as the driver opened the undercarriage door and we gathered our things. Matt threw the bag of gifts over his shoulder like a young Santa Claus.

The bus pulled away and left behind nothing but darkness. The taillights became dots, the motor's hum faded in the distance, and suddenly all I could hear was the trickling of water through the irrigation ditches that ran the length of the colony. The rows of tall willow trees lining the ditches swayed in the breeze. The town was so quiet I could hear myself breathe.

Mom looked up and down the highway, and I watched her expression melt from expectation to disappointment to weariness to acceptance. Lane obviously wasn't coming. "He probably didn't get my messages," she mumbled with a sigh. "It's no big deal. We can walk home."

She balanced Aaron on her hip, threw her purse strap over her shoulder, bent over to pick up the suitcase, grabbed Audrey's hand, and prepared herself for the mile-long walk home. The rest of us followed silently, watching and listening as Mom took a wide step over the highway shoulder and onto the dirt road, the gravel crunching beneath her footsteps, the sound of home.

As we walked past the adobe homes that led to the farm, I envied the bright and buttery glow emanating from the few that were wired for electricity. Interspersed among those warm, well-lit homes were houses where the light flickered and ghostly shadows bounced against every wall. These were the homes with kerosene lamps, homes like ours.

But ours wouldn't even have flickering lights at the moment. It would be utterly dark, distinguishable only by Mom's broken-down van parked outside.

Alejandra's house was on the other side of the property, farther from town than our own. As we walked that night, I could see through the bare peach trees and across the alfalfa fields the faint light from my stepsisters' bedroom widow. I was always curious about my stepsisters' lives, but that night their kerosene lantern was too dim to reveal much.

We reached the long gravel driveway leading to our house. I could hear the water flowing through the irrigation ditch, the small house standing cold and dark on the other side. The windows were so black they gave me a feeling of emptiness. I dreaded going inside.

Mom handed me Aaron, his wet diaper squishing against my waist. She and Matt pulled the gate open, and we all moved out of the way except Audrey, who just stood there bending her upper body forward and moaning with her fingers squeezed tightly together. On instinct, I moved some distance away, but when Mom walked back and patted Audrey softly on the back, the moaning stopped and Audrey stepped out of the way of the gate.

Mom was the first to jump over the ditch. She climbed onto a soggy dirt mound, lifted Aaron from my side, wrapped both her arms around him, and jumped. Aaron's head bounced and his hood fell off when Mom's feet landed safely on the other side. She wobbled a little but righted herself to avoid falling backward into the mud.

She looked back at us, her glasses perched on the end of her nose. "Let Audrey go," Mom insisted. "Go ahead and jump, Sis," Mom told my sister in the kind, patient voice she always used to address Audrey. Audrey hunched her head forward, straightened her rigid legs, leaped, and landed smack in the middle of the ditch. The cold water reached all the way up to her knees. She moaned as Mom helped her out of the muck. The rest of us were well practiced, so we safely cleared the ditch and made our way to the house.

The smell of wet alfalfa was strong as we walked around the Microbus and approached the black wooden side door that led into our kitchen. It didn't have a real lock, just a long, bent nail that hooked over the inside doorknob. Still, it kept the door closed and could only be opened from the inside. Matt had to climb through the one unlocked window into the kids' room at the back of the house. He yanked the window open, jumped inside, and soon we heard the nail twist away and the door opened.

We stepped into a dark, frigid kitchen, which reeked of mice droppings. Audrey's teeth chattered as she rocked from left to right, and Aaron started to cry. Mom passed him to me while she went to retrieve the pair of kerosene lamps and matches she kept in her bedroom. She set one of them in the center of the kitchen table and lit it, the smells of sulfur and kerosene masking the mouse stench. The lamp's flame brought light to the gas refrigerator and the stove, our white table and the four plastic chairs that surrounded it.

My stepfather seldom completed any of his projects. The inside of our house hadn't even been finished before the outside began to crack and crumble. The house had been intended for Lane's original second wife, who had taken their two children, left him, and moved to the States a few years before Mom married into the family and became Lane's second second wife.

Even though it was just two days before Christmas, no decorations were in the kitchen or any other room. In better times we'd bought Christmas trees in El Paso and brought them down with us, but this year we had neither the money to buy one nor a working car to transport it.

I felt fresh mouse droppings squish under my feet as I followed Mom into the kids' bedroom, where she set a lamp on the small, white dresser we all shared and pulled on it with all her might until the top drawer came open. She found a flannel nightgown and helped Audrey change into it before wrapping a white cotton diaper around her bottom, securing it with two pins, then covering it with a pair of clear-plastic underpants.

I opened my drawer, took out a red-and-black flannel nightgown, and shook off the mouse droppings. I shivered as I put it on over my head. Like the rest of the house, the kids' bedroom was unfinished. The two outer adobe walls hadn't been stuccoed inside or out, and small animals and insects lived in and crawled through the holes between the dirt bricks. That night, the chilly wind whistled through the cracks and made our clothes, which hung from a silver pipe attached to wires in the wooden ceiling, sway in the breeze. The wind hardened my skin with goose bumps and rattled my bones. I slipped cotton socks over my feet and ankles and put my jacket back on over my nightgown.

While Mom dressed Aaron for bed and nursed him to sleep, Matt brought a kerosene lamp back into the kitchen and sat it in the center of the oval table so we could all play a game of Go Fish. The lamp's small flame created tall, bouncing shadows that played on the bare white walls, and I had to squint to see the numbers on my cards. A dark purple sky was visible through the uncovered, wooden-framed window above the table, and dim moonlight shone down on us.

Audrey shuffled the cards, of course, and stacked them into a perfect pile before dealing them to Matt, Luke, and me. For some reason, she never needed help with Go Fish. She knew all the rules, how to pair her mates, and never forgot who had the cards she needed. She also seemed calmer when we played card games, although her concentration would periodically waver. Sometimes I'd look up to find her staring straight ahead at nothing in particular, and Matt had to call her name or tap her shoulder to remind her it was her turn. He always had the most mates on the table by the end of the game; then he would often throw his head back and laugh fakely with one eye closed, acting superior as if to remind us that he was the smartest.

With Aaron now asleep in his crib, Mom made us quesadillas with the rest of the tortillas she'd bought in Casas Grandes and with her own white cheese made from the milk of our cows. The cheese was stringy and always melted perfectly; the grease oozed from between the tortillas onto our fingertips and mismatched plastic plates. As Luke chewed his food, he opened his mouth and grunted, a dinnertime habit. "Lukey, eat with your mouth closed," Mom said for the thousandth time, but he never learned.

The night grew darker and colder. Given that, and how tiring the day had been, Mom decided that we should all go to bed. Audrey and I tramped back to our room, where I lay down next to her, still in my coat. My head was at her feet and my legs prickled with goose bumps as they slid across the cold plastic bedcover that protected the mattress from Audrey's leaky diaper. I moved next to my sister for warmth.

The bed that Matt and Luke shared was opposite ours, up against the windowed outer wall, although Matt preferred to sleep on the green-and-white couch in the living room on nights when the wind howled through the walls of our bedroom. The wind didn't blow through the living-room walls the way it did in our room. Matt took the lamp with him when he left, and for a time the three of us lay in pitch-black darkness. Soon, thanks to the heat from Audrey's body, I stopped shivering and took my jacket off. I listened to the sounds my home made, of Aaron's whimpering on the other side of the single plastered wall, of the whistling outer walls as the winter breeze blew through them. I held my pillow tightly, pulled the blankets over my head, and drifted off to sleep.

THE WALLS WERE whistling again when I woke up on Christmas Eve morning, my legs freezing and damp from Audrey's leaking diaper. I had barely opened my eyes when I heard a bloodcurdling scream from the living room. Throwing off the blankets, I bolted over Audrey's sleeping legs and ran in the direction of Matt's voice, my feet almost burning from the cold of the cement floor.

My brother's eyes were still shut and he was shaking his head from side to side. "There was a mouse on my head!" he screamed. "There was a mouse on my head and he was chewing on my hair!"

"Where is it?" I yelled as my eyes scanned the floor.

"It ran into the kitchen."

Now Luke was up, and the three of us ran in that direction. Matt grabbed a broom and swept its handle wildly under the oven.

Luke's face was panic-stricken as he begged Matt to stop. "Don't hurt it!" he cried.

"What the heck are you guys doing out here?" Mom asked as she walked into the kitchen in her old, blue robe. "The baby's still sleepin'. You're gonna wake him up."

"Mom, he was chewin' on my hair!" Matt said.

"I heard. Quiet down. I'll pick up some mousetraps when I go to the store later." Mom took off her glasses, exposing swollen, tired eyes. "You and Luke—go bring in some wood and start the barrel heater."

"I don't want you to kill de mouse, Mommy," Luke said meekly. He didn't always pronounce every word correctly or speak in complete sentences. Mom was already out of earshot, silently padding to her room in search of our ragged, old cotton sheet with little yellow flowers. She attached it to the walls between the kitchen and the hallway so that the warmth from the barrel heater would concentrate in the living room and the kitchen.

The heater was a rusty, fifty-five-gallon petroleum barrel into which Lane had cut a circular hole so we could load it with wood. He'd also attached a makeshift door that half covered the hole and made several coin-size holes in the barrel so the fire could breathe. A silver metal tube rose from the top of it and up through a hole in the wooden ceiling, the hole being at least a quarter inch larger in diameter than the tube. As a result, we always kept a silver milking bucket next to the heater to catch rain when it fell into the house.

The ramshackle heater stood in the far corner of the living room to the left of an old upright piano that Lane had originally bought for the wife whose place Mom had taken. Even though it was out of tune and most of its glossy black finish had faded and flecked away long ago, I loved that piano and played it more than anyone else. My grandmother LeBaron, my dad's mom, gave me piano lessons twice a week at her house, which was about a mile from our house.

Within minutes, my brothers had come back inside with chopped wood in their arms. Matt filled the barrel and wiped his dirty hands on his faded jeans. Then he stepped back as Mom poured kerosene over the wood, struck a match, and threw it into the barrel. Flames burst out of the hole before she closed the round door, and Mom reminded us for the umpteenth time to watch Aaron so he wouldn't burn himself on the heater.

The smell of burning wood filled the living room. The entire family was up now, sitting on the couch or the living-room rug, all of us snuggled under blankets. Knowing we were still chilly, Mom lit the oven and left its door open while she made breakfast. She filled a pan half-full of wheat berries that she kept stored in a gunnysack, then covered the berries with water and boiled them until they were soft and round. We ate the chewy, hot cereal out of plastic bowls at the kitchen table with milk, cinnamon, vanilla, and sugar.

After breakfast, once everyone was dressed and ready for the day, Mom placed Aaron into his round, hard-plastic walker in the living room as far as possible from the heater. While he rolled around on the rug, she put on her heavy wool coat and told Matt and me to watch the baby and Audrey while she walked to the Conasupo. The Conasupo, about a mile and a half away, was another convenience store run out of someone's house and sold staple food items and toiletries.

The hinges on the kitchen door creaked as Mom left. I was practicing "Mary Had a Little Lamb" on the piano, my rough, tuneless playing accompanied by the rhythmic squeaking sound Audrey made as she rocked on the couch. She picked at the bottom edge of her pink cotton turtleneck, pulling little pieces of thread from the material with her fingertips. A bit more of the pasty-white skin of her skinny belly peeked out with each thread that fell to the floor.

I played the song over and over, faster each time, as Aaron made his baby sounds. Matt and Luke played checkers on the rug, and Matt laughed teasingly at every wrong move our brother made. Suddenly, the bouncing springs on the couch went quiet. On instinct, I stopped playing. I turned to find Audrey on her feet, squeezing her hands together just as she had the night before, although now her lips were spread wide, exposing clenched teeth. Her upper body began to jerk from left to right. We all just watched for a second, not sure what to do. Even the baby looked at her, wide-eyed, his mouth open, drool falling onto his chin.

Audrey was older, bigger, and stronger than the rest of us, so Matt stood up from the rug slowly and positioned himself in front of her, an arm's distance away. "Audrey," he said calmly, staring at her with kind but fearful eyes. "Settle down, okay, Audrey? Sit back down on the couch and settle down. Mom will be back in a few minutes."

Audrey threw herself back down so hard the whole couch shook. Matt returned to the rug but kept one eye on Audrey. She stared straight ahead, gazing blankly at something that only she could see. She cocked her head forward, clenched her teeth, and started to moan loudly from deep inside her throat. In an instant, she shot to her feet again, still staring at something. Matt and Luke scooted away and scrambled to the other side of the living room.

Her moaning grew louder as Audrey began rocking forward and backward, her pale lips spread apart like a wild animal's. She then bent forward all the way to the ground without bending her knees. She grabbed the checkerboard with both hands, lifted it up, and slammed it back down with a crash. Red and black disks flew in every direction.

"Audrey, settle down, 'kay?!" Matt was pleading now. "Sit back down. Okay, Audrey?"

No response. She just continued to moan and stare. Matt inched closer, trying to grasp her forearm to lead her back to the couch the way Mom would have done. But the second his hand touched her, her head jerked forward and the moaning grew louder.

Matt looked panicked. He turned back to Audrey, and then, as commandingly as he could, told our sister to settle down and sit back on the couch. His voice startled her—her head spun around in his direction.

"Settle down. 'Kay, Audrey? It's okay. Mom's coming back in a few minutes."

Audrey blinked and turned her head abruptly away. Then, in one violent motion, she jerked her arm away from Matt's grip and attacked him, grabbing fistfuls of his hair in her hands. She jerked his head sideways from left to right, making him lose his balance and fall to one knee. Then, with almost superhuman force, she threw him onto the floor. He landed with a thud, flat over a sea of checkers.

I screamed and my body went stiff. I had seen Audrey get violent, but never like this. Matt picked himself up off the rug, his face crimson, a red checker stuck to the center of his forehead.

Aaron squeezed his eyes shut and started to cry as loudly as if he'd been the one who'd been hit. Now Audrey's head swiveled in his direction. I knew what was coming and raced for the walker, but she arrived first, grabbing it with both hands and shaking it as hard as she could. The baby wailed and Audrey turned the entire contraption upside down, slamming Aaron's head into the rug. I knelt down to pull him upright, but Audrey grabbed my hair, pulling me sideways and throwing me down onto my back. I quickly rose, but she yanked the sleeve of my shirt, pulled me close, and bit down on my arm. Her jaw was so tightly locked on it that I couldn't pull away. I shrieked with pain.

"Matt, help me!" I cried.

"Ruthie, we gotta get out of here!" I looked over and saw Matt and Luke standing in front of the open door to the yard, Matt now holding Aaron. "Hurry, Ruthie!"

I pushed so hard against Audrey's forehead I saw my fingerprints white on her pink skin, and still she wouldn't let me go. I lunged for my sister's head, pulling the top of her hair back. She screamed, and

I felt my body thrown forward, propelled by Audrey's hard slap on my back. I teetered but didn't fall. I ran out the door and slammed it behind me.

"Hurry, Ruthie, keep running!" Matt yelled.

I looked over my shoulder. The living-room door was open again. She was coming. I ran faster, my heart pounding and my breath as thick as smoke in the cold morning air. I stopped and turned. Audrey was planted in the front yard, her feet hip distance apart, shifting her torso from left to right and gripping her hands together.

"Why isn't she following us?" I said.

"Ruthie, hurry up! Run!" Matt yelled back at me with Aaron still crying in his arms.

I did, and soon enough I caught up to my brothers, who had slowed down once they realized that Audrey had stopped. I was still in my nightgown, sweating and freezing at the same time. The calmer I became, the more I shivered.

Aaron was still crying a few minutes later when a beat-up, white Ford pickup rounded the corner. Matt sniffled and wiped his red, runny nose with the sleeve of his wool sweater. "Is that Lane's truck?" He craned his neck. "It *is*! And Mommy too!" We ran toward them.

"What the heck are you guys doing out here without your coats on?" Mom said, rolling down the window and popping her head out. Matt talked so loud and fast he almost collapsed.

Lane reached his head over the black steering wheel and raised his light brown eyebrows at us curiously. "I'm glad you guys are all okay," he said. He looked at me and smiled, the lines of long crow's-feet visible at the edges of his blue eyes. His sandy-blond hair was longer than he usually wore it and was combed away from his face. His sideburns reached almost to the edge of his jawbone.

Now in Mom's arms, Aaron had stopped crying and began to chew his thumb. She scooted next to Lane on the bench seat and put both of her feet on the driver's side of the stick shift as if she couldn't quite get as close to him as she needed to. I crowded in between her and my brothers. The truck smelled like the manure that was crusted on the sides of Lane's work boots and the black grease that always stained his calloused and cracking fingertips.

As we drove past the gate, Mom gasped. Audrey was still standing in the muddy yard, rocking from left to right, picking nervously at her turtleneck, which had a hole now the size of a grapefruit. Her teeth chattered, her face was pale, and her lips had turned a purplish blue. Mom pushed all us kids out of the way so she could jump out of the cab. Aaron still on her hip, she approached Audrey and reached for her hand. As soon as Mom touched her, my sister stopped moving. She blinked, her head slowly turning in Mom's direction. "Mom," Audrey said in a monotone voice through chattering teeth, "I'm cold." Mom took Audrey by the upper arm and led her through the open living-room door.

My brothers and I followed my stepfather into the house as he carried the groceries in through the kitchen door. Lane always walked with his left toes pointed out and a slight limp, the legacy of an old knee injury. He set the groceries on the kitchen table and poked his head through the entryway into the living room. "I'm going to tell Alejandra that you're back now and I'm stayin' here tonight," he said to Mom, his voice matter-of-fact, smooth and deep. "I'll be right back."

"Sounds good," Mom said, sighing.

4

Count your blessings;
Name them one by one.
Count your blessings;
See what God hath done.
Count your blessings;
Name them one by one.
Count your many blessings;
See what God hath done.

Lane strummed his acoustic guitar after a Christmas Eve dinner of boiled beans, cottage cheese, and warm corn tortillas. With the barrel heater in the living room blazing, his voice rang deep, smooth, and loud over the rest of ours. If my family had had a theme song, "Count Your Blessings" would have been it. My siblings and I knew the lyrics by heart, and Mom and Lane would sing it to us anytime we complained. It represented a core belief of theirs: we should be grateful for every little thing God had given us. That Christmas Eve, the words reminded me of the boy in the box and the other children I'd seen in Juárez the day before, and the lyrics rang true. They made me feel almost righteous for living without, as if being poor were the same as being humble and good.

Whatever our financial situation, Mom always found a way to buy us gifts. That afternoon she had wrapped the presents she'd purchased in El Paso and stacked the candy-cane-striped packages under the window in the living room. Every Christmas Eve began with Mom's reading the story of Jesus's birth aloud to us. Lane didn't believe that December 25 was Jesus's real birthday and therefore didn't see any reason to celebrate the holiday, not unlike many other members of our church. But in keeping with the traditions of her American family, Mom celebrated Christmas with us kids every year. This year, because Lane was with us, Mom asked if he would read the story for her.

Mom had trimmed his sideburns and cut his hair. She sat next to him with Aaron on her lap, and her hand massaged Lane's back in time with the rhythm of his voice. Audrey sat on the couch next to Mom. The rest of my siblings and I encircled them on the floor. My upper arm still ached from Audrey's bite that morning, and I started to feel sleepy until Lane read the part where Joseph sat Mary "upon her ass" before their trip to Bethlehem. I think Mom must have said a different word when she read the story. I was certain she had never read the word *ass*. Matt and I looked at each other, red in the face, and burst into giggles.

"Knock it off," Lane said sternly. "The story of Jesus isn't something to laugh at." I put my hand over my mouth to cover my smile and swallowed my laughter. Lane continued reading.

Soon Mom pulled out the mismatched-socks box from our bedroom to prepare for Santa Claus. I picked the biggest sock I could find, inserted my fist all the way to the toe, and carefully examined the sock for holes. I gave it to Mom and she attached it with clothespins to one of the wire hangers that she'd hung from the back of our plastic kitchen chairs.

"The real meaning of Christmas isn't about presents and stockings and candy," Lane said. I turned around and saw he had picked up his acoustic guitar again. Whenever he did that, another round of "Count Your Blessings" couldn't be far behind. "It's about the birth of our Savior, Jesus Christ, the Son of God."

He cleared his throat and sang solo while we readied ourselves for bed:

> *Count your blessings;*
> *Name them one by one. . . .*

The only blessing I could think of was what might be coming the next morning, when I hoped I would discover an old sock so heavy with candy it would hang elongated and distorted from the chair.

That night, unable to get the sock out of my mind, I lay awake for an hour. I had to pee but I fought the urge for as long as possible. When I could hold it no longer, I got up, walked to the kitchen, put a stool up to the refrigerator to retrieve the red plastic flashlight and roll of toilet paper that we kept on top, and made my way to the kitchen door.

I hated few things more than getting up in the middle of the night and walking alone to the outhouse, but at least on this night the moon was half-full; the dark blue sky was clear and dotted with stars that brightened the cold air. Long before the flashlight's beam found the outhouse, the smell of stale urine guided me toward the eight-foot-tall, unpainted wooden box that rose out of the ground like a dead tree trunk. I knew it would be completely dark inside except for the light that streamed through a small crescent moon carved into the door. Its knob was a piece of wood nailed to it, and its hinges were made of rubber cut from recycled tires, which made the door rigid and hard to open.

One step up onto a small wooden floor and there I was, standing over a hole while I held my breath to keep from sucking in the stench that would make me retch. I turned around, crouched down, and placed my behind over it, supporting myself with my palms to guard against splinters in my cheeks. One interminable moment later, I hurried out of the rickety door, sucked in the cold air, and walked quickly back to the house, my heart pounding inside my ears.

CHRISTMAS MORNING, ALL of us ran for our stockings, unclipping the clothespins way before Lane and Mom woke up. The socks were indeed stuffed, though mostly with peanuts, which didn't feel like a treat as we always had peanuts around the house. I was happy to find two mini Almond Joy bars and an orange mixed among them.

Count your blessing;
See what God hath done.

After we emptied our stockings, Matt sorted through the wrapped gifts, read whom each one belonged to, and handed them to us. We had two each. While we felt and shook our packages, Mom and Lane got up. My stepfather, already dressed and ready to feed the animals and milk the cows, peeked into the living room, bid us good morning, and made a quick exit. Mom came in soon afterward and announced we could open our presents. I tore into my biggest one first and ripped open the red-and-white candy-cane paper to reveal a previously opened cardboard box that had been taped shut. Inside was a white plastic Ferris wheel, its Fisher-Price sticker faded and peeling, with four little boy and girl figurines. These, plastic and dull, looked as if they had been left out in the sun. The figurines' round bottoms still nested easily into dusty round holes on the Ferris wheel. One figurine looked like me: she had light freckles on her cheeks and was dressed in navy blue, her hair pulled back into a blond ponytail. I would have been jealous of her long hair—Mom always cut mine short—but her ponytail had somehow been chewed off and tooth marks were on her head.

Luke also received a weather-beaten Fisher-Price toy—a red farmhouse with a farmer figurine, a horse, a cow, and a little, pink pig. They had little, round bottoms just like my figurines, and the whole thing was identically tattered. Once we realized that our figurines were interchangeable, we played with our new used toys for hours. Luke opened and closed his plastic farmhouse door over and over, and each time it closed, a loud *moooo* came from inside the door, and he laughed out loud with watery eyes as if he had never seen anything so amazing. I liked the way a cow could go straight from the farmhouse to a Ferris-wheel ride and back again. We were thrilled by our new toys, exhausted as they were.

> *Count your blessings;*
> *Name them one by one.*
> *Count your many blessings;*
> *See what God hath done.*

— 5 —

By the following summer, I had turned six and I decided I was old enough to help my brother Matt with his farmwork. The alfalfa fields glowed green under the hot desert sun, and the peach trees were covered with green leaves and small, unripe fruit. A dense pecan grove created several acres of cool shadows behind our farm, and although the house still smelled of mice, it was brighter and warmer in the summer light.

That summer had seen two exciting developments on the farm. First, electricity had finally stretched to our corner of the colony. Lane had dug narrow, shallow trenches and buried electrical wires to ferry the current to his shop, where it powered his tools and the irrigation pumps on our farm. He promised that it wouldn't be long until he would wire our house and Alejandra's. He had also installed a toilet inside our house. The bathroom was the first door on the left in the hallway, a narrow, gray room that smelled like wet cement. The toilet itself was not new, naturally. The seat was scratched, the tank was missing its flushing handle, and a five-gallon bucket filled with water sat nearby. This, we were instructed, was how we could flush the toilet until Lane could locate a functional handle.

At nine years old, Matt could milk a cow himself. He had been assigned a relatively benign brown ruminant. One evening at dusk, I decided to go with him to the corral behind Lane's shop, which was about fifty yards from the back of our house, right next to the corral. I wanted to see milking firsthand. "Why are you followin' me?" my brother said, annoyed by my presence, squinting over his shoulder with mock-menace. "Go back inside and help Mom."

"I don't want to. I want to help you milk the cow."

He ignored me, looking straight ahead, and began to walk faster.

I picked up the pace and could soon hear Lane's cows mooing and the buzz of the flies that swarmed around the five filthy animals and feasted on the manure-covered ground beneath them.

As I approached, I inspected the cows' movements with caution, my shoulders tense. Directly in front of the corral lay a large, open well, which also made me nervous. I had always been afraid of it; the black surface of the water was far below ground level. I could never watch when the boys would run straight for it, scissoring their legs wide as they leaped from one crooked edge to the other. Loose dirt would fall into the hole, and it always took a few seconds to hear the hollow sound of a splash.

Resigning himself to my presence, Matt warned me to stay away from the cows' swinging tails. I watched as he tied his cow's two back legs together with thin baling wire so that she wouldn't run away while he milked her. He sat down on top of an overturned bucket and made a big show of his competence, reaching confidently toward the cow's swollen, pink udder. Then he stopped and looked up at me, his chin pointed out, and his eyes peering from underneath his cap.

"Ruthie, don't ever stand behind the cow," he said with a sternness beyond his years. "If it gets scared, it'll kick ya in the teeth and knock ya flat on your butt. Its legs are skinny but they're real strong, and its hooves are solid bone—"

"I know, Matt." I sighed. I concocted an offended face and refused to look at him, sighing again as I waited for the sound of milk to hit the bottom of the empty bucket. Instead, I felt a stream of warm liquid spray my forehead and drip down my sunburned nose and cheeks. I whirled around and slapped Matt, who couldn't stop laughing, which incensed me further. My face was hot; sticky milk had seeped under my eyelids. I yelled as loud as I could for him to quit it.

"Oh, stop being such a big baby." He laughed as he returned his attention to the milking bucket.

Eventually, the sting left my eyes and I sat and stewed in silence. Every once in a while I would glance at Matt out of the corner of my eye as he squeezed milk into the bucket. Soon it was three-quarters full and covered with frothy bubbles.

The bright blue skies outside the corral had grown darker, and the clouds above looked as foamy as the milk. The sun had at last set behind yellow bales of dry hay that created a cool, triangular shadow over the cows. Matt outstretched his right arm to balance the weight of the bucket in his left hand as he walked slowly back to the house, taking care that the milk didn't slosh on his jeans. This made it easy for me to keep up.

Lane's truck was parked in front of his shop. My stepfather had left the door to the shop wide-open and was sitting inside on an empty paint bucket, his shoulders hunched forward over a wooden workbench. He was welding, something he did all the time now that the shop finally had electricity.

The leather gloves he wore had grease-stained fingertips, and the sleeves of his checkered shirt were tucked inside the gloves. A large, gray welding mask obscured his face, protecting it from blue, orange, and yellow sparks. Matt gave the whole scene a quick glance as he trudged onward with his milk bucket, but I couldn't resist stopping to watch.

I didn't say a word, but Lane somehow sensed my presence anyway. He pulled his torch away from the metal and peered at me through

the helmet's rectangular glass, his eyes smiling. He extinguished the
torch's blue flame and lifted up his mask to rest it on his head. He
smiled again, his eyes tired and puffy under the mask's gray rubber
strap wrapped around his forehead.

I never knew my father, and Lane was only an occasional presence
in our house, so having grown men around was strange and vaguely
frightening, but Lane's smile was friendly, so I walked inside. The shop
was dark and reeked of grease and gasoline, which smelled sweet and
appealing compared to the corral's manure-and-cow stench. "What are
you making?"

"I'm building a funnel for our grinder motor," Lane said gently,
describing the shape in the air with his hands. "Your mom needs this
so she can grind corn and wheat. That's how she makes our bread. I'll
bet she'll show you how to use it when I'm finished, and you can learn
how to make bread too." He picked up a hammer and pounded a few
times on the cooling metal. "Everybody needs to learn how to help out
with the family. Ya know what I mean?" Lane took off his mask and set
it on the dusty cement floor.

"Can I milk a cow like Matt does?" I blurted out.

Lane raised his eyebrows in surprise as he peeled off his gloves. "So,
you want to help with the cows, do ya?" He sighed. "Well, milkin' cows
is hard work. Maybe you can have your own cow to milk when you're
about ten. By then, your hands will be big and strong enough to squeeze
all the milk out of a cow. You know, Ruthie, if you don't get all the milk
out, it'll dry up inside the cow and it won't be able to give milk anymore." He threw his gloves on the ground. "But your mom might need
help with other things."

I nodded.

Lane smiled again and patted his faded jeans. "Come sit on my lap."
The words were tinged with a definite sweetness, but also something
else, and whatever that something was, it kept me frozen in place from
fear or unfamiliarity, my hands clasped behind my back.

A fly buzzed on my ear in a spot where milk had dried. I shooed it away. "But maybe I can just try it, practice to see if I can do it," I said shyly. "I'm pretty sure I can milk a cow *and* help my Mom too."

Lane laughed heartily and jumped up, as if the joke had given him energy. In one motion he reached over and picked me up by the belly. My shirt rode up and his calloused hands felt rough against my skin. Then, he sat back down on the bucket and cradled me—one arm around my back and the other under the back of my knees. I felt my bare lower back against the denim of his pants as he bounced his legs up and down as if I were a baby. A nervous knot grew in my stomach, but I wasn't quite sure why.

"Well, now. Let's see." The bouncing had stopped and he turned his head to look at me. "Maybe you and Luke can come outside in the mornings and afternoons to feed the chickens and pick up the eggs in the chicken coop till you're both old enough to milk cows." He put his arm around my neck and brought my face closer to his. His whiskers dotted his jaw, chin, and upper lip. His nose looked bigger and wider up close, shiny, and covered in little white dots.

"What are we s'posed to do with the eggs?" The words nearly got trapped in my throat, blocked by the knot that had formed when Lane put me on his lap.

"Take 'em to your mom. She can separate them so that you guys can have some, and Alejandra and her family can have some too." He broke into a hollow chuckle. "You have to be careful not to break them, though, because we've got lots of mouths to feed around here." He gave that chuckle again. I felt his arm lift my neck and my face rose even closer. His whiskers grazed my cheek, and I smelled cheese curds on his breath. He looked straight in my eyes, and his voice was barely audible.

"Can I have a kiss before you go back inside?"

I jerked my head back and tried to wriggle out of his lap, only he held me tighter, so tight I almost couldn't breathe. I suddenly felt sick too, sort of like I'd felt when I'd gotten the flu. But this was a different kind of sick, a kind that I had never before felt, and I didn't understand where it came from.

"Just one little kiss before you go inside. Come on now, it's no big deal."

I stopped wiggling. It wasn't doing any good. Instead, I closed my eyes, took a deep breath, and kissed Lane on his rough, unshaved cheek.

I felt his grip loosen, and this time when I pushed, he let me go. I jumped off his lap and scampered away. From behind, I heard that chuckle yet again. "Ya see now, that wasn't so bad." Then the chuckle turned into a full-blown laugh. "See ya later, alligator."

Fearful that he might ask me to sit on his lap again, I put my hands in my pockets and walked quickly out of the garage. The night air made my skin feel cool, and I realized I was dripping with sweat. I made a silent vow to stick closer to my brothers and Mom over the rest of the summer.

6

Mom smiled from ear to ear as she made the announcement: she was pregnant again and the baby would be born in December. Her belly and bosom began to grow even though her hips and legs remained slender, an incongruity I first noticed on a hot midmorning in August. The two of us were walking together hand in hand out to Lane's shop, her fingers warm and swollen in mine. We weren't even halfway there when I noticed sweat running down Mom's forehead and the front of her neck. She carried a stainless-steel bucket in her free hand, and I carried one in mine.

As Lane had predicted, the baby's impending arrival meant that I would indeed need to take on more responsibilities around the house. In a few months I learned how to make cheese and butter from the milk Matt lugged back to the house each day. I learned how to whisk eggs, oil, and lime together in precise ratios to make mayonnaise. And most important—now that Lane had finished building our electric grinder—I learned how to make bread.

The shop door was locked when we arrived, but Mom had a key to the padlock, and soon we entered Lane's world of heat and grease. The stink reminded me of my stepfather and made me queasy. A string hung lazily from a ceramic light socket screwed to the wooden ceiling; Mom yanked it, instantly flooding the room with a harsh, naked light. We made our way through a maze of toolboxes and buckets of bolts and an old, rusted washing machine lying on its side, its guts spilling out onto a grease-stained white towel. At last, in the shop's back corner, we found them: several black barrels lined up against the wall. Each was twice my size and looked just like the heater in our living room. I asked Mom why we kept beans and wheat in the shop.

"So we'll have food to last us when hard times come," she said, "after the United States is destroyed." Lane regularly rotated the barrels, she told me, so that the oldest grains were the most accessible; the newest were always stored here, in the shop's far corner.

A cloud of tiny particles rose up like smoke from the barrel when Mom pried off its lid and dipped a pale plastic pitcher into the pile of wheat berries. Then, pounding the lid back onto the barrel with the meaty part of her hand, she told me to follow her out of the shop, where she locked the door before leading me over to the grinder. The contraption was bolted to a small, white table. On the ground below, at the base of the shop's gray cement wall, a hard, black plastic tube stuck out of the dry dirt—the end point of an electrical wire that Lane had attached to a line on a neighboring farmer's property, with whom we shared the costs of electricity.

The tube sat open to the air, as did a bare wire bent into a fishhook shape that stuck out of its tip. Mom held the tube-and-hook in one hand, and the loose wires of the grinder in the other, motioning for me to watch closely. I crouched down, my hand on her back.

"Ruthie, always make sure that when you hook these wires together, you don't touch any of the bare ones," she said gravely. "You have to be very, very careful. The pieces that aren't covered with plastic will shock you, and they could hurt you real bad." She paused for effect. "Do you understand me?"

I nodded slowly and seriously before Mom broke into a gentle smile, her face bright red and dripping wet as she wiped it with a towel. "The black tube has electricity coming through it, but it won't hurt you if you only touch the hard plastic part. But promise me you'll never touch the metal bits."

"I promise," I vowed.

Satisfied that I understood, Mom stood up and flipped the brown switch Lane had welded to the grinder, which emitted a gentle squeaking noise that made the thin metal table vibrate. I placed my bucket under the grinder's nozzle while Mom poured the whole grains into the funnel. The grinding began, and a tan-colored dust soon spilled into my bucket, creating clouds that made me sneeze right into the flour. Mom giggled as she reminded me to cover my mouth, then shook the flour from her polyester pants, turned off the grinder, and wiped my face clean with her towel, now soaked through with sweat. She disconnected the grinder, set the black tube with its bare wire on the ground, wiped the grinder clean, and headed back to the cool safety of the house.

Bored, I sat with my elbows on the table while I watched Mom make the bread dough, which seemed to take forever. After several hours of letting the dough rise, kneading it, and letting it rise again, she finally kneaded it one last time, separated it, and placed it into our special bread pans—juice cans shorn of their labels. Mom placed the pans upright in the oven and baked the bread. The smell of it seemed to transform our little house, as did the perfectly round slices of bread it produced. My siblings and I ate a delicious dinner of warm bread, honey, and milk out of cereal bowls that night.

By the end of summer, the peaches had grown ripe on the trees and then overripe, plunging to the damp earth below. Alejandra's eldest children and Matt climbed silver ladders to pick the fruits that remained on the branches, while Luke and I scooped the rest from the ground. In late summer, we'd devour bowls of peaches smothered in fresh cream and sugar, a welcome change from bland meals of wheat and beans. But fruit was always left over, and all of us had to help preserve what we couldn't eat.

Learning how to boil peaches in quart jars was the last lesson in my summer of domestic education. As Matt, Luke, and I carried the many, many glass jars to our bedroom, where we'd been instructed to place them on shelves up against the wall, I felt the winds of change begin to blow. I was tired of homemaking and excited about starting school.

IN EARLY SEPTEMBER, after the limbs of the peach trees had been picked clean and their light green leaves began to turn golden yellow and dark red, I was ready to start first grade. I hated having to sit and watch as Matt and Luke set off each morning for Primaria Miguel Hidalgo, which was just across the highway from the LeBaron bus stop. Mom told me that the school, which taught only grades one through four, was where I would learn to read, write, and do math. I couldn't wait. I had always been fascinated by how a sound could be suggested, an *A* or a *B,* by a single squiggle on paper. Plus, I wanted to play with new friends and get away from Audrey and her unpredictable tantrums.

On the last Sunday evening before school began, Mom gave us our weekly baths after she cut our hair. Thinking about starting school the next morning, I was especially embarrassed by my bowl cut, which felt shorter and looked even more boyish than usual. I wasn't allowed to grow my hair long enough for pigtails or a ponytail, no matter how many thousands of times I begged for them. Long hair had too many tangles, Mom insisted, and she had enough work to do without having to fight with my hair every morning.

Even though Lane had put a toilet in our house, we still didn't have running hot water, so Mom had to place our biggest stainless-steel pot under the faucet that came up from the kitchen floor, fill it, then set it on top of the stove. The tub, which was kept in the almost-finished bathroom, was round, made of galvanized steel, and could only hold one of us at a time. We would wait our turn in the kitchen while Mom traipsed back and forth from the bathroom, her hands protected by red oven mitts as she gingerly transferred the boiling water to the bath.

Audrey went first since her hair was the thickest and took the longest to dry. Next came Aaron, who always fought the bath and threw his head against Mom's chest, kicking his feet against her round, pregnant belly. After that it was my turn. The warm air smelled like Ivory soap and fogged the window. Our bathroom didn't yet have a doorknob, but Mom had stuffed a sock in the hole where the knob should have been to give us a little privacy.

I looked at Mom's face as she helped me into the bath. She looked so tired. I gripped both sides of the small tub to support myself while dipping my body into the murky water. I had to sit upright with my legs crossed to fit in the tub. Mom picked up the pot from the floor, turned the nail away from the door, and went back into the kitchen to heat up more water. My shoulders and upper torso shivered from the cold, but she came right back and filled a tall plastic cup with water, poured it over my head, and massaged pink strawberry shampoo into my hair. I loved the comforting feel of Mom's fingertips rubbing my head and the luxury of having her undivided attention.

Only at moments like this did I feel a longing for the comfort of other girls. I missed my girl cousins from California. I wished they had stayed in LeBaron so I would have had other little girls to play with. Mom had read Disney's version of *Cinderella* to us out of an oversize children's book, and I used to have dreams of pretending to be princesses with my cousins. We'd wear beautiful gowns and dance with princes at formal balls. But then I'd wake up and find I was stuck with a bunch of boys and an older sister who scared me.

"Why don't my cousins and aunts go to my dad's church anymore?" I asked as soap suds rolled down the sides of my face.

Mom considered my question for a few seconds. "You know they moved to California after your dad died. They left the church. And, actually, Grandma never believed in your dad's teachings, not even after Grandpa joined the church and moved us to LeBaron." Mom paused, searching for the words to explain this to me. "Grandma was a Baptist, and they believe that polygamy is bad. She didn't have much say when Grandpa decided to move our families down here, but after your dad was killed, they all lost faith in his teachings."

"Why?"

"Because not all of what your dad said would happen came true. And, well,"—Mom took a deep breath—"Grandpa once told me that he worried about his daughters livin' polygamy, that they were so poor with so many little kids. Maybe he regretted gettin' involved with your dad's church." She lifted her eyebrows and shrugged her shoulders. "But I never have."

I still didn't quite understand why they left. Life in LeBaron didn't seem so bad to me. Mom washed the rest of my body in silence, then held out a damp towel for me with her arms open wide. I fell into them, savoring the warm feeling of her arms squeezed tight around me.

7

A rooster's crow woke me up the next morning. In the half darkness, I stepped over Audrey's legs and made my way across the chilly cement floor to a dresser full of musty-smelling, unorganized clothes. I picked out a simple white blouse with a heart-shaped patch that matched its red, short sleeves and a pair of elastic-waist jeans. I headed to the bathroom to dress myself before anyone else needed it. "A freckle-faced boy," I said aloud to my reflection in the mirror.

Mom shuffled by in her house slippers, and soon the smell of boiling cornmeal wafted my way. I heard the familiar splatter of its bubbles as I entered the kitchen and found Mom smiling, standing over the stove in her navy-blue robe.

"You ready for school, Sis?" Then she gave me a second look. "I like your pretty blouse."

I looked down at the wrinkled cotton. "I'm ready," I said, my voice still dry and raspy from sleep. I sat at the table with a nervous stomach and swung my tennis shoes back and forth underneath my seat. My nerves went away when I dipped my teaspoon into the mush, which

Mom had made sweet by adding honey and cinnamon. But I felt queasy all over again when I found a tiny black fly lying dead and upside down at the bottom of the bowl. I hated few things on the farm more than finding flies in my food.

The sky was blue and cloudless when Matt, Luke, and I stepped out of the kitchen door, my brothers in their T-shirts and jeans, Luke's hair standing up in an unruly cowlick. Mom bid us good-bye at the doorway, wished us good luck, and waved us on our way. For almost half an hour we walked along a dirt road in silence, each of us carrying identical woven-plastic schoolbags with rubber handles. My heart began to beat fast when we reached the two-lane highway and the gray, rectangular cinder-block building just on the other side, with its metal-framed windows, slanted tin roof, and four classrooms for each of the four grades that were taught there. Fifth-grade students took a bus to a nearby town.

As we waited to cross the road, a semi pulling a trailer with a crowded load of cows rumbled past us, the cattle squished in together randomly, facing all different directions like an unfinished jigsaw puzzle. As the truck rumbled past, it blew dust into our faces and my hair into my eyes. I cleared my forehead, certain that my first day of school had been ruined.

The dry, sun-baked schoolyard was filled with a mix of light- and dark-skinned children playing together. But no one else had skin as light as mine; Casper would not have felt whiter. A basket-ball bounced with a *hamp-hamp* against a cement court filled with kids. One boy with dark, curly hair threw the ball up, aiming for the hoop—nothing more than a netless, rusted rim. I saw no swings, slides, or any other play equipment, only girls playing hopscotch and jump rope in the dirt, repeating Spanish chants and kicking up dust at their feet.

From behind came the sound of a heavy metal door scraping a cement floor, and all eyes turned to find a Mexican teacher calling students in Spanish through a megaphone. I stood frozen while each child bolted for one of the four classroom doors and got in line. Using the children's heights as a guide, I found the right line, and soon our teacher stepped out to welcome us. A serious but friendly woman, she had dark hair and large curls that surrounded her face and made her look as if she were wearing a football helmet. She wore a purple dress with nude stockings and gray high heels, dark red lipstick, purple eye shadow that matched her dress, thick, black eyeliner, and mascara. She waved us inside.

The classroom smelled like Pine-Sol and had twenty wooden desks in lines on a cement floor that looked brand-new, smooth and shiny like the film over Mom's glossy photographs. I scanned the room and chose a desk in a far corner beneath a window, which is when I realized that going to a Mexican school meant being taught in Spanish.

"*Buenos días, alumnos. Me llamo Señora,*" the teacher said.

The words blurred together in fast-paced sentences. I never even caught my teacher's name; it was forever lost in the torrent of her opening speech. My body went stiff and the blood rushed to my face as I looked at my classmates and watched wide-eyed as they reached down into their plastic schoolbags almost in unison. I followed their lead and took out my new spiral notebook, which Mom had given me as a special present for starting school. Meanwhile, the teacher walked the aisles and made marks in her notebook with a sharp, yellow pencil, smiling and greeting each child individually.

When she reached my desk, she stopped, knelt down until we were eye to eye, and smiled. She said something to me in Spanish, and all I could do was stare at her and hold my breath in fear. She smiled again, then called someone over, a little girl on the other side of the classroom who promptly picked up her supplies and moved to the desk next to mine.

The girl had long, straight brown hair pulled back by a barrette, just as I had always wanted, not to mention her straight bangs cut evenly over her green eyes. She had light pink skin with dark brown freckles on her nose. I thought that maybe I'd seen her in church, but I wasn't sure. I was certain that her yellow dress was brand-new, or almost. It was definitely freshly washed and perfectly ironed.

The teacher looked back at me, smiled one more time, then continued her walk down the aisle. The little girl in the yellow dress turned to me, grinned, and said hello, in English.

"My name is Natalia," she chirped in a quiet, welcoming voice, her English clear and perfect. I felt my body relax into the hard chair beneath me. "The teacher wants me to sit by you so I can help you." She smiled again. "Is your name Ruthie?"

"Yeah. How do you know my name?"

"I saw you at Sunday school, and my mom told me who you were."

"You know everything the teacher is saying?"

"Almost everything. She talks real fast, though."

The teacher, back at the front of the room, appeared to be asking for quiet as she began writing with pink chalk on the dark green chalkboard. Natalia turned her attention to the front of the room as she opened her notebook and picked up her pencil, so I did the same.

Then she whispered something so softly I was sure I had misheard her. "Hey, did you know that we're sisters?"

I tilted my head and just looked at her. "Are you sure?"

"I think so. My mom said that your dad is Joel the prophet."

"Yeah. He died, though."

"I know. Joel was my dad too," Natalia said.

"Really?"

She pointed to a little girl in the front row. "She's our sister too. She lives right by me." My mouth dropped open as I stared at a second sister. Her black hair was shoulder length and curled under at the ends. I was surprised when the girl whipped her head around and smiled under big brown eyes. "Her name is Brenda," Natalia said. "She can talk in English and Spanish too."

The teacher stopped writing, looked at Natalia and me, and shushed us. We both sat up straight and turned our attention back to the front of the classroom. But my mind was a million miles away, too excited and shocked that I had sisters at school, and nice ones at that. Besides, I didn't understand a word the teacher said.

I knew I had half siblings all over the colony, but who they were had always been a mystery. Now, in school, it occurred to me that almost every child in LeBaron could be related to me.

Natalia introduced me to Brenda at recess. She was really nice, but she and Natalia looked so different that I realized they must have different mothers. They showed me how to play hopscotch: how to draw out the squares and the circles in the sand with the tip of my forefinger and the importance of choosing a unique stone.

When we returned to the classroom, Brenda sat with Natalia and me in the back of the room, and at lunchtime we ate together. Natalia had a whole-wheat sandwich like mine, although hers was square and mine was round. Remembering the fly at the bottom of my bowl that morning, I lifted the bread of my peanut-butter-and-honey sandwich to inspect it.

The smell of green, spicy peppers filled the air the minute Brenda opened her bean-and-cheese burrito with pickled jalapeños, and when I couldn't resist trying a bite, the morsel exploded in my mouth and burned all the way down my throat. My eyes watered and my lips burned. The girls giggled at my reaction.

"Make sure to drink lots of milk when you eat peppers," Brenda said in a thick accent that convinced me that Spanish was her first language and that her mother was Mexican. "It will take the burn away. Water makes it worse."

At the end of my first day at school, I rushed home to tell Mom about my two new friends who were also my sisters. While stirring cheese curds on the stovetop, she explained that Brenda was the

daughter of my dad and his first wife, and the youngest of their thirteen children. Natalia was the youngest of three children born to my
father and his sixth wife, who was another one of Lane's sisters. With a
laugh, Mom said she felt sorry for the man who tried to draw our family
tree.

It had been a long and confusing first day of school, and I couldn't
wait to go back.

8

As the school year progressed, so did I. By December, I was singing the Spanish alphabet, I knew how to pronounce all its exotic vowels, and I could even read books if the words were short. The once rapid-fire sentences began to slow down in my mind, and when I didn't understand what was being said, I didn't worry about it too much. Much of this progress I owed to my half sisters. Because of them, I woke up excited for school every morning and walked there as fast as I could with quick, light steps.

Winter arrived with gloomy gray clouds, and the skies became damp and dim. Getting ready in the morning now meant the smell of burning wood from the barrel heater and mud-caked shoes that had once been white. Going to school meant walking past round-piped chimneys that billowed out smoke like giant steel cigarettes, and air that had grown thick with the scent of burning wood.

Meanwhile, Mom's lap became smaller and smaller as her belly grew larger and larger, and in mid-December she gave birth to a baby girl in the same Casas Grandes hospital where I'd been born. Mom's cheeks were ghostlike when she came home, and her eyes were swollen and red, but she had had fewer complications than with Aaron, and Mom brought Meredith home the day after she was born. Everyone called the new baby Meri, and we all wanted to hold her from the moment our pale-faced mother came through the door.

Meri was beautiful, with porcelain skin like Snow White and a tiny, molelike birthmark on her upper lip that made her look like a movie star. Her eyes were crystal blue, and she had long, dark eyelashes that curled up just below thin, blond eyebrows. When Mom placed the little bundle that was Meri into my arms, they naturally folded around my sister, who, from that moment forward, always seemed to rest comfortably in my lap. For this reason, Lane decided my Christmas break should start early. I was needed at home to help with the baby while Mom recovered.

The season's other new arrival was electricity in our home, at last. Lane took the same black tubing that brought current to the shop and extended it from there along the barbed-wire fence and into our house. The cable carried 220 volts of electricity, too strong for light-bulbs and appliances, so Lane connected it to a transformer, a metal box placed outside the kitchen door next to the cement porch. Next, he strung an electrical cord from the transformer through a corner of the kitchen wall and then tacked it along the beams of the wooden ceiling until it reached a white, ceramic light socket with a bare lightbulb. Cords snaked over the ceilings and walls of our home like plastic veins. But we finally had lights—bare-bulbed and bright—in every spot except the living room, which had an actual lamp with a shade.

Lane had also fixed the old-fashioned washing machine that had been lying on the floor in his shop for months. Mom said that it was from the 1940s and was older than she was. It certainly looked it, with a metal box that swiveled between two open tubs, one for washing and one for rinsing. I liked helping her push the washed clothes through the rolling pins, and squeezing the rinsed clothes into a basket, but they took a whole day to dry on the clothesline when the weather was wet and cold.

Once he'd finished the improvements on the house, Lane began going to the States more and more often. He had bought a semitruck so that he could haul loads of various types and sizes throughout the southwestern United States. He was gone for most of Meri's first months while Mom and Alejandra ran the farm. When spring came, just as the weather was turning beautiful, Lane announced he was taking a third wife, Susan. She was one of Mom's closest friends in the colony. I was surprised she and Lane were getting married. She already had eight children with a polygamist whom she had recently divorced. The church discouraged divorce, but it was common anyway. It was an easy process because most polygamists' marriages weren't legal in the first place.

Mom said she had suggested Susan marry Lane. Knowing that Lane would probably take another wife anyway, Mom decided it would be best to find a sister wife she liked. Susan and her children lived a half mile down the road from us, in a small adobe house we passed every day on the way to school. After Susan and Lane got married, she and my mom got together every other afternoon.

Between his new wife and his new hauling business, Lane had little time for Mom when he was in LeBaron. His repairs and improvements to our house came even more slowly than before, which became more and more embarrassing to us as ours was one of the only homes without hot water. We still used the stove for heating bathwater and everything else.

We were all excited when we found out that Mom had finally persuaded Lane to install electrical wiring in the bathroom to heat water for a shower and grew even more excited when we saw silver tubing running up the bathroom wall for that very purpose. We counted the days until we could take our first hot showers at home. The only thing we needed was a showerhead.

One rainy spring weekend, Lane announced that he would be

spending a night in Casas Grandes with Alejandra at her parents' home there. Mom saw this as a chance to have him pick up a showerhead. She dipped into her welfare check and gave Lane the money to buy the fixture while he was in town. It would be shower time by the beginning of the next week. We couldn't wait.

The following evening, I found myself in the living room with our oversize children's Bible lying heavily in my small lap. It was open to a page I didn't yet know how to read, but because neither Aaron, Luke, nor Audrey knew that, I took the opportunity to perform a melodramatic reading of the Noah's Ark story. I recited the tale I had heard told many times in Sunday school, waving my arms dramatically as I described the animals boarding the boat in twos while the waters rose around them. As I told my siblings about all the wicked people who had foolishly laughed at Noah only to find themselves drowning in the floods, Lane drove up in his white Ford pickup, a rusty camper mounted on its bed.

The sun had gone down outside and storm clouds were gathering. The kitchen door scraped open and hard-soled workboot footsteps clomped on the floor on the other side of the wall. Lane said hello to Mom, I heard the light smack of a quick kiss, and then he popped his head into the living room. He wore the same red polo shirt he'd had on the last time I'd seen him, and his hair was wet and combed back behind his ears. His face was freshly shaved except for his sandy-blond sideburns, which looked hard. His mouth was closed and expressionless. I stopped my performance, and we all stared back at him for a moment.

"So, what's for dinner tonight?" he asked Mom.

"I haven't decided what to make yet. Where's the showerhead?"

Silence.

"Did you buy it when you were in Casas?"

"Well, yeah, I bought it," Lane said, perfectly matter-of-fact, "but I decided to give it to Alejandra. She wanted one too."

Silence again, then Mom called for me to help get a bottle ready for the baby. Meri was four months old but had had trouble latching onto Mom's breast, so we'd resorted to feeding her bottles of goat's milk. I slapped the Bible shut over my lap as thunder roared through the dark, cloudy sky, shaking the whole house. We soon heard rain start to fall on the tar and gravel rooftop. Mom had Meri's head over her shoulder while she bounced the baby lightly and patted her back. She glared at Lane, who now sat at the kitchen table silently, his arms folded and elbows resting on the table. I could feel the tension between them as I opened the refrigerator, unscrewed the gold lid of a mason jar, and poured the goat's milk into a small saucepan on the stove.

"I gave you money to buy me a showerhead—last Thursday. From my welfare check, that I saved so we could finally finish the bathroom."

I turned to look at Mom as I reached for the red box of matches. She was biting the corner of her lower lip, looking at Lane as if he were a child, like the mother in *Jack and the Beanstalk* after she discovers that her son traded the cow for beans.

Lane sighed. "Hey, Alejandra needs a finished bathroom too," he said calmly, as if the whole thing might blow over with just a shrug of his shoulders. "Get me a glass of water, would ya?" he asked casually.

I turned back to the stove and lit the burner. The smell of butane burst out with a soft hissing sound before blue flames erupted under the saucepan. Out of the corner of my eye I could tell that Mom hadn't stopped looking at Lane. She hadn't moved to get him a glass of water either. Her mouth was stern and she was patting Meri's back faster and faster. Rainwater began to drip from an open hole in the wooden ceiling. She took an empty pan from the stovetop and placed it on the floor to catch the water from a hole that had been intended for the round metal chimney of a wood-fired stove, one that had never materialized.

Matt burst through the kitchen door at that moment carrying a bucket of fresh milk, his hair and clothes soaked from the rain. He paused in the doorway, his eyes wide as if he already knew something was wrong.

"Close that door, Matt!" Mom snapped, walking the baby into the bedroom and laying her down in the crib. "You're lettin' all the cold air in." In an instant she was back and made a beeline for Lane. She pulled a chair out from under the table and sat across from him.

"That money was *my* money," Mom said seriously, her freckled forearms stretched flat on the table as if half reaching for him, her fingers interlaced. "I saved it so that we could finish *my* bathroom before the summer. You promised you'd have it done by now."

"Well, Alejandra needs a bathroom too," Lane said, still calm. "She's my first wife, and she has more kids than you. Do you think it's fair for you to have your bathroom done first?"

Mom leaned almost across the table, her eyes squinted in anger. "I gave you *my* money to buy *my* family a showerhead." She threw her arms out and then brought her fingertips back to her chest. When she spoke again, her voice was louder. "How can you even try to excuse using *my* money to buy something for *her*?!"

Now Lane's voice matched Mom's. "What makes you think the money was yours? What comes into this family is for everyone to use. *I'm* the one who decides what to do with *our* money."

They stared at each other, both bodies cantilevered across the table. Suddenly I smelled burnt milk and turned to find it boiling over into the blue flames.

Mom twisted around in her chair. I turned the stove off and lifted the pan from the burner, but even as I did, I heard the legs of a chair scrape against the floor. Mom tore the long, black handle out of my grasp with one hand and squeezed hard on the thick part of my upper arm with the other. "You stupid kid!" she said through clenched teeth. "Can't I count on you to do *anything* right?" I felt a pinch on the inside of my arm where her fingertips pressed together. "Get away. I'll take care of the bottle."

Matt looked at me, his brows raised in sympathy. My eyelids stung with the beginnings of tears and my throat hardened. Mom hardly ever yelled at me. I was shocked.

She knelt down to the spigot that rose up from the floor, turned over the pot of burnt goat's milk into the drain underneath it, scrubbed it clean, rinsed it, and refilled it.

Aaron walked into the kitchen. He stopped, looked at Mom, then took a seat at the table as if he thought it was dinnertime.

"Why are you making such a big deal about this?" Lane said to her. "We'll get you a showerhead after I get paid for my last load. You're gonna get more welfare money. Stop complaining about it!"

Mom made a sound from somewhere deep inside her, as if she'd been angry a long time.

"*Complain about it?!*" Blotches of red began to appear on her neck and upper chest. "That's not the point. *That was my money.* Money that *I* saved." Mom took a deep breath, trying to calm herself. "Did you even stop to consider how I might feel about this?" she asked quietly.

Lane cocked his head and stood up. "It's not your money, and you don't have any reason to feel bad about this. You're overreacting." His palms rested on the table, but now he glared at Mom. "Like I already told you, the money that comes into this family is for *everyone in this family.*" He pressed his grease-stained index finger into the table so hard the entire tabletop shook. "*I* decide what happens to it." Now Lane's teeth were clenched too. "*Now you need to shut up about it . . . or I'm gonna take my belt off to ya.*"

"No! You go *get* that showerhead from *that woman* before she puts it up in her bathroom. It's *mine*! *I* paid for it."

Droplets of spit flew from her mouth as she screamed, some of them landing on Lane's face.

"The shower is already all hooked up and working in her bathroom, and I'm not going over there and taking it out. *You can wait your turn.*" He jabbed a finger into her collarbone.

Luke was standing in the kitchen entryway, big eyed with his mouth agape. I could hear Audrey too, still sitting in the living room, now moaning and rocking faster than ever before. The base of the chair slammed against the living-room wall again and again.

All I heard after that was screaming. Mom was yelling at Lane, and he yelled right back at her. She slapped his finger away from her chest and then, without warning, threw Meri's warm bottle of milk at him. We all watched it bounce off his shoulder and land on the table, then roll onto the floor, where the nipple exploded, splattering milk all over the entire kitchen, even the stove and the fridge.

Thunder continued to roar above us, and rain dripped into the pan on the floor next to the table.

"Who do you think you are?!" Lane bellowed, reaching over and grabbing Mom by the short layers of her hair. He whipped her head toward the floor and twisted her neck sideways. Mom shut her eyes tight and gritted her teeth, desperately reaching for the table so he wouldn't throw her on the floor. She tried to pull his hand away but he jerked her violently again, pulling her face toward his.

"How many times do I have to tell you not to talk back to me?!"

As our parents fought, the table shook against Aaron, who raised his arms for me to pick him up. But before I had the chance, Lane slammed Mom's body hard onto the kitchen floor. I heard the dull sound of her head hitting the cement and saw her glasses fly into the puddle of milk.

She screamed, and her hand reached for the place on her head that had made contact. "What the hell are you doing to me?" she shouted. *"What are you doing to me?"* Her eyes were swollen; she crawled frantically across the wet floor. "Kids, please help me find my glasses." She continued to sob as her cotton blouse, now twisted up, revealed the elastic of her nursing bra and a purple scar from her C-section.

Lane's hands shook as he lifted his shirt, revealing a pale, round belly that hung over his brown leather belt. His face, as red as his shirt, stared down at his trembling hands as he reached underneath his stomach. Unfastening the silver buckle, he pulled his belt from the loops on his jeans in one motion.

"If you're gonna act like a big fat baby, then I'm gonna treat ya like one."

He pushed Mom back down and straddled her bare belly, slamming his knees against the floor. I watched in shock as her shoulders were thrown backward and her head hit the cement again. Aaron began wailing with his mouth wide-open and his eyes closed tight.

"Stop it!" Mom yelled, lifting her head up. "Stop it, Lane. You hear me? Stop it right now!"

His eyes and lips open wide, his teeth bared like a snarling dog's, he pulled her back down by the hair. Matt picked up Aaron, and we all backed into a corner of the kitchen.

To our horror, Lane lifted his belt and began lashing Mom's bare belly, the leather exploding like gunshots as it snapped against her arms and shoulders. *"I'll stop it when you do what I tell you to do! You hear me?!"* He whipped her again and again.

Suddenly, Mom quit struggling. She covered her face with her hands and her body went limp, even as the lashings continued. She sobbed and screamed but no words of protest could be made out.

It was a long time before the beating ceased, and longer still before Lane got off her. For an eternity he just sat there, red-faced and breathless. "That'll show you who's the boss around here." He straightened his knees and stood straight up, still hovering over Mom's motionless belly. As he wiped the sweat from his brow, she kept her face covered and wept loudly, her body shaking from the sobs.

Lane put his belt back through the loops in his jeans and looked down at her one final time. "You shut up when I tell you to shut up. I gave the showerhead to Alejandra, and she's gonna keep it."

"Get out of here! Get out of here, and don't come back!" Mom cried out from underneath her palms. As if to obey her, Lane stepped over Mom's body, walked right past us without so much as a glance, and slammed the door. The dark, wet sky rumbled with thunder while Mom lay on the kitchen floor and wept.

We were all still frozen. Aaron's screaming had turned into a sniffle. Audrey's rocking had stopped. The house was quiet except for the sound of Mom crying, the rain falling, and the roof leaking.

Finally, she sat up on the floor and looked around, still without her glasses. Matt picked them up, rinsed and handed them to her. They fit more tightly on her now-swollen face. She thanked him weakly and pushed herself up from the floor, righted the fallen chair, and slid it under the table. She picked up Aaron, carried him from the kitchen, and called out to us over her shoulder in a hoarse voice.

"You kids have bread and milk for dinner. And, Ruthie, will you bring me a bottle for Meri?"

With that, she lifted up the tattered sheet and walked down the hall to her bedroom.

9

The potholes filled with rain overnight, and Matt, Luke, and I kept our heads down as we sidestepped muddy puddle after puddle during our long walk to school the next morning. None of us had seen Mom since she'd left the kitchen, and no one said a word about the incident the night before. We didn't even look at each other. Mom and Lane had argued before, but he'd never beaten her like that.

At morning recess, I couldn't concentrate, not even while standing in line for hopscotch. I kept throwing my stone marker outside the lines, hopping in the wrong circle or square, and had to keep repeating my turns. Natalia and Brenda asked if I was okay, but I couldn't bring myself to tell them what had happened. As I fumbled my way to the end of the hopscotch line one more time, I found myself behind a stocky, blond girl who turned around and smiled as if she knew me. She was taller and in an older grade. I had seen her on the playground before.

"Is your name Ruthie?" she asked in a sweet, high-pitched tone.

I looked up, a little taken aback that the girl knew my name. The sun had started to peek through the clouds, and I had to squint to keep the light out of my eyes while studying her.

"Yes."

"Is your mom's name Kathy?"

"Yes," I said, not feeling much like chatting but curious nonetheless. "How do you know my mom?"

"My mom knows your mom."

"Oh." We moved up the line. It was almost my turn again.

I watched as the tall girl put her hand over her eyes, spying something off in the distance. It was Luke playing basketball. He looked as clumsy and disoriented as always, taking wide steps across the court with his tongue sticking straight out of his mouth, his muddy shoelaces untied, only half of his blue T-shirt tucked into his jeans. The tall girl giggled with her hand over her mouth. For the first time, I felt embarrassed to have a brother like Luke.

"Hey, Ruthie," she said, laughing, "is it true that your mom has lots of retarded kids?"

I turned away from the game and stared back into the sun. "What do you mean?"

"My mom told me that your mom has lots of retarded kids," she repeated slowly. "That they're kinda stupid and have lots of problems."

I blinked, rubbed at my temples with my fingertips, and tried to count the number of problem kids in my family. Audrey must be one, and maybe Luke was another. Meri was too little to tell, but Mom did say that Meri had trouble knowing how to suck. To me, Aaron seemed pretty smart for a little boy. He was learning to talk and he always made Mom laugh. Matt was definitely smart. He could read. Then again, he might be retarded too because he got carsick a lot. I didn't know.

"Oh, my gosh, Ruthie." The tall girl giggled again and slapped her leg. "Are you retarded too?"

It stung, hearing that, and I thought I would cry. Maybe I *was* retarded. The thought of it terrified me and made me wonder about the times Mom had called me stupid and how everyone seemed to understand Spanish except me.

"Hey, Ruthie, it's your turn," yelled someone from behind me. I turned around and pushed my feelings deep down. No way was I going to cry in front of my friends. "Hurry, Ruthie. It's your turn," someone else said. I hopped forward, stepped on the line, and was out right away. The tall, blond girl laughed at me. I went back to the end of the line and folded my arms across my chest. I didn't want to play anymore.

As if on cue, the sound of a sputtering engine startled me out of my thoughts. Tracing the noise to its source, I was surprised to see Mom's Microbus stopped across the highway from school. I couldn't believe the bus was working! I couldn't remember the last time Mom had driven it. When the traffic cleared, she sped over the highway and into the school's muddy driveway. Her tires splashed water everywhere as they came to an abrupt stop. From the playground I could see Audrey in the front seat and Aaron standing in the back, waving at me and smiling with bright red cheeks and his thumb in his mouth, still wearing his baby-blue pajamas. Meri was in her car seat next to him, wrapped in pink baby blankets. All the schoolkids turned around to look at the Microbus. We weren't used to having people drive up in the middle of the school day.

I looked for Matt and Luke on the basketball court, caught their eyes, and we all started to run toward Mom. She didn't even turn the engine off. She just opened her door, stood up with her feet on the running board, and popped her head out over the van's white roof.

"Kids," she yelled. "Get your stuff. We're leaving."

"Mom said to get our stuff," I reiterated to the boys. We hurried into our classrooms, grabbed our pencils and notebooks, threw them into our plastic schoolbags, and ran back out to the van. I was so glad to get out of school, I splashed right through the mud puddles, and when I threw open the sliding door, it felt lighter than ever before. My shoes, socks, and pant legs were soaked, but I didn't care.

I picked Aaron up, scooted him over on the other side of Meri, and took his seat by the door. Matt and Luke jumped onto the seat behind me, and I slammed the door closed. The tires splashed through a puddle as Mom sped out of the driveway. I waved good-bye to Natalia and Brenda and looked at Mom's reflection in the rearview mirror; her face looked sticky, red, and swollen. She had obviously been crying more.

I looked at Audrey, who had a deck of worn-out playing cards in her lap. Then I knew we were going on a trip. "Hey, Mom, where we gonna go?"

She glanced at me through the rearview mirror. "We're gonna go live with Grandma and Grandpa for a while." Her voice was scratched and weak. "Do you kids want to go live with Grandma and Grandpa in California for a while?"

"Yes!" my brothers and I screamed simultaneously.

Mom never slowed down, not even for the wet potholes, and I had to hold on to the door to keep myself from being knocked to the floorboards. "When are we gonna leave, Mom?" I asked.

"Is Lane coming with us?" Matt added.

Her voice was stern. "We're leaving *now*. I want you to get your clothes ready right when we get home."

"Is Lane coming with us?" Matt asked again.

"No, he's gonna stay with Alejandra and Susan. I'm leavin' him." At this, she started to cry and fished out a tissue from the blue Kleenex box between the seats. "They can have him. He doesn't love me, and I'm nothin' to that man but a baby-makin' machine." Tears now streamed down her cheeks from underneath her glasses, and she blotted them with the tissue.

"Thank God Lane's not comin'," Matt said with a nervous, quick laugh while he chewed on the nail of his pinkie finger.

"Don't take the Lord's name in vain, Matt," Mom said.

"Yeah, Matt, don't take the Lord's name in vain," I repeated.

"Oh, be quiet, Ruthie," my brother shot back.

As soon as we got home, we crammed our clothes into plastic bags and threw them into the back of the van. Mom flattened the gray vinyl seats and packed them with quilts so we could lie down if we wanted. She bolted out of the driveway as if she couldn't get away from that house fast enough, and within a few short minutes we were on the highway headed for the Texas border. I gave Meri a bottle while I lay on the quilts and looked outside the window. I couldn't stop thinking about how we would get to see my cousins more often. They wouldn't be as far away from Grandma and Grandpa as they were from LeBaron. A rainbow rose from a mesquite field in the distance and split the gray clouds in the sky. I imagine it had been there all morning but I'd been too sad to notice it. Seeing it now, I took it as a sign from God, a sign that everything was going to be okay.

PART II

BABYLON

*Clockwise from left: Luke, Matt, Audrey,
Meri (on Mom's lap), Aaron, and me.*

10

Magically delicious. That's how I would later come to think of the time we spent in Strathmore, the tiny San Joaquin Valley town where my grandparents lived. I first heard the phrase from the Lucky Charms leprechaun on TV, who ended each commercial for his cereal with "They're magically delicious." I agreed! Before we went to live with my grandparents, I had started each day eating mush. Suddenly, pink hearts, yellow moons, orange stars, and green clover marshmallows were among my oats in the morning.

Once we pulled out of LeBaron, Mom drove continuously, all that day, night, and well into the next morning, straight through Texas, New Mexico, and Arizona, until at last the Microbus was enveloped in San Joaquin's thick, white fog. Matt and I pressed our faces against the chilly windows, seeing nothing but white as the ebb and flow of farming smells indicated a succession of rural communities along the two-lane highway. Here and there, what looked like giant, gray robotic chickens would appear—Mom said they were oil derricks—pecking at the earth before disappearing into the mist.

When we arrived in Strathmore, it felt as if we had dropped into a town in the middle of an orange grove; the air was thick with the scent of sweet orange blossoms. The neat, orderly rows of small, rectangular homes looked like an Emerald City, and at its center was my grandparents' olive-green, three-bedroom house. The manicured, lime-green front yard had two oak trees that framed the house perfectly. Grandma kept a flowerbed of orange and yellow marigolds next to the front door, along with neat green shrubs, and pink roses under the living-room and guest-room windows. From the first time I saw it, I felt warmed from the inside out.

Mom balanced Meri on one arm and reached for the shiny silver screen door, but before she could knock, Grandpa surprised us by pulling it wide-open. His gray eyes twinkled as he gazed at what must have been quite a sight—seven nomads, dirty, hungry, and exhausted.

"Well, hello there." His smile was wide enough for us to see the full extent of his perfectly straight dentures, and his voice was raspy from an old smoking habit. What little hair he had was greased back from his forehead, gray streaks across a pink landscape. "Come on in!" His shoulders shook with a short laugh, and his eyes flashed like a playful child's. His voice was tinged with hints of a Texas twang, a legacy of his boyhood in Plano, where he'd been one of ten children in a monogamous Mormon family.

Grandpa gave Mom a one-armed squeeze and welcomed each of us as we walked through the door. Then he leaned forward, gently grasped Meri's opalescent face with a red, leathery hand, and kissed her forehead. "She's a pretty baby, Kathy." He patted Mom on the back gingerly.

My grandpa kept the thermostat at seventy-five degrees minimum, so their house was always warm—so different from the barrel heater and drafty walls we had known in LeBaron. My grandparents' brown-and-white-speckled carpet—as opposed to our cracked concrete floor—made us feel cozy, insulated from the outside world. The house even smelled warm, like a breakfast of maple syrup, waffles, butter, and coffee.

Grandma stood in the kitchen, where she had been preparing breakfast, her thin forearms crossed over a pale blue housedress that she wore with matching slippers. Behind her, morning sunlight streamed through the window and lit up the big, white curls on her head like a halo. She met Mom where the living room started and the kitchen ended and said, "Well, hello there," echoing Grandpa. She closed her eyes behind silver-framed bifocals while she hugged her daughter. They separated, and for a moment Grandma held Mom at her shoulders and seemed on the edge of giving a speech. Instead, her arms went limp and dropped to her side. "You must be tired, Kathy." Grandma took Meri from Mom's arms and Mom started to cry, her shoulders shaking. She dropped her purse to the floor, collapsed onto the living-room couch, bowed her head, and rested it in her palms. I watched her and didn't understand how she could be crying when I was so happy.

Grandma's eyes resisted a glance in her daughter's direction and remained fixed on Meri. Grandma's eyes were watering too. "Oh my gosh, Kathy, this little baby girl looks just like a movie star. She even has a mole over her lip like an actress in an old movie." Now tears rolled down Grandma's cheeks, though she still refused to look up. "I swear she's one of the most beautiful babies I've ever seen, and I'm not just sayin' that because she's my grandbaby." Grandma bent forward and buried her face in the bundle of blankets that swaddled Meri.

I watched as Mom patted her eyes with a Kleenex one final time before putting on her glasses. She seemed unable to look at anyone else in the room, her head hung forward, her shoulders slouched. Grandpa sat quietly in his leather La-Z-Boy chair with his head in his hand, his eyes wide and vacant, as if he didn't have a clue what to say.

11

The following Monday morning, we woke up to Grandpa's alarm clock instead of a rooster's crow. Its soul-shattering buzz didn't so much wake us as shock us to life. Then, another shock: we had to go to a new school. The house already smelled like hot coffee by the time I was out of bed. I dressed and went to the kitchen for breakfast and found Grandpa slumped over the oval, faux-oak kitchen table with a mug of coffee at his side and his face hidden behind the newspaper. Grandma looked hunchbacked as she fried her husband an egg on the stove. Toast popped out of a white plastic toaster. My grandparents looked at us and said good morning with smiles. Grandma asked each of us what we wanted for breakfast. I chose cornflakes with sugar and milk.

"Pass the *lechee,* please," giggled Grandpa, who never tired of mispronouncing *leche* if he thought it might get a laugh, which it always did, at least from those of us under the age of ten.

Not until I'd almost finished my second bowl of cereal did Mom stride into the kitchen with her navy-blue purse straps already over her shoulder. She had on mascara and pearl-pink lipstick, and her hair was curled back. "You kids ready to go school?" she asked as she bit her pearl-pink lip. Matt, Luke, and I stood up from the table, picked up our jackets off the arm of the love seat, and followed Mom outside the front door.

I had to squint to keep the bright California sun from stinging my eyes as we made our way to Strathmore Elementary, which sat directly across the street from Grandpa and Grandma's. The walk hardly took a minute, but it was long enough to catalog a lifetime of differences between our new home and our house in LeBaron. In LeBaron, our walk to school had been along dirt and gravel roads lined on each side by sharp barbed-wire fences with crooked wooden posts. My brothers and I had walked with our heads down as we avoided potholes, kicking stones with the tips of our tennis shoes. We'd watch cows graze in green fields of the surrounding farms, picking up friends as we got closer to school, and walking with them the rest of the way. We didn't know anyone but Grandpa and Grandma in Strathmore. Instead of pastures and cows, we saw sidewalks, shiny chain-link fences, a crosswalk with bright white stripes, and stop signs so new they looked glossy.

Mom held my hand and Luke's as Matt walked on ahead, his skinny body quickly lost in the shadows of a building as wide as two city blocks. Our new school was covered in stucco and painted a neutral cream color, which somehow made its tall trees look taller and its grass greener.

At the end of a wide cement staircase lay bronze doorknobs and double glass doors. Inside the doors, phones rang, smartly dressed people talked professionally, and women with long, well-maintained fingernails tapped on typewriters. The registration office was bigger than my entire Mexican classroom had been, and it was crowded with framed photos, trophies, plaques, and green potted plants on every desk and in every corner. I was so busy looking around that I hardly noticed when Mom announced she needed to get back home to the other children and kissed us good-bye.

A school secretary walked me to the first-grade classroom, which was adjacent to the most elaborate playground I had ever seen: it had two swing sets, a teeter-totter, a monument of a slide, two tetherball poles, and a set of monkey bars. As we entered the classroom, I noticed it smelled serious—all crayons and pencil shavings—and was filled with individual wooden desks and big, round tables surrounded by shelves crowded with books. I heard my teacher's voice behind a wall of cubby compartments before I ever saw her. I liked her from that instant, and not just because she spoke English.

"I'm Mrs. Tabousky," said a tall woman with short brown hair sprayed stiff with a thick coat of hair spray. I took note of her light, lavender lipstick and black mascara and the bright pink blush on her cheeks, as well as the way her soft, warm hand confidently gripped mine. Understanding every word she said made me feel smart, and the desk I was assigned fit perfectly. I settled into it, ran my elbows over the shiny, smooth surface, and smiled.

The days flew by, and before I knew it, the school year was almost over and I had turned seven. I woke every morning to the protection of thick, warm blankets, and in the mornings when Audrey's diaper leaked, I'd never be wet or cold for long because I could always take a hot shower. After breakfast, I'd skip across the street to the playground and play with my classmates. They were nice and welcoming, not at all wicked the way church elders in LeBaron had said Americans always behaved.

One afternoon in June, the week before school was out, Mom folded her arms over her belly, narrowed her eyes, and inspected me. "Did you get into trouble at school, Ruthie?"

The suggestion surprised me. I shook my head and tried to think of what I might have done.

"Your teacher wants to meet with me after school tomorrow."

I couldn't sleep that night, I was so nervous about Mom's meeting at school. The next day was even longer. At last the final bell rang; I stayed at my desk as my classmates filed out. I spied Mom waiting in the doorway, tugging at the bottom of a tight, pinstripe blouse like a nervous schoolkid waiting to talk to the principal. Once it was quiet, the two women greeted each other.

Mom fixed her hair with her fingers, acting as nervous as I felt. "Ruthie's not in any kind of trouble, is she? I know she really loves your class. She comes home talking about it every day."

"No, no, not at all." My teacher turned to me. "Ruthie, I'm going to talk to your mom in private for a little while. Do you have anything to work on while we talk?"

"Can I color when I'm finished with my math?"

"Yes. I just copied some new color-by-number worksheets. You know where they are."

Mom observed the exchange in silence and followed Mrs. Tabousky up the aisle, where the two sat at students' desks to talk. Mom's large breasts nearly covered the cream-colored desktop, and her bottom hung off the sides of the chair. My teacher showed her a pile of papers, pointing out certain parts with the tip of her ballpoint pen. Gradually, Mom's body began to relax into the chair to the extent it could; she even seemed happy, happier than I'd seen her in a long time. At last, the women got up from their desks and my teacher waved me over.

"Ruthie, your mom and I think it's a good idea if you spend the next school year with me. Would you like that?" Mrs. Tabousky asked.

"Do I get to stay in this classroom?" I asked excitedly.

"Yes, you will be in this classroom with me for all of next year. We're going to work on your pronunciation, and I'll help you practice your reading every day."

I couldn't have been happier about the idea of repeating first grade. I loved Mrs. Tabousky, and after all our going back and forth between LeBaron and El Paso, staying in one place sounded good to me. I was dreading the approaching summer break—I couldn't imagine why all the other kids were so excited. I had an uneasy feeling that summer wouldn't be much fun.

"I like your teacher, Ruthie," Mom said as we walked home hand in hand. "Are you happy to have her again next year?—*Oh, no!*" Mom screamed before I could answer. She dropped my hand in the middle of the crosswalk. I followed her gaze to my grandparents' yard, where Audrey was running, naked from the waist up. Matt was chasing her with a pink cotton blouse.

"I think Audrey's gonna make us all nutty," Mom said to herself, her voice grave. A car honked for us to cross the street, and Mom ran toward the house as Audrey ran in the opposite direction on the sidewalk. Even though she still wore diapers and didn't talk much, Audrey's body had begun to change. Suddenly she was almost as tall as my mom and had some of Mom's curvy softness. Audrey's breasts bounced when she ran, and her nipples looked like brand-new pencil erasers.

"What the heck are you doin'?" Mom yelled. "Put your shirt back on!"

Audrey stopped short and blinked several times, her face expressionless. I felt frozen when she acted that way, and I didn't know what to do. My instincts told me to keep away from my older sister, and I stayed back at the corner while Mom and Matt approached Audrey from different directions, Mom having snatched the blouse from his hand. Even after they had practically tackled Audrey, the shirt barely made it over her head.

"Lift up your arms, Audrey. We gotta get this shirt on ya, Sis. Be still."

I made my way to them, close enough to see that Audrey's blank expression had been replaced by a delirious smile. Her moaning was emanating from deeper in her throat than ever. Her tongue licked her upper lip and lapped up the mucus that streamed from her nose. Her body was rigid as she refused Mom's commands.

"Audrey, put your arms up!" Mom said.

Completely isolated in her own world, my sister kept her arms stubbornly straight at her sides, her hands in tight fists as she rocked back and forth and stamped her feet—first left, then right, left, right. Mom kept struggling with her and finally got Audrey's blouse over her head. Matt stood behind her, body-blocking Audrey in case she tried to make a run for it. Frustrated, Mom's pale pink lips stretched taut as she pulled the blouse down past Audrey's breasts and belly.

We heard laughter from across the street. Three boys were standing on one of Strathmore's pristine sidewalks, snickering with their hands over their mouths. I recognized them as some of the boys Matt played basketball with at school. My brother's face was bright red with humiliation. He smiled, trying to make it seem as if the whole scene hadn't been a big deal, but I could see that he was blinking as he tried to hold back tears. He pulled down the brim of his cap, bowed his head, and walked back to the house with his arms across his chest. Mom panted, her chest expanding and contracting furiously as she pulled Audrey toward the door. I wished summer were over, a summer that hadn't even begun.

School had been out less than a week when Mom announced that she had found us a home of our own, a rental she would pay for out of her government assistance checks. The old house was on the other side of the railroad tracks from my grandparents' neighborhood, but well within walking distance. We were ecstatic. We knew what it meant: we were in the magically delicious land of California for good!

The house had a tan exterior and dark brown trim. In the center of the front yard was a gigantic oak tree, much taller than the house itself, with thick roots that extended across the entire lawn, making it look lumpy and brown. It was more like a tree with a house than a house with a tree. The shade of the branches helped cool our kitchen and living room all summer long.

The cement porch was the red of the fancy ladies' toenails I had seen on the TV in my grandpa's living room. The front door was dark brown with thick, glossy paint that reminded me of chocolate, and it even sounded sticky when we opened it. Inside, we discovered a spacious living room and kitchen surrounded by three bedrooms, and one bathroom—but not a stick of furniture. I thought houses came with that sort of thing. What did come with this house was a musty smell of wet wood. Our empty home looked huge, large enough to hold two families, at least by LeBaron's standards.

Mom looked happy with her choice, in part because it gave her a reason to spend each Friday evening of the summer, pen in hand, scanning the local *Gazette* for garage sales where she might find furniture, electronics, and small appliances for our new house. One of her first bargains was a secondhand TV, which she plopped down on the carpet in the living room against a bare white wall. It was the first time we ever had our own television set. From that day forward, we spent hours and hours in front of it. Mom told us we were only allowed to watch cartoons, but often she'd sit with us in the evenings and we'd all watch family sitcoms together. She'd sit with Meri resting over her shoulder, laughing at Mr. Drummond, Arnold, and Willis on *Diff'rent Strokes* and Mrs. Garrett on *The Facts of Life*. We could tell that Mom loved watching TV almost as much as we did, but she'd get angry whenever we tried to watch something violent or grown-up shows she called "inappropriate."

Not only was life different in Strathmore because of the TV, but in California we didn't have to go to church anymore. There wasn't a church close by that taught the same things we believed. Mom said she missed going to church, but I didn't. I was having too much fun.

Mom didn't have a lot of rules, and the few rules she did have, she didn't always have the time or energy to enforce. The house could get loud and chaotic. The days of grinding our own wheat, making bread and cheese, and milking cows seemed far behind us. Mom loved chocolate ice cream with nuts in it as much as we did, so there was always plenty of that in the house, along with all sorts of other junk food she'd buy at the grocery store just down the street. We only occasionally had beans and rice and never had to eat mush for breakfast anymore. On Saturday mornings, we'd sit in the living room in front of the TV eating bowl after bowl of cereal that Mom bought in large, clear-plastic bags. So compelling was the Saturday-morning cartoon lineup that none of us even noticed when Mom slipped out to go to her garage sales. Mom would leave seven-month-old Meri with us, and she'd sit on the carpet for hours and stare up at the ceiling while we watched TV.

Mom worried about Meri. She thought she should be crawling or at least rolling over. Meri couldn't even hold her head up. Around the time we moved into our new house, Mom's Medicaid application came through, so we spent a lot of that summer taking Meri to doctors to try to find out what was wrong with her. But it seemed that no one ever had any answers to Mom's questions.

One bright Saturday morning in the middle of July, Mom opened the door of my white, bare-walled bedroom and startled me. "Do you want to go yard selling with me, Ruthie?" she asked in a whisper.

Still half-asleep, I couldn't decide whether I wanted to miss watching cartoons. The sky outside my window was still pitch-black, and I was warm and comfortable in my very own twin bed. Finally Audrey and I were sleeping in separate beds, and I woke up dry every morning.

"I'll give you a dollar to spend," Mom said, sensing my hesitation. As I came to, I began to get excited about going shopping all morning alone with Mom. She never asked Audrey or the boys to come with her, and she hardly ever gave us our own spending money. I rose quietly and tiptoed out the door, wincing as I passed Audrey's bed and caught a whiff of her urine. Mom smiled apologetically. Whatever influence she'd once had on Audrey had been lost and Mom knew it. Audrey now refused to use the toilet and wore diapers day and night.

Mom drove us to the bigger neighboring towns of Lindsay and Porterville, where the streets were wider and the homes larger. The garages were so big it seemed as if we were shopping at huge department stores.

"The real yard sales have nice stuff," Mom told me as we drove down one quiet, tree-lined street. "But in some of them, people are just reselling what they bought at other yard sales, trying to get a higher price." Mom prided herself on being able to detect garage-sale wheat from chaff even from a distance. She'd slow the car as we approached every sale, but often we would speed away without even stopping, Mom having already seen that it was mostly overpriced junk. That was my signal to put an *X* through the corresponding ad in the newspaper while she unfolded and refolded an area map and found her way to the next stop.

Absent the usual distracting noise from the television, enjoying a quiet moment as Mom drove from house to house, I was reminded of the mean girl at my old school who'd talked about all the "retarded" people in my family. I started thinking about Audrey and her diapers, the way Luke wouldn't pronounce words the right way, and how Meri still couldn't roll over. I had wanted to ask Mom about the girl on the playground for a long time, but I needed a private moment to do it—and private moments in my family were rare.

"What does *retarded* mean?" I asked after a deep breath.

Mom seemed irritated by the question—she cocked her head back and looked at me with an exaggerated wince. "Where'd ya hear *that* word?" Her nose scrunched up beneath the bridge of her glasses.

"A girl on the playground in Mexico told me we had lots of retarded people in our family. She said her mom knew you and that you have lots of retarded babies."

"Who was it?" Mom demanded, turning into a new neighborhood so fast I had to hold on to the door handle.

"I don't know. She asked me if I was retarded too."

"What did she look like?" Mom was almost yelling now. She pulled over to a curb while I stumbled through a description of the girl.

"I don't know who that is." Mom realized we were lost and angrily unfolded the map. "Did she say who her mom was?"

"No."

Mom switched off the van's engine, took a deep breath, and sat back in the seat with her hands folded over her lap, exhaling slowly through her mouth. "Ruthie, your teacher says that you're real smart. She sees lots of kids, so she knows. That little girl was just bein' mean. If somebody asks you a question like that again, you don't pay any attention to them. You tell them it's none of their business and turn around and walk away." Mom looked up at me from the map with red, wet eyes. The anger had been washed away from them, and I felt emboldened.

"Why is Meri going to so many doctors?"

Mom tossed the map into the backseat, started the van, and pulled away from the curb before answering. "Meri is sick. The doctors think she was born with a birth defect, but they don't know what it's called. It's kind of like what Luke has, and they don't have a name for his either." Mom made a U-turn in the middle of the street while she fished a tissue out of her purse to blow her nose. "They have to do lots more testing on Meri to find out what's wrong and how they can help her."

"Is she gonna be sick for a long time?"

"I really don't know, Sis. I *hope* she's gonna be just fine." We drove a bit before she said, "All families have problems." She stared intently at something just over the horizon. "We just have to have faith that everything's gonna work out and be okay." She looked at me, shrugged her shoulders, and smiled. "Don't ya think so, Ruthie?"

"Yeah," I replied, not convinced.

The next yard sale was a good one, with many newer items and almost nothing broken or falling apart, although everything cost more than a dollar, so I kept mine in my pocket. Mom bought an entire box with BOYS CLOTHES written on its open flaps. She also lingered for a long time in the book section with her head bent over a box filled with beat-up, old volumes going for five cents apiece. She gathered up an entire stack of coloring books, stood up, and flipped through each to find the ones with the fewest already-colored pages. She settled on a tattered pile of treasures.

"I'll give ya a dime for all these," she said to the proprietor. They settled on a quarter, and when we were safely out of earshot, Mom confided that she had gotten a good deal. She was even happier about all the little-boy pants she'd found without holes in the knees. These were rare finds, she said, because boys played rough and usually wore out their clothes before they could be sold.

Thanks to a string of Saturdays with good sales, Mom had the entire house fully furnished before school started again. Thanks to welfare and SSI checks from the government—compensation for Audrey's and Luke's disabilities—we had a ready supply of food too, and American breakfasts soon led to American lunches and dinners. By fall, meals of beans and rice were a thing of the past. Now our favorite foods were macaroni and cheese, peanut butter and jelly, hamburgers, and french fries. I sometimes missed a few things about LeBaron—mainly Brenda and Natalia—but I loved strawberry milk shakes and having my own bed.

When first grade began again in August, I found myself in an unexpected situation: I was the tallest girl in my class. Sometimes I played with my former classmates at recess or lunch, bragging about the fun I was having in my second year of first grade and making them wish they'd been held back too. Because we were no longer living across the street, my brothers and I began taking the bus to and from school, which I thought was an adventure. I was glad to be back at Strathmore Elementary, and even gladder to be out of the house, where Audrey was acting scarier than ever.

Now twelve, her attacks came more and more frequently. Her patterns shifted constantly, so we could never know when an attack was coming or how to stop it. Mom began to suspect that what was troubling Meri was the result of an injury Audrey had caused, that maybe Audrey had picked Meri up and thrown her to the ground when no one was looking. Audrey was more than a decade older than Meri, yet Mom was changing Audrey's adult-size diapers more often than Meri's.

I looked for every reason in the world to avoid the little home Mom had made for us, and when my number one excuse, school, failed me, I took refuge at my grandparents' house. Throughout that fall and winter, I went there every day after school. I was always welcomed by Grandma's homemade corn bread, fresh out of the oven.

One afternoon in late fall, I stopped by their house on my way home from school, and Grandma was just taking a cake pan of corn bread out of the oven. I sat down with Grandpa at the kitchen table, and Grandma served us both a square piece on white saucers with tall glasses of milk on the side. She had already smeared honey and butter in the middle of mine, but Grandpa liked his plain. He crumbled his piece up into his glass of milk and started eating it with a teaspoon. Grandma stood at the kitchen sink in her light blue housecoat washing dishes.

"How come you guys didn't come to visit us when we lived in Mexico?" I asked. I loved being with my grandparents, and they seemed to love being with us, so I couldn't figure out how come they had never come to visit when we lived in LeBaron. Did they only love us if we lived in California?

Grandma stopped scrubbing the cake pan and glanced over her shoulder at me as if she wasn't sure how to respond. Grandpa set his spoon onto his saucer. "Well, it's kind of a hard place to get to from here, Sis," he said with a serious but caring tone.

"But didn't you guys used to live there too? When my dad was alive?"

Grandma dried her hands on a yellow hand towel, served herself a piece of corn bread with sliced raw onions on the side. Grandma liked raw onions with everything. She pulled a chair out from under the table and sat next to Grandpa, across from me. "Living in Mexico has been hard on your mama," she said with a hint of disappointment. "It's hard to make a livin' for a big family like yours. When we used to visit, your mama already had three little kids and was pregnant with you. She lived in a tiny, little one-bedroom trailer with no electricity. Had nothin' to eat but beans out of a big, dusty gunnysack. She never had any money and had to ask for eggs from her sister wives, or anything else she needed for that matter." My grandmother had always been open about her disapproval of Mom's way of life, but I had never heard her describe it with such sadness. "Ruthie, it broke our hearts to see your mom livin' like that."

"When your dad was alive," Grandpa added, "all of our daughters lived in Mexico. Three of them were married to polygamists."

"Your aunt Kim almost married one of your uncles who had a bunch of other wives too, but luckily she decided not to." Grandma shook her head and bit into her onion slices. The whole kitchen smelled like sharp, tangy onion and sweet corn bread. Kim was Mom's youngest sister; she left Dad's church when she was only eighteen.

"Your mama and her sisters were all livin' in tiny trailers or adobe homes, and their husbands were hardly ever home. Your mama was alone most of the time. So young and on her own with all you kids." Grandpa looked down at his glass of corn bread and milk, and the look on his face made it obvious that the memory made him sad.

"Your daddy had too many wives, and he kept marrying more, women even younger than your mama, and she was just a teenager." Grandma shook her head and a hint of bitterness slipped out of her mouth with her words. "We just couldn't believe it. There was no way he could take care of all those wives and all their little kids. And his American wives were collecting welfare in the States. It just wasn't right."

"When we joined your dad's church," Grandpa added, "we had no idea how hard a polygamist's life would be. I grew up in the LDS Mormon Church, and I always believed in its teachings. When your dad and Ervil showed up in Utah where we were livin', they asked all the right questions about Church doctrine, and I really believed they were right. And when your dad preached, it felt like anything was possible, like God was speaking right to you."

"Oh, I never believed in any of it," Grandma interrupted. "That ol' Ervil; I never liked the crazy look in his eyes. If you ask me, he was always a big nut. But he knew every scripture in the Bible and the Book of Mormon by heart. He was a big talker and he could argue any point about religion anyone ever asked him. He was like a genius." Grandma sighed, as if remembering something sad. "And your dad had so many wives and kids competing for his time. But your mom was never the squeaky wheel. She was the easiest baby and the quietest child. She never complained. Never asked for anything. Never. Bless her sweet heart. Everyone around her was always askin' for stuff, whinin' and complainin', but not your mama. She always got lost in the background, and I think sometimes she got overlooked, and somehow, for some reason, she just didn't think she deserved any better than what those worthless old men gave to her, which wasn't much."

"Awe, Tressie. Come on now. That's Ruthie's daddy you're talkin' about," Grandpa said, trying to shush Grandma. He always wanted Grandma to be more careful about what she said around my siblings and me, but Grandma was outspoken and opinionated. It was part of what made me interested in what she had to say. Grandma was always talking about how terrible my dad's church was. We all knew she disagreed with his teachings. Grandma vowed that she never converted to fundamentalist Mormonism, although once Grandpa became a convert, she had acceded to his demand that Mom and her sisters be raised in the Church of the Firstborn.

"Well, it's the truth, and you know it is." Grandma looked me straight in the eyes. "We shoulda never let her marry your dad. She was too young. Only seventeen years old. But she wanted to marry the prophet, and we had no idea how much sufferin' and hardship that was gonna bring her. We didn't want her to marry Lane either, but she was dead set on it. All her sisters had left and stayed away from the Church. We all tried to talk her out of it. We would have done anything to help her. But after she married Lane, we figured the best thing was to let her get on with her life. So I guess that's why we stopped visitin', Ruthie."

Hearing all this, I couldn't help but feel sad. Sure our lives in LeBaron had been hard—our house was cold and small and nothing in it ever worked—but we were living for God's purpose. I didn't like that my grandparents didn't believe what my mom did. What if when they died, they didn't get to go to heaven? I thought about how sad that must make Mom, and I made a silent promise to try to be better for her. She didn't ask for my dad to be killed, but he had been, and now her family had left the church. I vowed I'd be better about listening to her and doing what she asked, even when that meant cleaning up after and taking care of my siblings, which wasn't much fun.

Grandma stood up and took the dishes to the sink. "Ready to read, Ruthie?" Grandpa asked. I loved going to Grandma and Grandpa's house after school because, in addition to my talks with them, Grandpa would read to me. He and I had just started *Joseph and the Coat of Many Colors,* a book I had chosen from the Scholastic Book Club because of its shiny purple cover.

As Grandpa began reading to me about Joseph's older brothers selling him into slavery, the phone rang in the living room. Grandma answered it.

"Hello. . . . Oh, hi, Kathy. How's it goin'?" Grandma smiled and winked at me from behind her bifocals. "Yes, she's sittin' right here with Grandpa. You wanna talk to her?" Grandma didn't hand me the phone. "Well, all right, I'll tell her." She hung up. "Ruthie girl, your mama wants ya to go on home now."

Mom didn't usually make me go home that early, so I knew something was going on. I got a sick feeling in my stomach, one that stuck with me during the half hour it took me to walk back to the house. Was Meri okay? I wondered. Had Audrey thrown another tantrum? As I rounded the corner onto our street, I told myself that I was probably just imagining things, that there was nothing to worry about.

Then I saw Lane's white truck parked in the driveway.

— 13 —

I had to will my body across the porch, with its flecks of red paint peeling off the cement. I could hear *Scooby-Doo* playing on the TV, and sure enough I found Matt, Luke, and Aaron inside, sprawled out on the living-room floor. I walked right past them, deciding to put my school things in my room. The house smelled like Mom's sweet spaghetti sauce and chocolate cake. It couldn't be cake, I thought. Mom never baked unless it was someone's birthday. As I passed Mom's room, I could hear giggling from behind her door. How could she be happy to see the man who had beat her? I felt sick.

"Ruthie?" Mom called out. "Is that you, Sis?" I stared at the door. "Come on in here. Your daddy wants to say hi to you." I wanted to run as far and as fast as I could. Instead, slowly, and full of dread, I pushed the door open. She was lying on her bed with Lane, the two of them entwined on top of her wine-colored comforter. Meri was sleeping soundly at the foot of the bed.

Mom had her hair curled back and was wearing her mascara and pearl-pink lipstick. She rested her head on Lane's chest, nuzzling his blue-and-gray-plaid cowboy shirt, which barely covered his belly. My eyes fixated on his belt, which I had last seen landing on my mom's bare stomach with a skin-splitting smack.

"Hey, how ya doin'?" Lane asked casually, smiling so wide his crow's-feet wrinkled back into the sides of his short, damp hair. It looked as if Mom had just cut his hair and trimmed his sideburns. She and Lane were acting as if nothing were different, as if we had never even left LeBaron.

"Good," I replied vacantly. "I'm gonna go put my stuff away, 'kay?" Mom nodded. I couldn't get out of that room quick enough.

My confusion and discomfort were even worse at dinner, which Mom treated like a celebration. A fresh chocolate cake with thick, creamy frosting sat on the kitchen counter next to an empty box of Betty Crocker cake mix. Mom mixed a large pitcher of orange Kool-Aid and dramatically placed it in the center of the table. My brothers and I just looked at each other. We were each given large plates of spaghetti with side salads made of bagged iceberg lettuce with shredded carrots and blue-cheese dressing. I felt as if my mom had gone crazy.

The dressing made the salad smell like mold, and my already queasy stomach was doing backflips. "I'm not hungry," I said to Mom. "Can I be excused?"

Lane answered for her. "No, you may not. You eat everything on your plate. It's a sin to waste food, Ruthie."

I looked over at Mom, who had now finished dishing out everyone's supper. She smiled as she set the remaining spaghetti in the center of the table by the Kool-Aid, then she sat right next to Lane at the head of the table. He bowed his head to thank the Lord above for the food, this wonderful healthy family, and for blessing him with so many wives and children, amen. I didn't know what to think. I couldn't remember the last time we had said grace.

We opened our eyes and picked up our forks. Only Audrey did not participate, bobbing back and forth in her chair and staring at some spot over my shoulder. The Kool-Aid sloshed in our glasses each time her rib cage slammed into the table. Lane stared at the unused fork by her plate as if it were a personal affront.

"That's how she always is now," Mom said quietly. It was true. By then, it had become a struggle just to get Audrey to drink a glass of water. Mom had been making regular trips to the hospital to get Audrey fed intravenously.

Lane told Mom that Audrey was just being stubborn. "I'll handle this," he said, and directed Mom to switch places with him.

"Sit still and eat your spaghetti, Audrey," Lane said to her as though she were just a typical unruly child who could be coaxed into right behavior with firm treatment. Audrey stopped rocking for a few seconds, but then resumed banging the table with more force than before. Lane grabbed her arm roughly, as if to force her to stay still. Audrey stared down at his hand. She never liked being touched, much less like that, and she clenched her teeth, spreading her lips wide-open and expelling her familiar moan.

"Hey, now, you knock that off!" Lane shouted. Everyone went still, the tapping of forks against plates coming to a sudden halt. Then, noticing that everyone at the table was watching him, Lane let Audrey's arm go and switched to a less threatening approach. "Take just one bite of your spaghetti, Audrey. You need to eat at least some of your dinner." He picked up a piece of garlic bread and held it to her lips. "Come on, take a bite. It's not gonna hurt ya."

Audrey pursed her lips and her face remained blank. She didn't even look at the bread. "Take a bite, Audrey!" Lane said louder. He glanced over at Mom.

She nodded knowingly. "I told you. She won't eat anything. I don't know what I'm gonna do with her." Mom went back to her salad, took a bite, and shook her head.

Next, Lane lifted a forkful of sauce-covered spaghetti to Audrey's mouth. Nothing. "I said to take a bite!" he yelled into her ear. Audrey began to bob forward and backward again. Lane shot up from his chair, positioned himself behind Audrey, and held her motionless by wrapping one arm around her neck and shoulders so he could use the other to shove a fork between her closed lips.

"Take a bite!" he screamed again. I couldn't watch, but when I closed my eyes, all I heard was the sound of metal poking against teeth. Then a chair slid back from the table and I looked up again. I was dumbfounded: Mom was rushing to help Lane, not Audrey.

"Kathy, you take the fork and try to feed her," he directed, passing Mom the fork. My brothers and I watched as the two of them tried to force spaghetti down Audrey's throat. Lane grabbed Audrey's hair and pulled it back. She had to squint from the bright light above the table.

"I don't know what to do, Lane," I heard Mom say.

"I'm gonna try and open her mouth. You feed her." With the violence of a strangler, Lane tried with all his might to pry Audrey's jaws apart, his big fingers obscuring her face as the muscles in his own tightened. He wrenched my sister from side to side with so much force I thought he'd pull her head off.

Audrey won't ever open her mouth, I said to myself.

After a few more seconds, Mom moved the fork away and Lane let Audrey go. Her skin looked flushed, and she had droplets of blood on her lower lip where the fork had punctured it. After a moment of silence, Lane attacked Audrey with a suddenness that took everyone by surprise, Audrey included. He pulled her head back and shoved the fork in front of her eyes. "Take a bite or I'm gonna smack ya with this!" he yelled. "You hear me? You're not leavin' this table till you take a bite."

Audrey recoiled and her mouth came open. Lane stabbed the fork between her lips. Her teeth clamped closed on the metal, she let out a painful moan, and then all at once and without chewing, she swallowed the spaghetti. Mom pulled the fork out, and after that Audrey's face returned to its customary blank stare. I looked at Matt and searched for some assurance that what we'd witnessed was okay because maybe Audrey wouldn't remember. He nodded and lowered his eyes to his plate.

"Now, that's a good girl," Lane said, his voice slightly shaky. He glared at me and said, "Finish your salad." I looked at my plate, then quickly shoveled the whole mass of moldy-tasting lettuce down my throat, washing it down with the sticky, sweet Kool-Aid.

Lane stayed with us for three days. The morning before he left, he said that he needed to see me in the backyard. I hesitated but decided I'd better do as I was told, making my way through the kitchen with my head down as he followed behind me. I opened the back door, took one step down, and sat hunched on the top step with my arms folded over my knees. The sun burned through the fog, casting an eerie light on the brittle leaves of the lemon, orange, and avocado trees. Lane walked past me, then returned and sat beside me on the step.

He began by resting his arm on top of my shoulder, but I must have flinched because he quickly took it away. "Listen, your mom and I have been talkin'," he said in a soft, want-to-be-fatherly voice. "We think it's best for you to start comin' home right after school and helpin' your mom with Meri while your mom takes care of Audrey."

My heart sank, my chin collapsed into my hands. "My grandpa is reading me a story after school," I said, attempting to mimic Lane's genial tone in the hopes that he might reconsider. "Can I wait till he finishes it?"

He chuckled and patted my back, a gesture that made my skin crawl. The forced smile slipped from my face, although his was still intact. "Your mom needs help. Audrey's a handful, and we don't exactly know what's goin' on with Meri, either. Your grandpa can finish the book another time."

I remembered my vow to be better to my mom. Maybe I should start coming home after school to help out. Mom always seemed over-whelmed and exhausted. Her face was perpetually pale, her eyes red, and her voice raspy from lack of sleep. But the other part of me refused to obey Lane. He was not my father. He slipped in and out of our lives without warning, bringing disruption and terror with him every time. I looked at him with contempt.

The next thing I knew, he put his arm around my shoulder, pulled me toward him, and tried to shake the expression from my face. "What's the matter? Come on now. Your mom needs you." I nodded, which prompted him to pull me closer and kiss me on the cheek. I wiped my face with my sleeve, my brows twisted into a scowl. Lane got up and left me there, chuckling as he walked back into the house.

The next afternoon, I rode the bus home from school with my brothers instead of going to my grandparents'. Lane had already left by then, off to haul a load of railroad ties to Oklahoma. The phone was ringing when I walked in the house, and I continued walking while Mom answered it and explained to Grandpa that I would be coming straight home from now on. Mom then told Grandpa about some of Audrey's and Meri's latest episodes. The conversation continued for a few minutes, and as I disappeared into my room, I found myself perplexed by what Mom hadn't mentioned: Lane's visit. Of that, of the disturbing scene at dinner, of his arrival or departure, Mom said nothing.

— 14 —

Meri and Audrey spiraled downward simultaneously, and even Luke seemed to struggle a little more as he grew into a rambunctious little boy. Audrey's hostility increased by the day, while Meri's physical limitations got worse. Her body was steadily growing heavier and longer, but her head was growing even faster. The doctors told Mom that my sister had water on the brain, though they weren't sure why. Mom explained that Meri had hydrocephalus, which was why she still couldn't crawl, walk, or talk, even though she was more than a year old. Still, I adored my baby sister and loved taking care of her, especially when I gave her a bath. Her disabilities were obvious, except when she was in the bathtub. In the water, Meri seemed normal. She kicked her chubby legs enthusiastically and laughed as the water splashed in her eyes. In those moments, I recognized myself, not as the fourth of six kids in a chaotic family, but as Mom's little helper. I was a partner with a purpose, one whom Mom noticed and needed. I would hover over Meri in the tub, getting splashed in the face, laughing along with her.

Like Audrey, Meri had feeding problems. We would feed her spoonfuls of mashed bananas and watch as her tongue sloshed them round and round in her mouth until they finally slipped down her throat. The problem with sucking that she'd had since birth also worsened. I watched Mom closely as she smiled nervously and carved larger holes in the nipples of Meri's bottles, knowing that it would mean a flood of milk onto the floor or our laps when we fed her. Eventually, I perfected a technique for tilting Meri's head at just the right angle so that enough milk would run down her throat to keep her satisfied, but not so much that she choked.

Now in the third grade, Luke needed extra help at school and had started going to a special class. Mom spent extra time with him on his homework, helping him to read little words and write basic letters. His disability showed up most when he was in front of the television. He didn't know how to separate himself from the emotional intensity that played out during a cartoon's most dramatic moments. He'd lie on the floor directly in front of the set with a pillow underneath him. Anytime a character was in trouble, he'd groan from deep inside his throat while squeezing his pillow tightly or biting the edges of its pillowcase.

Other times, he would go wild, jumping up and down or thrashing around on the carpet. None of us could do anything to stop him. When *Scooby-Doo*'s heroes were chased by villains, the truth about them hidden behind ghost masks, Luke would throw himself down as if his life depended on whether the Mystery Machine made it to safety. It was like nothing I had ever seen. Matt and I used to watch Luke, look at each other, then laugh. Sometimes, his outbursts were so intense that he'd cry, especially if an animal was hurt or killed, and Mom would insist we turn off the TV, which Matt, Aaron, and I hated to do.

Meanwhile, Audrey, had become a teenager. When not visiting Meri's doctors, Mom was taking Audrey to her own battery of physicians and psychiatrists, who became increasingly convinced Audrey was suffering from multiple disorders. Not long after that horrible night when Lane forced her to eat her spaghetti, we noticed that she had started experiencing hallucinations. Audrey's doctors told Mom they thought she might be schizophrenic, but her reaction to the medications they prescribed were baffling. The doctors said that Audrey became more aggressive and violent when they gave her drugs that should have made her calm and subdued.

Audrey's behavior reached a crisis point on Valentine's Day when I was in my second year of first grade. That morning, I went to school excited about the pink-frosted, heart-shaped cookies my teacher promised she'd be serving, and the thick stack of valentines my classmates and I had been making and delivering to each other all week. Sure enough, I received more cards and candy than either of my older brothers, both of whom begged me to share.

When we got home, Aaron and Audrey were sitting at opposite ends of the sofa watching *Scooby-Doo,* as always, and the house was filled with the aroma of peanut-butter cookies. My brothers and I threw our things to the floor and bolted to the kitchen. Mom wasn't there, and we took full advantage, each of us scooping up a handful of cookies straight from the tray and devouring them before Mom could catch us.

A knock at the door stopped us in our tracks. Visitors to our house were rare, so we didn't know what to do. My brothers and I ran to the door. We opened it to find . . . no one. Luke spotted something on the porch, though, a white envelope covered with heart-shaped stickers and with a handful of Hershey's Kisses poured on top to keep it from blowing away. When Luke picked it up, we saw the letters *M-A-T-T* on the envelope. Matt ripped it open. "It's from Mom!" he yelled. Then we heard another knock, this time on the back door of the house. We opened it and found another envelope on the back porch, this one with Luke's name on it. He hadn't yet even opened his letter when we heard another knock at the front door, where we found a letter for me. The shuttling between doors continued until everyone had a valentine.

Then Mom walked through the front door. "Did you save me any chocolate?" she asked, out of breath and smiling coyly, like a little girl. We surrounded her and competed with open hands to share our chocolate kisses. "I'm just teasing." She laughed. "There's leftovers in the kitchen. That's what's good about being the Mom—I always get to eat the leftovers."

It wasn't the first time Mom had played the door trick on us for Valentine's Day, but we still managed to be surprised each year. Mom loved Valentine's Day. She celebrated it with so much gusto that I never understood why we didn't get the day off from school. In our house, Valentine's Day felt every bit as important as Christmas and Easter.

By dinnertime, we were all stuffed with chocolate and cookies—everyone except Audrey and Meri. That Audrey would refuse even sweets made her seem stranger than strange to me. But something else about her was different that day. It wasn't her rocking movements on the couch—she did that every day—but her face seemed different somehow. She kept her dry, chapped lips pressed firmly together, her cheeks pale and sunken, her eyelids puffy and red. My sister looked like a monster.

The effect was heightened by the purple and blue circles under her eyes, and her habit of scanning the living room, going from person to person, as if monitoring enemies. A quiet moan emanated from her, and when it had grown loud enough to reach the kitchen, I saw Mom peek her head into the living room and tell her to settle down. The sun had set and a February chill had descended over the house. When Mom called us to the dinner table, I stopped off at my bedroom first and put on my wool sweater.

The kitchen smelled like baked potatoes and the steak Mom had fried on the stove, but no one really noticed because Audrey was so agitated. She just stood in the entryway to the dining room, squeezing two bright red hands together. Suddenly she uttered a shrill scream. Clearly rattled, Mom led Audrey by the elbow until she was across the table from me. Audrey sat and started her usual bouncing and moan-

ing and clenching of teeth, but Mom had an unusual look of worry
on her face as she went to the kitchen to prepare Meri's baby food.

"Here we go again," Mom said, mostly to herself.

Although Audrey hadn't eaten a normal meal in months, Mom
continued to set her a place at the table and had cut up her steak into
bite-size pieces, as if my sister might one day snap out of it and just dig
in. I noticed how carefully Mom had arranged the pieces of meat, how
thoroughly she had mashed the potato inside its skin. Then I looked
up at Audrey, at her blank, unfeeling expression. She continued rocking
and moaning.

"Audrey you need to settle down and eat," Mom said firmly, walking from the dining room to the living room with Meri's bottle in her
hand. We usually fed Meri on the couch, her head propped up on a
pillow. Mom said she found it too exhausting to eat with such a large
child hanging limply in her arms.

Audrey did settle down, staring straight ahead, but this time she
clearly saw something, or thought she did. Her hazel eyes squinted, and
she shook her head at some figure in the cold air. "Uh-oh, somebody's
in *trouble.*" She spoke loudly but in a monotone voice. The window
behind me rattled. "Uh-oh, somebody's in *trouble.*

"Uh-oh, somebody's in *trouble.*

"Uh-oh, somebody's in *trouble.*

"Uh-oh, somebody's in *trouble.*

"Uh-oh, somebody's in *trouble.*"

Each time Audrey said the sentence, it came a little faster than the
time before. She bounced violently, her chest hitting the table. The
dishes rattled. Matt looked at me from across the table, his eyebrows
raised in alarm.

"Audrey, who's in trouble?" Mom asked, trying to stay calm on the
couch in the living room.

"Uh-oh! Uh-oh! *Uh-oh!*" Audrey shouted. She licked her flaky lips,
biting at a loose piece of dry skin at the corner. I had to turn my head.

A constantly empty stomach had left her breath so rancid it made me queasy.

"Audrey, nobody's there. Who ya lookin' at?" Mom asked again.

Audrey's voice grew louder. "Uh-oh, somebody's in *trouble*." Her body went rigid, and she shivered.

Mom tiptoed into the dining room. She immediately noticed something different in Audrey's face, something that frightened her.

"Audrey, there's nobody there," Mom said again quietly, hoping to charm some calm out of her. "You need to settle down now, Sis." Once more, Audrey seemed to settle as soon as she heard the word, and Mom walked over to her, smiling now, trying to make light of the situation. "It's okay, Audrey, there's no one there." Mom's voice was so soothing, and I began to settle down too. "Please settle down now, Sis."

Satisfied that the storm had passed, Mom gently placed her hand on Audrey's shoulder. Audrey reacted immediately. Staring at Mom, Audrey lurched backward, her back curved like a cobra's just before it strikes. A moment of utter stillness swallowed the room whole. Then, with explosive force, Audrey leaped from her chair, her hands lunging for Mom's hair. Gripping it with tight fists, Audrey jerked Mom's head back and caused her to lose her balance and fall to the floor. Audrey fell down on top of her, Mom's hair still firmly in her grip. Matt and I jumped up and each grabbed one of Audrey's arms.

"Audrey, let go! Let go!" Mom cried. "You kids—*get away from her.* Leave us alone! This is between me and Audrey." Mom's voice was as loud as Audrey's moaning.

Mom was determined to win this round. First, she yanked Audrey's hands from her hair and then flipped her onto her back, still holding her wrists. I couldn't help but notice how alike they looked. Both Mom's and Audrey's faces were red and blotchy in the exact same places, their lips spread the same distance apart, their teeth similarly clenched. Finally, Mom let go of Audrey's hands and rose to her feet. Audrey stood up and lunged for Mom's face, but Mom grabbed her forearms before she had the chance. Mom pushed her backward and their bodies fell to the floor again, Audrey's back hitting the choco-late-colored carpet with a loud, hollow thump.

Mom panted and pressed her face close to her daughter's. They gasped for breath. "Audrey, you can*not* treat me this way. I'm your mother!" Mom's posture was so aggressive that her glasses flew to the floor, and she began to cry hard. "You better settle down . . . or else," she wailed between gulps of air.

Audrey sat up and gently put her hands on Mom's cheeks, almost as if she felt remorse for the pain she'd caused. Then her hands tight-ened and she pinched Mom's cheeks between her fingers, harder and harder until Mom hurled Audrey's body back onto the carpet. This time, Mom got on top of her, straddled her waistline, forced her arms apart, and pinned her wrists to the floor. But Audrey wasn't yet ready to give in. She fought to free herself, kicked her legs wildly, and lifted her head off the floor.

Then something happened that was even more frightening than Au-drey's violence. Suddenly Mom's face turned scarlet and her eyes went wild. Her whole body shook. She seemed to have found a new strength within and used it to pin Audrey down even tighter. Mom's neck stretched from her collar until her face was within inches of Audrey's, and a voice both low and hoarse rose from deep within her.

"Get the devil out of you!" Mom wailed. "Get out of my daughter, whatever you are! Leave her alone. *Leave this family alone.* Get out! Get out of her!"

The room went silent. The clock ticked on the wall behind us. At last Audrey was in the presence of a force she didn't dare challenge. Her head and body relaxed into the carpet, her face still red and ex-pressionless. Eventually, Mom let go of Audrey's wrists and pushed herself up heavily from the floor, all the while keeping a watchful eye on her daughter. Audrey's body remained limp as Mom backed away and took a deep breath. Then she leaned down again, wiping tears from her eyes as she picked up her glasses.

"You kids go back into the kitchen and eat your dinner," she instructed us in a half-dead voice. All of us save Audrey marched into the kitchen and no one said a word.

That was the last time I saw Audrey for a long time. The next day, Mom took her to the hospital, where doctors decided that aggressive intervention was needed. Mom spent the whole day and evening at the hospital, and when she finally returned home, she was alone. She explained that she'd decided to have Audrey taken to the state mental institution. Mom couldn't take care of her anymore.

Mom never spoke to us of what happened at the hospital, of how it felt to be a mother who couldn't give her child what she needed, who felt forced to entrust her daughter to the care of strangers. While I knew I should have felt sad that my sister no longer lived with us, a great sense of relief slowly washed over the house once Audrey was gone.

15

A few days after the hospitalization, Mom took Audrey's soiled mattress to the dump, and for the first time in my life I slept in a room that didn't smell like urine. I was especially excited to have a bedroom to myself, which felt like an obscene privilege in my family, where privacy was virtually nonexistent. My brothers and I had been raised to believe not that Audrey was sick, but that whatever made her behave the way she did was of the devil, that she had been possessed by an evil, destructive, and violent spirit. Once that evil was out of the house, we all felt a little calmer and more relaxed.

One year later, I was a happy, healthy second-grader. I was getting better and better at reading and started reading books on my own. My siblings and I spent a lot of time on the school playground, playing tetherball or kickball for hours on the weekends and after school. We had dinner every Sunday night with my grandparents, and Grandma always made a delicious pot roast with vegetables, and blackberry cobbler fresh out of the oven with vanilla ice cream for dessert.

Most of my siblings were thriving too. Matt was on the honor roll every month, and he and Luke had friends at school they were always playing basketball with. Aaron was still Mom's smartest child. His blond hair and bright red cheeks made him stand out, and he had the kind of personality that attracted attention. His clever comments always made the adults laugh.

Still, at times Mom would reveal a deep dissatisfaction with our lives. Over that year these moments came more and more frequently. She still hadn't found a church she liked, which bothered her. Mom didn't agree with the philosophy of the Christian or Mormon churches around us, and she was never an outgoing, social person who had a lot of friends. She said she had no one to talk to about her religious views except Lane, who had started showing up unexpectedly every few months and staying for a few days each time. Mom still didn't tell my grandparents about his visits. Instead, Mom started complaining about our lives in Strathmore. She'd say that the processed foods we ate and the culture of violence and immorality we were exposed to by watching TV were standing between us and our connection to God.

In March 1981, when John Hinckley Jr. fired six shots outside the Washington Hilton Hotel and almost killed President Reagan, Mom's concerns about living in the Babylon that was the United States seemed to be coming true. But it wasn't only the assassination attempt that convinced Mom to leave Strathmore and move us closer to LeBaron, which she'd often spoken of over the previous months, especially after Lane's visits. "You kids need a healthier environment," she'd say. "You need a father figure, and we should be going to a church where people believe what we do." That the president had almost been killed was a clear sign that the long-predicted destruction of the United States was at hand.

"Did you hear about the president, Sis?" Mom asked when I came home from school that afternoon. She popped her head into the living room with puffy, red eyes and a red, sniffling nose. It looked as if she'd been crying. "Someone shot him."

I nodded. I already knew what had happened. The teacher had

brought a TV into my class, closed the mustard-colored curtains, and showed the special news report of Reagan's near-murder in an endless loop.

That evening after dinner, Mom said she needed to speak to all of us in the living room. My siblings and I piled on the couch and faced her. "I think it's gonna be time for us to move somewhere closer to Le Baron soon, probably at the end of this school year," she said as Meri flopped on her lap. The setting sun created long shadows on the brown carpet. "With the president being in the hospital, there's no tellin' what might happen to this country next. I'm afraid it's gettin' closer to the Last Days, and your Grandfather LeBaron's prophecies are startin' to come true. I think you kids need to be close to our people now, to the people who believe the way we do."

Mom's confidence that disaster was imminent terrified all of us. She paused and patted Meri lightly on the back, staring at each of us in succession. "Plus, there's nothing here for you to do but watch TV all day. I want you to learn how to work on the farm and do things that really matter. And you need to be close to your dad. It's important to have a man around the house."

Mom continued talking for several minutes, explaining how living in LeBaron would protect us from the doomsday to come. I stopped listening after I heard Lane's name. To me, going back to LeBaron seemed as bad as staying in California while disaster struck, maybe even worse. But my brothers and I couldn't protest or ask for further explanation. We just shrugged our shoulders and accepted Mom's decision. How could we argue when the destruction of an entire nation was at hand?

A DIFFERENT SCENE played out the following Sunday evening in front of Grandpa and Grandma. We arrived for supper and found Grandpa sitting in his big brown chair with a leatherbound Book of Mormon open on his lap. Grandma was in the kitchen, and the table was already set. I felt an uncomfortable quietness throughout dinner. The air was heavy all through the meal, even when Grandma served her warm blackberry cobbler with huge scoops of melting vanilla ice cream. "Just like Mama used to make," Grandma always said.

After dinner, we went back to the living room to watch *Hee Haw* on TV. Every week, Grandma would close the heavy, sage-green drapes behind the beige love seat and we'd all gather on the rug and couches. Mom sat in the rocking chair, rocking Meri back and forth quietly, as if waiting for the perfect moment to spring the news on her parents. Grandpa's eyelids began to hang heavily.

"Are you gettin' tired, Daddy?" Mom asked sweetly. "Why don't you go and lie down. Don't worry about us."

"Oh, I'm all right." She'd startled him back to life and he sat straighter in the chair when canned laughter erupted from the TV.

"You all right, Kathy?" Grandma eyed Mom skeptically through her bifocals, the lenses reflecting the images from the TV.

"Oh, I'm doin' real good," Mom said unconvincingly, readjusting Meri, who lay in the middle of her chest. "I want to let you guys know that I've appreciated all your help." She cleared her throat. "And that I've decided to move to El Paso to live close to the colony again. Lane's been comin' to see me and the kids, and we're gonna try to make our marriage work."

Neither of my grandparents said anything for a moment, but then Grandpa got up from his La-Z-Boy, turned the TV off, and returned to his seat. I looked at his face, then to Grandma's. They seemed disappointed but not surprised.

"Well, I—" Grandma stopped and reconsidered her words. "Well, we heard the kids talkin' about Lane, so we figured he was comin' around to see you guys." She fidgeted in her seat. "We figured it was just a matter of time before you went back to that place."

"Well, we can't go to the colony right away. Lane's not makin' enough money with his trucking business yet, and Meri needs to see all these doctors. We have to figure out what's goin' on with her before we move back to LeBaron. But El Paso's close enough to travel there on weekends and during the summer."

"But you got everything you need here," Grandpa said. "The kids are settled in a good school. Meri has a good group of doctors, Audrey's close by. Now why would you want to uproot everyone?"

"I don't feel like we belong here, Daddy. I want my kids to grow up around the people who believe like I do, close to the church and close to their dad."

At this, Grandma folded her arms over her chest and shook her head. "For the life of me, Kathy, I don't understand why you keep goin' back to that man. He has all those women and all those kids. How's he supposed to support all of you too?"

"Well, Mom, we believe that it's not all about the money, that it's God's will for a husband and wife to bring new life into this world even if we're not rich."

Grandma met this with a sneer and leaned forward. She knew perfectly well what her daughter believed. "There's no way that it's God's will to have one man bring so many kids into the world that he can't take care of, Kathy. You're not even legally married. You're not his wife, you're his concubine." I didn't know what *concubine* meant, but I could tell the word upset my mom.

"In my church, polygamy is a commandment from God," Mom said defensively. "I was married in that church, so I'm Lane's wife whether you like it or not." She seemed to regret her words almost immediately and turned to Grandpa. "You can't call yourself a Mormon, Daddy, and just ignore that. Joseph Smith believed in polygamy, he taught that it was the right way to live."

"Times have changed, Kathy," he said wearily.

"God doesn't change His mind, and we don't get to change His rules."

Grandma couldn't take any more. She erupted, yelling, "The Bible says that a man will leave his family and a woman will leave her parents and *the two shall become one*. It doesn't say three or four or five shall become one."

"What does the Bible say about Moses and Jacob? *They* had more than one wife." Mom gave Grandma a ferocious stare, turned, and gave Grandpa the same look. "Daddy, you once believed that Joel was the prophet. You believed in plural marriage. He was a prophet. He wasn't crazy. You both know he wasn't crazy."

"I should have never gotten my family involved with that church or that man." Grandpa shook his head. "I should have never given you my blessin' to marry him."

"You don't believe that," Mom spat back.

"But now I see how my daughters suffered, livin' that way."

"I *always* knew we shouldn't get involved in that church, but nobody listened to me." Grandma's eyes bored holes in the carpet. "And that ol' Ervil was definitely a nutcase."

"We're talkin' about Joel, not his brother," said Mom.

"Makes me sick to think about all those old men bringin' so many little babies into the world." Grandma shook her head furiously. "All those children, those little bastards runnin' round all over the place with no one lookin' after 'em—"

"Callin' those kids bastards is callin' the kids in this room bastards," Mom fired back. I could tell she was on the verge of screaming.

"Well, if the shoe fits . . . ," Grandma said.

"Oh, come on now, Tressie," Grandpa said, trying to pull everyone back from the brink.

"Now, Leo, you know it's the truth." Grandma shot him a look that stunned my grandpa into silence.

Mom sprang from the rocking chair. "Ya see? That's exactly why I have to leave here. No one believes like I do anymore." She hoisted Meri onto her shoulder, yanked a pink cotton blanket out of the yellow diaper bag, and wrapped the baby in it tightly. "I know I'm right, and in the next life, you will too. And by the way, I'm not askin' for your blessin' or permission. I'm just lettin' you know what I'm gonna do." Her head pivoted in our direction. "You kids get your shoes on. We're goin' home."

"Now, come on, Kathy. You don't need to leave," Grandpa said weakly, looking over at his wife, her eyes ablaze with anger. "Let's turn the TV back on."

But Mom was already halfway out the door. "Thanks for dinner," she called out, pushing us toward the van.

16

As much as I hated the idea of leaving California, I was comforted knowing that we weren't scheduled to move until school was out, in two months' time. But two weeks later, Mom announced she was pregnant again, and that meant we'd be leaving as soon as possible.

A few days later, Lane's white pickup rolled into our driveway. Rather than sporting its usual camper top, the truck was pulling an old wooden trailer. I ran to my bed and dug my head in a pillow as deep as I could. I didn't want to hear any enthusiasm that might come with my stepfather's arrival.

It was dark when we had finally packed up our things in the truck. The following morning we embarked on yet another journey. I trudged to the microbus, opened the sliding door, and stepped up into it.

"Ruthie, you come ride with me," Lane said.

The offer took me by surprise, and I looked up at Mom to save me. Already starting up the van, she smiled and reassured me, "Oh, go on. Go ride with him."

"I don't want to, Mom." My body was frozen in the van's doorway.

"Don't be silly. Go ride with your dad. Go on, and stop bein' a baby."

I flashed Lane a scowl as I retreated from the van. I was relieved to find Matt already sitting in Lane's truck, but when I opened the passenger door to get in, Matt told me I had to sit in the middle.

"Ruthie," Lane said, "Matt needs to sit by the window in case he gets carsick." Matt got out to let me in, and Lane motioned for me to slide my body to the middle. The seat was cold, the black dashboard was covered in jagged cracks from sun damage, and mud was caked on the rubber mats on the floorboards. I noticed on the floor half an avocado that had long ago turned black, and wilted envelopes containing letters of apparent importance were scattered below the windshield. I rested my left knee against the stick shift as I dug my fingers into the crack of the seat in search of my seat belt, finding only dirt and crumbs in its place.

"It's broken. The buckle doesn't work. Here, scoot over this way so I can change gears." Lane extended his arm around my upper back and pulled me until I was right up against him with both my legs on his side of the stick shift.

We had a late start, Mom announced, and would only have a few minutes to stop and say good-bye to Grandpa and Grandma. As we pulled up along the front yard and parked in the street, I stared at the vibrant pink roses and the orange and yellow marigolds in the front yard and wanted to cry. I swallowed and held back the beginnings of tears. Grandma emerged from the house, her eyes cast down, the tears already spilling. A sob burst from my chest the minute I saw her. I was surprised to see that Matt was crying too, just as hard as I was. He hadn't complained about leaving as much as I had, but he was clearly just as upset.

I got out of the truck and threw my arms around Grandma's shoulders so hard I thought I'd knock her down. She steadied herself, and I pressed my crying face into her neck and wanted to disappear into it.

I embraced Grandpa the same way. "Don't you worry, Sis," he whispered in a broken voice. "You'll be all right. I'm sure we'll be seein' ya soon." His eyes were wet and red when I pulled away from him.

Lane kept his distance at the end of the manicured lawn and stared down at his army-green work boots. Mostly he went ignored, but Grandpa eventually looked in his direction.

"How ya doin'?" Lane asked, trying to sound respectful.

Grandpa just nodded.

Within minutes, we were gone, Grandma and Grandpa waving at us through forced smiles and wet cheeks.

THE SOUND TRACK to our 968-mile road trip from the center of California to the southwestern tip of Texas was Kenny Rogers's *Greatest Hits,* a cassette tape that played on an endless loop. Lane seemed to have a special love for "Lucille." " 'You picked a fine time to leave me, Lucille,' " Lane wailed. " 'With four hungry children and a crop in the field.' "

But things were worse when he didn't sing. Lane tried to catch us up on everything we'd missed in LeBaron. He reported that he had three new sons, twin boys with his first wife, Alejandra, and another with his third wife, Susan. "They don't look anything alike," he said of the twins with a proud smile, his grease-stained fingers wrapped tightly around the steering wheel. "One of 'em—Alex—you can barely tell he's mine. He's got this dark brown hair and skin just like his mother." Lane let out a quick, jolly laugh. "The other guy is a little version of me, a white boy with blond hair, so we call him Junior." He looked over to see if he'd impressed us. I tried to smile. "My wives have blessed me with fifteen kids now, and your mom's new baby will be number sixteen. That's not including all my stepkids. I see it as a retirement plan. I have lots of people to take care of me when I'm old." He laughed at his own joke and seemed surprised that we didn't laugh too.

"Can we turn on John Denver?" I asked.

Lane cleared his throat and the smile vanished from his face. "Look"—he gripped my left thigh—"I know you like livin' close to your grandma and grandpa, but I think the family's better off livin' in El Paso. It's right at the border." He patted the top of my leg above my knee.

I glared at his hand until he put it back on the steering wheel.

"Your grandfather LeBaron and your dad set the colony up as a safe place for all of our Heavenly Father's people to run to when the destructions come." Lane stared off at the endless expanse of road in front of us. "We have no doubt that it will, we just don't know exactly when. We gotta at least try and be prepared." He looked over at Matt and me with a satisfied smile. "Believe me, when that time comes, your grandparents are gonna be sorry they ever left your dad's church. Our way is a harder way of life, but it's the Lord's way."

Lane continued steering with his left hand on the wheel and swept his right index finger through the air as if he were conducting an orchestra. "They're gonna be sorry, all these born-againers in the States, only havin' one or two kids per family." He made number one and number two signs in the air. "It's so selfish I can't believe it. We have to sacrifice lots to have the big families we have, but it's the right thing to do. There are millions of souls in heaven still waitin' to come to this earth and prove themselves to the Lord. Our Heavenly Father will take care of us. Our blessings will come in the celestial kingdom." I hoped this was the end of his sermon, as I had heard it all before. But he was just getting wound up. "All the lazy American men sittin' around TV sets, drinkin' beers and smokin' marijuana, never doin' anything good with their lives. I know your mom doesn't want that kind of life for you two."

Out of the corner of my eye, I saw Lane glance at us, but I kept staring straight ahead. "Even the LDS Mormons here in the States don't have all the kids they should have. They don't even live polygamy. They wanna say Joseph Smith was the prophet and then wanna forget what he preached, that plural marriage is one of God's most important commandments. It don't make no sense." He shrugged his shoulders.

Lane continued to ramble for the better part of an hour. I did my best to disappear inward, occupying myself with thoughts of the life I'd left behind. I thought about my school and the friends I had made in California. I thought about how sad I was not to be finishing second grade. And I thought about Grandma and Grandpa and how I'd miss Grandma's freshly baked corn bread and reading stories with Grandpa. At last Lane was winding down.

"Can we turn on John Denver?" I asked again.

This time Lane grunted in response and switched the cassette tapes. Soon he was singing along, belting out "Country Roads." *Take me home to the place I belong.* Exactly, I thought, if only Lane would turn the truck around.

— 17 —

Eventually we pulled off in a small town in the middle of nowhere. We stopped to have lunch at Safeway, the only grocery store we could find. Mom and Lane had carefully apportioned our food stamps so they would last until the end of the trip. Alleviating Matt's car sickness by rolling down the windows had left my hair in a mass of complete tangles, and as soon as I could, I asked Mom if I could ride with her. She smiled at the rat's nest on my head and said that would be fine, she needed help with the baby anyway.

Luke didn't complain when Mom told him to take my place in Lane's truck. I lay in the back of the van next to Meri, and soon we were back on the highway. We made it to Arizona by nightfall, and the air turned cool. Meri was curled up in a wool blanket next to Aaron, so I crawled up into the passenger's seat and sat shotgun, a privilege usually granted to my brothers.

The yellow moon that night cast a dim light over the sandy, cactus-covered landscapes. Here and there, mesquite trees and tumbleweeds appeared on the sides of the road and then disappeared. Like the valley of LeBaron, it was a place of desolation but also of beauty. I started thinking about my father. Mom hadn't talked much about him while we lived in Strathmore. As much as I preferred Strathmore to LeBaron, I knew my father had believed in his visions and wanted his followers and families to live in Mexico, even though it was a harder way of life.

This highway, smooth and wide, was nothing like the ones in Mexico. In the side view-mirror, a quiet, endless line of headlights stretched for miles along the rolling hills behind us like a flowing river of lights. It was serene and exhilarating, exactly what I imagined my life would have been like if my dad were still alive.

I looked over at Mom, drinking water out of an empty yogurt cup, hunching exhausted over the steering wheel, her life like a constant trip with no arrival point.

"I wonder about my dad," I said.

"Wonder what?" Mom's mind was obviously somewhere else.

"What happened to him?"

"You know what happened, Ruthie."

"No, I don't. Not really."

"I've never told you? I must have told you."

I shook my head. "I heard in Sunday school that Uncle Ervil shot him, but that's all. Everyone says Uncle Ervil was a mean man, that's why his name is so close to *evil*."

"Well, that's part right, but Ervil didn't exactly pull the trigger." As cars continued to rush past, Mom groped for a bag of sunflower seeds on the dashboard, handing it to me and holding out her palm. I poured a few seeds into it while she kept her eyes on the road. It was a habit of hers on long car trips: cracking sunflower seeds in her mouth and fishing out the center kernel kept her awake and attentive.

"Ervil was the second-in-command of your dad's church, and—"

"Why was Ervil a part of the church if he was such a bad person?"

"He wasn't always that way. For most of their lives, Ervil and Joel were the two closest in the whole family. When they were little, people used to think they were twins, they looked and acted so much alike. And they were only eighteen months apart. When Grandfather LeBaron died and left his priesthood to your dad, he and Ervil worked side by side to build the Church of the Firstborn together with your dad as the prophet. Ervil was a missionary too. He was a good man till he and your dad disagreed about how to run the church, and your dad removed him from being patriarch."

"But if he was good, then why—"

"It wasn't an easy decision for your dad to make. He let things go on for a lot longer than he would have if Ervil hadn't been his brother. People in the church started noticin' that Ervil was spendin' lots of money on himself, wearin' nice clothes and drivin' nice cars even though he had thirteen wives and all his kids to support. There was no way he could afford those things on the money he was makin'. Everyone knew that."

"He was takin' money from the church?"

"That's right, Ruthie, and the church didn't have much of it to begin with. Heck, my sister wives and I were survivin' on a gunnysack of pinto beans and some eggs—that was it. I was livin' in a one-bedroom trailer with three little kids. *And* I was pregnant with you."

I thought of Mom living off gunnysacks of beans and remembered how Grandma had once said that Luke's and Audrey's disabilities were likely the result of poor nutrition. I heard her voice in my mind again: *Makes me sick to think about all those old men bringin' so many little babies into the world and not takin' care of 'em.* My grandma seemed smarter than my mom.

I poured some more water into Mom's yogurt cup, and she chugged it down before continuing.

"Once he was removed from office, Ervil started preachin' that *he* was the real prophet and that your dad was a *false* one. Your dad was never a fanatic and encouraged his followers to make choices for themselves. Ervil was the opposite. Your uncle started claimin' that he had the authority to shed the blood of anyone who didn't do what he told them to do. Your dad told him that there was no way they had the right to start killin' people. By the time you were born, Ervil and your dad just couldn't get along anymore. Ervil went and started his own church with those people, and he took a few Firstborners with him."

"Why did the people believe Ervil if he was a bad man?"

"Well, Sis, people didn't know that at the time. Ervil was real smart and he was a big talker. He was tall, had these huge hands, and he towered over everyone he talked to. He knew all the scriptures and knew how to twist them to make your dad look bad. Plus, members of the church were gettin' discouraged because there was never any money, the farms we were plantin' were young and not producin' much of anything, and most of the men had to take construction jobs in the States to support their families in Mexico." Mom opened her mouth wide in a yawn, sucked in the dry air, and covered her mouth with a flat palm. She shifted in her seat and rubbed the side of her forehead with her fingertips as if she had a headache.

"We heard rumors that Ervil had been threatenin' your dad during his church sermons, tellin' his followers that your dad needed to be removed so that the church could fulfill its purpose." Mom took in a deep breath and shook her head. "Your dad knew somethin' could happen, but of course he had no idea when or where it would take place."

Mom yawned again and her eyes glistened in the darkness. She inhaled deeply, her belly expanding until it reached the steering wheel. "We were on our way to LeBaron for church conferences. Your dad had been preparin' for them for weeks. He was drivin' a big truck with a camper on the back with me and my four kids and my sister wife Lisa and her five kids. The older kids were all piled in the back. Lisa and I both sat up in the front with your dad, and I had a nursin' baby."

I did a tally on my fingers—twelve people in one truck. "I was there?"

"You were the one I was nursin'." Mom laughed. "I was holdin' you on my lap, sweatin' like a pig, it was so hot. Your dad told us he'd promised to stop by and help a friend fix his car. But when we got there, it was clear that nobody was livin' there. The place was completely empty. That was our first clue that somethin' wasn't right."

I sat mesmerized by Mom's voice while I studied jagged cracks in the black dashboard that looked like lightning bolts.

"An old, broken-down car was in the front yard with two men sittin' in it, young Mexican boys who belonged to your dad's church. They nodded their heads hello, smilin', and tipped their cowboy hats at us. Your dad asked if there was a car here that needed fixin', and they said, yes, this one here, but they'd accidentally left the keys for it at a house down the road. They asked my sister wife and me to go with one of the young men in his truck and fetch the keys. Your dad told all of us to go with the boy and we did." She exhaled a long time. "That was the last time I saw your dad alive."

"What happened?"

"Everybody hopped into the guy's truck—Lisa, me, and all the older kids, except for Lisa's son, Ivan. He stayed behind to help your dad. Poor kid. He was only about ten or twelve, I think. We drove around with the Mexican guy for what felt like an hour. Lisa and I looked at each other. We didn't know what was goin' on. Finally, the guy said he couldn't find the house he'd been lookin' for and asked if we wanted to stop at a little taco stand for lunch. Lisa and I didn't have the money to buy everyone tacos, so we left the guy there.

"We walked all the way back to the empty house, and all along the way these cars passed us on the road going real quick. When we got back, the place was surrounded with flashin' lights and police cars, police takin' pictures and holdin' back this huge crowd."

Mom yawned again. Lane was just ahead of us now, and she flashed her headlights off and on to get his attention. She was too tired to drive any farther.

"Ivan ran through the crowd of people cryin' and said that your daddy was dead, that they shot him and that he was dead." Mom shook her head and flashed the lights again. Lane hadn't gotten the message. "I couldn't believe it. I didn't believe it. Lisa talked to the police. She was a lot older than me and she knew how to speak Spanish pretty well. I had to see what happened for myself. I had you in my arms and pushed my way through the crowd. I walked into the front door but he was gone. They'd already taken his body away.

"The house had green walls and all of them were bare. There was nothin' in the place but a broken chair in the middle of the floor next to a pool of blood. Ivan had been waitin' in the broken-down car for your dad. He said he heard the two shots that killed him, said that your daddy put up a fight to the very end. And Ivan said he saw three of Ervil's followers leave through a side window. We later heard that Ervil was sittin' in an air-conditioned movie theater, watchin' a movie while his murder plan was carried out."

I couldn't believe that my life had begun with that kind of story. I felt so sad for Mom, thinking of her with all of us and a dead husband. And I felt so sad for myself because I never got to know my dad.

"Ervil was arrested in Ensenada," Mom said. "He was found guilty at first, but then they let him go. The judge said that they didn't have enough evidence against him. Our people believe that Ervil bribed the judge, but no one knows what really happened."

A blue sign announced a rest area. Mom turned on her blinker and sped up to pass Lane. "It wasn't long after that when Ervil and the Ervilites started threatenin' us. He started havin' his people murder polygamist leaders all over Mexico and the US. He even wrote letters to the president of the United States, threatenin' him if he didn't recognize Ervil as God's prophet. It was just unbelievable."

As Mom passed Lane's trailer and truck, she gripped the steering wheel with both hands and leaned her body forward, squinting her eyes at the yellow headlights that cut through the darkness.

"Ervil is finally in jail now in Utah. They caught him after seven years of killin' people and finally found him guilty for murder and attempted murder. The reporters on TV called him the 'Mormon Manson.'"

"What does that mean?"

"It means that Ervil never pulled the trigger himself but ordered his followers, even his wives and kids, to kill people, over twenty-five of them. Your dad was the first victim. But Ervil's followers are still out there, so we still have to be careful."

She took the off-ramp toward the rest area that was quiet as we wound our way toward the parking area.

"I loved your dad," Mom said suddenly, as if interrupting herself. "I never wanted anything more in my life than to marry him. I got to spend the night with him on my twenty-fourth birthday, the day before he died. I was so tickled." She looked at me and smiled. "I didn't get to spend a lot of time with him. He had so many kids and wives and was workin' in the church almost all the time. And even when he wasn't, people were always stoppin' by one of his homes lookin' for him. I never saw him turn anyone away." The Microbus came to a stop and she turned off the ignition. "Believe it or not," she said as if to end the story, "being married to your dad was a lot harder than being married to Lane."

"Really?" That seemed impossible.

Mom parked the van and Meri started to squirm under the blankets behind us. "Oh, yeah. Seems like I was always cravin' your dad's love and attention. I couldn't get enough of it."

Lane appeared at Mom's window and she rolled it down. "You want to stop for the night here?" he asked.

"Yeah. I'm too tired to keep drivin'."

"That's fine with me. I could use a break too."

He stepped away, and Mom opened her door. "I'll get the beds made up."

Everyone had blankets and a spot to sleep when she was finished arranging the van and moving sleeping bodies around. Matt and I lay in sleeping bags on top of cots in the open air as the traffic whizzed by. I stared up at the stars and wondered what it meant to crave attention. What was so important about it that Mom actually looked for it in Lane?

We arrived in El Paso in late afternoon. The May air was hot and thick with the smell of asphalt, but it was much better than the air in the Microbus, which was like a furnace. By the time we drove off the highway, into a neighborhood, and then into a driveway alongside the camper that would serve as our temporary home, my hair was drenched in sweat.

The camper we pulled up next to would have fit snugly onto the bed of a pickup truck. The lightweight tin was painted white, and its edges had rusted into reddish brown dust. It wasn't designed to sleep seven people. Lane's brother Gary lived in El Paso, and Lane had unloaded the camper onto a slab of concrete behind Gary's convenience store. Lane explained that this was his "little home" when his work brought him to El Paso. All I could think about was how happy I was that people couldn't see the dilapidated heap of metal from the street.

A short, narrow hallway was just inside the door with a two-burner electric stovetop on one side and a compact fridge on the other. Thanks to electrical hookups, they both worked. But the toilet didn't, so it was back to primitive living and a five-gallon paint bucket for us. I thought that with Audrey's departure my days of living in a urine-scented room had passed, but the stench from the little bathroom permeated the entire space.

The sun had set, and Mom told us we only had time for a quick bowl of cornflakes before bed, which was fine with me. I couldn't imagine there was much else we could do in that cramped tin can. Matt and Lane unscrewed the white tabletop and laid it between the foam plastic seats, creating a full-size bed that Mom covered with a quilt. This was where Matt, Luke, Aaron, and I would sleep.

Meri slept with Lane and Mom on the top bed, a mattress inside a narrow compartment that ordinarily hovered over the cab of the truck. Lane waited to turn out the light until everyone else was in bed and undressed to a pair of tight, white briefs. He stepped over us to pull the thin string connected to the bare lightbulb overhead. Seeing him in that moment, the deep farmer's tan on his arms, the pasty whiteness everywhere else, made me fell that familiar nausea in my gut.

Still, nothing prepared me for the next morning, when we got our first glimpse of what would become our new home. Mom said Lane had found a single-wide trailer that he was hoping to purchase with money borrowed from Mom's parents. He drove us across town in the Microbus to see it. We arrived at a large, fenced-in lot that looked like a trailer-park graveyard. All around us were single- and double-wides with doors wide open and hinges falling off. On some, the roofs had been partially torn away, as if giant can openers had abandoned their work midstream. Others had broken windows and drooping, white tin walls with pink and yellow insulation that sprang from every crack.

For a moment, I thought that this might be the last straw between Mom and Lane, especially when I noticed the look of horror on her face. She sat in the driver's seat with Meri in her arms, her mouth open and her eyes wide under her glasses. I thought she had stopped breathing for a few seconds. "Lane," Mom said with a gasp, "what kind of place . . . are we movin' into? This looks like a junkyard."

"One man's junk is another man's treasure," he said, chuckling, not missing a beat.

Mom didn't smile and neither did the rest of us.

The Microbus stopped in front of a single-wide with solid-white outer walls and light brown trim framing the windows and roof. The front door was several feet off the ground, and even though no steps led up to it, it looked nice compared to the other trailers. But when Lane opened the front door, a strong smell of burned plastic and wood greeted us. The entire interior had been scorched almost beyond recognition. The plywood walls and linoleum floors were the color of charcoal, and fire had burned through the living-room carpet into whatever was underneath it. The ceiling was black too, and the only surviving overhead light fixture was covered in soot.

Somehow, Lane seemed excited. I didn't feel the need to see more, but he hoisted me up through the doorway anyway, and my white sandals landed in a pile of ankle-deep ash. "Don't get your clothes and hands all dirty," he cautioned as if it were avoidable.

Mom stayed silent, entering the trailer with one high step, Meri still limp on her shoulder. Black dust from the burned carpet rose from Mom's feet as she perused the living space, biting the corner of her lower lip. She was in shock.

"This . . . looks like it'll take . . . a lot of work and . . . money to fix up."

"Well," Lane said, still genial, "I can replace all the walls and floors and roll the linoleum down myself. I might need some help with the carpet, but it doesn't need that big of a piece. And I can fix any electrical problems this place has just like I did at my homes on the farm." My mind was flooded with memories of live wires sticking out of the ground and cords snaking up and down walls.

Lane motioned for Mom to come see the two bedrooms and bathroom, but she stayed planted in the living room. I studied her face as my hand brushed over pink insulation, which made my skin itch.

Still, Lane's confidence never wavered. In fact, he was beaming.

"Nice thing about this place is that the structure is still in good shape. I just have to build around it."

Mom's jaw dropped.

Lane tossed a sympathetic arm around her shoulder, caressing her back with his palm. "Think your parents will let ya borrow the money?"

"I don't know, Lane." She looked up at the filthy ceiling. "I don't know if this is a good idea."

He chuckled again. "Oh, come on now. Don't be silly. I can fix this place up real nice. Nothin' to worry about."

"Where will we move it to? We can't live here." She pointed out the door at the surrounding mess of homes.

"We can find a rental lot at a trailer park and get it towed." Now Lane sounded agitated. "People move trailers all the time. It's no big deal."

"Yeah, I guess you're right," she said, deflated. That afternoon, she called my grandparents from a phone in Gary's store, and they wired her the money the next day. Lane located a trailer park with an empty spot to rent and commenced work on the project. Meanwhile, we would live in a cramped, boiling camper for two weeks.

The school year was almost over, but Mom signed us up anyway. It felt as if no one wanted us there. I couldn't blame them: it was weird to be joining the second grade in a new school with only a few weeks left before summer vacation. The teacher barely said hello the first day I entered her putty-colored classroom. "You can sit there," she said, pointing at a vacant chair, her voice raspy and monotone. The air smelled like Vicks VapoRub. She cleared her throat, spit into a tissue that she then hurled into a wastebasket already full of soggy tissues, and went back to her work.

I looked over at the three other girls at my four-desk pod. They took their cues from the teacher, neither smiling nor acknowledging me in any way. I sat uncomfortably in my hard plastic chair. *This is going to be a* long *few weeks,* I thought.

At last our trailer was done, and Mom took us to see it after school on a muggy Friday afternoon. The mobile-home park, just off Alameda Avenue, a busy four-lane road, was a small neighborhood of clean, well-kept mobile homes. Each space had a swept and tidy concrete parking spot and, next to that, a small patch of lawn. As we pulled up to our trailer, I noticed that our lawn was the only dry and yellow one. A hammering sound came from inside, and as we climbed the new plywood steps, I dreaded what we would find.

Mom held the door open for me, and now it was my turn to gasp. It was astonishing. The inside looked brand-new, with only a faint hint of the old burnt smell. Lane had installed shiny glass fixtures on dark brown plywood walls, and the ceiling had been painted a blinding white. The new carpet was dark with brown, tan, and white speckles, and the new windows were open to the sunlight and a light summer breeze.

Luke and Aaron ran up and down the hall, opening and closing doors in all the rooms. Lane came out from the bedroom with a hammer, and his torn jeans and polo shirt were covered in white spots of paint. He smiled at us through bloodshot eyes and informed us that he'd been up all night working, saying that although there was still a lot to do, we could move in over the weekend. Mom's face lit up.

The period of remodeling was the longest time I ever remember Lane spending with our family at one time, and I was disappointed in Mom's excitement at all his attention. This was obviously not the end of their marriage. Worse, he also started to pay more attention to me. He seemed to be always looking for reasons to spend time with me alone. He needed me to ride with him to the hardware store, he said. He needed me to hold something while he hammered. And he needed me to sit on his lap, something he never asked me to do whenever Mom or my brothers were around. He began to kiss me on the lips when he said good-night. Aaron's bedroom and mine didn't have a door on it, so he'd just slip right in without my realizing it until he was at the edge of my bunk bed. It always startled me and made my stomach feel sick. I used to ask Mom if I could stay home with her when Lane wanted me to go with him, but she always just said, "Oh, go on. He needs your help," in a way that made me think all she wanted was for me to like him.

At the beginning of summer came unexpected good news: Lane had been hired to haul a load of something to Oklahoma and would be gone for several days. My sense of relief was overwhelming.

Mom then invited inspectors from HUD to appraise the trailer. This wasn't a coincidence. Her goal was to get the government agency to pay for at least part of the lot we had rented for it. She thought she had a better chance of succeeding if she applied as a single mother, which was what she had to pretend to be for the inspectors since she and Lane weren't legally married. I listened, confused and stunned, as my deeply religious mother told the men from HUD that she didn't know who the fathers of her children were. Mom would rail against us kids' lying, telling us what a horrible sin it was, but it was clear from her performance that she was good at it herself. She spoke to the inspectors with a straight face and made full eye contact. I don't think they ever suspected.

They were more suspicious of the trailer itself, which in spite of Lane's hard work was not up to code. It took a government agency to state the obvious: a two-bedroom, one-bath trailer was too small for a family of six, seven if you counted the baby on the way (Lane, of course, wasn't supposed to be living with us). Our trailer failed the inspection.

Lane returned from his trip and spent the first part of the summer building a new bedroom off the back door of our home. He did the best he could with the add-on—our trailer looked as if it had a square tumor—but HUD was satisfied, and we passed a second inspection.

Now we had a third bedroom, one large enough to hold a crib, a dresser, and a full-size bed. Aaron and I shared the back bedroom, which had bunk beds—mine on top, his on the bottom—and old sleeping bags Mom had repurposed as comforters by sewing a set of *Sesame Street* sheets over them. A curtain made from the same material was on the window next to my bed. My brother and I shared the built-in dresser on the opposite wall, and we each had our own closet.

Other than our home in Strathmore, that single-wide was one of the nicest places we ever lived. Lane's generosity when he built it was real, although not any more real than the nightmares he would later visit on me.

— **19** —

Eventually, our mobile home became sort of a truckers' rest area for Lane, a lot like the camper before it. In addition to his jobs, he was also visiting his other two families regularly. Mom must have known what his schedule was, but she never shared it with us, so I never knew when to expect him. He might suddenly appear at any hour of the day and create a whirlwind of activity around what he needed: a warm meal, clean clothes, a shower, and a haircut. Mom would drop everything for him, only to find that he was leaving the very next day.

One night that summer, Lane arrived home late and the entire house was asleep, or at least it was until the door's squeaky hinges woke me up. Groggy, I repositioned myself in the bed and caught slices of moonlight shining through the window. Then I heard the shuffling of footsteps. They grew louder and louder. I lifted my head just slightly, and there he was, standing at the threshold of my room. I heard Aaron's slow breathing on the bunk below me, and a soft spot in the floor squeaked as Lane walked into our bedroom. I laid my head back down slowly, then carefully pulled my comforter up until it was over my head.

My nose was pressed against it and my eyes were wide-open as I stared through the stitches and tried to see if he was coming.

My stomach tightened and my shoulders grew tense. I drew in shallow breaths and strained my eyes but couldn't see anything. I heard footsteps. They grew louder, then stopped at the edge of my bed. I flinched when I suddenly felt Lane's hot breath enter my ear.

"What are you doin' awake?"

I moved my head away from him but didn't answer.

"Hey," he whispered. He peeled the covers from over my head. I kept my eyes closed tight. He shook my shoulder in its pink cotton nightgown. "What's the matter with you?" He sounded as if he was chuckling, as if he was amused by my fear.

"You scared me," I said, trying to make myself sound as big and brave as possible.

"Don't be afraid. I'm not gonna hurt ya." His voice was reassuring, deep, gentle, and calm. "I just wanted to come in and say good-night before I went to bed."

I wasn't too young to know that I'm-not-gonna-hurt-ya could mean the opposite. I imagined myself making a run for it, pouncing over the bed frame, down the hallway, and into the night. Instead, I whispered, "I think you're gonna wake up Aaron," and hoped that Lane would walk away.

Lane ignored me, leaning over my bunk with his unshaven face and lowering it toward my lips. I closed my mouth tightly and sucked in. My resistance to his kisses had become like a game for him. I'd resist, and then he'd beg me, and then he'd try to kiss me again, and then he'd repeat the cycle until I gave in and kissed him back.

"You're not very welcomin'." His lips again pecked my closed mouth. "Aren't you happy to see me?"

I felt the comforter move and his fingers work their way along its edge till they'd reached my bare neck. It was July and the heat of the covers made me dizzy. Lane bent forward to kiss me again, and when he did, I felt his fingers reach under my nightgown until they found my tiny chest.

He drew in a deep breath. "Now that feels nice."

"Leave me alone," I whispered. I wanted to spit in his face, to run into Mom's room and scream.

"Feels like you're going to need a bra soon," he said, ignoring me, stroking my chest from one nipple to the other.

"Leave me alone." I grabbed his little finger and pulled it out of my gown, but my resistance only seemed to excite him. He freed his hand and slipped it back under my gown. "I don't like that, Lane."

"You might not like it now, but when you get married, you're going to love it when your husband touches you there," he whispered. "We should practice so you know what to do. You'll like it when he touches you here too." He reached down deeper, lifting up my nightgown, and put his hand inside my panties. His skin smelled like copper, as if he'd been sweating pennies all day. He scratched me with his calloused fingers as his hand slipped between my legs. "Does that feel good?"

"No!" I spat back in a loud whisper, tears rolling down my cheeks. "I want you to leave me alone!" I pulled hard on his hairy forearm, desperately trying to remove it. The bed creaked.

"Settle down, now," he shot back, suddenly nervous that he might be discovered. "You do what you're told. Be a good little girl. This will help you relax."

The next minutes felt like hours. Lane kept his hand between my legs, but all I could feel was the rapid pounding of my heart. Finally, when I could take no more, I said, "I'm gonna tell my mom."

The words hit their mark. Shocked out of his trance, Lane jerked his hand from beneath the covers. "No. You can't, Ruthie. She's too sensitive. You'll hurt her feelings if you tell her." Now it was he who struggled to keep his voice down, he who was desperate. Thinking quickly, he promised to buy me an ice cream cone the next time he was in El Paso, but only if I didn't tell Mom. "Does that sound good to ya?"

I didn't care about ice cream, but I knew Lane wouldn't go away until I vowed to keep his secret. I agreed that I wouldn't tell. As soon as he moved away from my bed, I heard him limping across the soft floor. But I promised myself that I would tell Mom what had happened just as soon as Lane left town. He opened Mom's bedroom door, and then it tapped closed behind him, and at last I knew the ordeal was over. My body wasn't convinced, though. I felt numb and tense. I put my head under my covers, curled my legs up, and wrapped my arms around them. Suddenly, my hands felt cold, *freezing* cold. I began to shiver. It was as if I'd been frozen from the inside out. I held myself and cried till morning.

Lane had already left town by the time I woke up. I walked into the kitchen and found Mom repairing her glasses.

She worked with a tiny screwdriver, her eyes squinting as she tightened an earpiece. She looked up at me. "Is that you, Sis? I'm as blind as a bat without these things. Good mornin', Ruthie. You look tired. Are ya feelin' okay?"

In the morning light, Mom looked like a fragile old lady. I hesitated. "Yeah, I'm fine."

"Are you sure?" Her voice was warm and soft.

At that moment, my brothers walked into the kitchen in their pajamas, stretching as they poured their bowls of Corn Chex.

I looked down at my sandals. "I'm okay," I said, not looking at Mom.

As the day went on, I began to have doubts about the previous night's events. My stomach twisted into knots when I thought about what had happened, and then I found myself questioning my memory. I went through the day with a sick stomach and a numb mind, my hands still freezing.

That night, as I always did when Lane was out of town, I lay in Mom's bed with a library book. This time I only pretended to read while Mom finished getting herself ready for bed. Eventually, she got under the covers, propped up her head on two pillows, and opened her book. My mom loved steamy romance paperbacks. The glossy covers always featured photographs of strapping, muscular men in the throes of passion with beautiful, thin-waisted, big-bosomed women wearing low-cut blouses and loose skirts that flapped in the wind.

As Mom read, I trembled inside. Finally, I turned to face her. "Mom?"

She lowered her book from her face, laid it open over her chest, and looked down at me from beneath her glasses.

"Uh . . . I have something to tell you." I bit the inside of my lower lip just the way she did when she was tense.

"What's that?"

I found myself hesitating the way I had that morning.

"Come on, Ruthie, spit it out. You can tell me."

I felt my mouth open. "When Lane was here last night . . ."

"Yes?"

"He-he-he . . ." I swallowed.

"He what, Ruthie?" Mom's eyes narrowed but her voice remained soothing.

Suddenly it all just tumbled out. "He touched my private parts." I sighed with relief.

Mom's eyes widened. She looked completely stunned. She closed her book, set it on the nightstand, and sat up straight in the bed. "Are you sure about that?" Her voice sounded higher than usual, questioning, uncertain. "Was it an accident? When did he do that?"

Mom's skepticism threw me off-balance and I began to question myself all over again. "Um, I think it was when he came home last night."

"Which private parts did he touch?"

"He touched me here." I pointed. "And here."

"Are you *sure* he did that, Ruthie?" Now she looked irritated, like someone who hadn't appreciated having her reading interrupted. Still, her body was frozen in place and hanging on my every word.

"I'm sure," I replied firmly.

She sat and stared at me for a bit. "Well, I'll talk to him when he comes home next time." With that, she whipped her body around, lowered her pillows, and turned the lights off. The discussion was over. I edged my body off her bed and walked to my bedroom. Aaron was already asleep in the bottom bunk.

A week later, Lane drove through El Paso on his way to LeBaron and stayed for the night. The next morning I was jolted from sleep by his hand on my shoulder. He needed to talk to me in the living room, he said. There, in a white undershirt and jeans, he sat on our burnt-orange couch beneath the tiled mirror and put on his tube socks, carefully avoiding looking at me.

"Your mom says that I hurt your feelings," he said in a flat, tired voice. "I just wanted to say that I'm sorry, and I won't touch you in those places again." With his head still down, he slipped on his army work boots and laced them up.

"Okay," I said, relieved that at least he hadn't denied his actions to Mom. Still, he hadn't said he did anything wrong. Was I making a big deal out of nothing? I wondered.

Lane stood up, shook his pant legs down over his socks and boots, and then—still without looking at me—asked for a hug good-bye. I walked slowly across the room. He bent over, wrapped his arms around me, and patted my back lightly. Then, he stood up straight and strode confidently out of the room.

PART III

ALONE

We are in the back of a small pickup truck that's going so fast I can barely hold on. The truck careens down a two-lane highway at a speed I've never before felt. They are all here, my cousins and siblings, pressed tightly up against me, my brother Aaron huddled at my bare feet, ducking from the violent wind, all of us holding on as tight as we can. But while they're somehow able to stay anchored, Aaron and I are inching closer to the tailgate.

"Don't let her take me," Aaron screams. He is holding on to my leg, clutching it for dear life with dread in his pale blue eyes. "Please!" he begs, his cheeks red from the cold, puffed from yelling. I nod so he won't be scared, but now my feet are up against the tailgate, and the witch is close behind us. Each time the truck screeches around a curve, she gains ground.

We hit a bump; my body hurtles upward and is carried away by a gust of dusty wind so powerful that I am ripped from Aaron's grasp. I grab for the truck's back bumper and hold on like a flag waving in the wind, the tips of my toes scraping against the road whenever we change direction. I can't see the witch but know she's there, and sure enough I hear a cackling.

I turn my head to see her flying ever nearer on her broomstick. I kick her away as the road beneath me passes in a blur, the yellow, dotted line an endless procession of minus signs.

"Help me! Help me!" I call out, but the wind is too strong for anyone to hear me, and now the witch's cold fingers wrap around my ankle. I see her evil face reflected in a taillight. She smiles with black lips and jagged, overlapping teeth, the tip of her crooked nose pointed. Her black eyes are mirrored like a cat's. They squint hard as she gives my ankle one last pull. "I'll get you, my pretty," her hollow voice cackles. I lose my grip.

I AWOKE WITH a jolt, slowly realizing that I was in my bed above Aaron, still safe under my *Sesame Street* sheets and only steps away from Mom. But I couldn't shake the dream, one I'd had over and over since Lane had first come into my room. My brothers and I had watched *The Wizard of Oz* at least a dozen times. It seemed as if it were always on TV. When I'd sleep, the Wicked Witch became my greatest nemesis. A recurring villain in my sleeping mind, she occupied all my nightmares, which felt real and terrifying. I took a deep breath as I stretched in the sunlight streaming through the window. I could hear Mom moving around her bedroom, so I shrugged off my covers and climbed out of bed to pour myself a bowl of cereal.

Later that morning, Mom called my brothers and me into the living room. We were greeted by the familiar smells of her musk perfume and Aqua Net hair spray, which I had started using on my own hair before school. She was dressed in her navy-blue polyester pants and a striped cotton blouse that fit tight around her pregnant belly. She had already curled her hair and feathered it back. So rarely did Mom fix herself up in those days, she looked like a little girl playing dress-up.

"I haven't spent time with Lane in a while," she said in a loud, excited voice. "Alejandra and Susan have both been on trips with him."

Mom's sister wives had spent nights riding shotgun with Lane as he made deliveries in his semitruck. Now he was heading to Oklahoma

City, a distance of more than seven hundred miles, and Mom and Meri were going with him. Left behind would be nine-year-old me, ten-year-old Luke, four-year-old Aaron, and twelve-year-old Matt—who seemed thrilled about having been put in charge. My big brother liked to think he could manage us and always looked forward to an opportunity to tell us what to do, which annoyed me beyond words.

Mom sounded exhausted. Pregnancies in the summer months were always the hardest, and this latest one had been particularly difficult. She slept whenever Meri did and suffered from migraines constantly, which were exacerbated by a houseful of screaming kids in a muggy, hot single-wide trailer.

She tossed a handful of socks into her hard-shelled, light green suitcase. "He's *my* husband too, and I don't think it's fair that I haven't had a trip with him in his truck yet." She looked at me for a second, as if waiting for confirmation that she was doing the right thing. I just stared at her, my face silent. I looked down at her fingers, snapping the gold latches shut on her suitcase; her nails had been chewed to nubs.

"You help Matt take care of the kids," Mom said, patting my shoulder and hurrying past as if she were late for a bus. "At least you won't have to take care of Meri."

Meri was two and a half and in constant need of tests and physical therapy. Despite the efforts of the best medical care Mom could find, Meri's condition was deteriorating. Her once-chubby body had grown lean and frail. The water on her brain was increasing, and with it, her motor skills were declining. She had also started to have light seizures, and when they occurred, Mom had to press a spoon in her mouth to keep Meri from swallowing her tongue.

I had been proud of my knack for feeding her, but that skill began to evaporate as well. Scared to see what mealtimes might bring, I felt like Mom in the final days before Audrey was institutionalized. It became almost impossible to determine the right amount of food to put in Meri's mouth. Sometimes her swallowing reflexes didn't work, and she'd gag and spit food back up in every direction. None of us could do much except make sure she was lying in a comfortable position and try the whole thing again.

Meri's mouth and eyes now remained open almost all the time, in a zombielike expression, like a child who sits in front of a TV all day. A sudden noise might make her eyes dart in a certain direction, but her head would never follow suit. Most heartbreaking of all, when she cried, tears poured down her cheeks, but no sound left her mouth.

"Make sure you make them last," Mom said, and handed Matt a plain white envelope with a few food stamps, after she took a few for herself. "Lane hasn't been paid in a while."

Matt accepted the envelope from Mom and asked when she would be home.

"I don't know," she said casually, shaking her head and shrugging her shoulders. "I'll call you from a pay phone when we're on our way back." With that, she put her diaper bag over her shoulder, picked Meri up from the couch, and walked out the door to Lane's idling truck, Matt behind her carrying her suitcase.

The odd thing was, although the prospect of Mom's leaving scared me, once she left, I felt liberated. Having the household managed by Matt had its perks. Babylon's excesses were welcomed with open arms. My siblings and I watched TV nonstop from the moment Mom left and ate crunchy-peanut-butter sandwiches for lunch and popcorn for dinner. We stayed up for hours past our usual bedtimes and—that first night—finally got to watch music programs that Mom considered so scandalous she had forbidden it. "Not with all those half-naked girls dancin' around all those crazy, shaggy-haired, ugly men," she'd say. "It's way too indecent for you kids. You have better things to be doin' with your time."

By then, Mom's oldies-but-goodies innocence had given way, at least in our minds, to pop and heavy-metal music. We were all fascinated by what Lane called "devil music," a term that most households in LeBaron took to mean any music from the sixties forward, which meant that rock and roll of any sort was not allowed. Having grown up loving music, Mom proved to be a little more liberal in this regard. She bought us vinyl records and cassettes as gifts, and as long as the music didn't have any cursing or references to sex, she let us listen to it as much as we liked.

I tuned in to Casey Kasem's *American Top 40* every weekend. Rick Springfield was my favorite. I tore his photos from teen magazines and Scotch-taped them all over my bedroom walls. I danced and lip-synched in front of the mirror, singing "Jessie's Girl" while pointing to my reflection.

The morning after Mom left, Matt and I realized that we were out of milk and cereal. Remembering the big bag of flour Mom always had on hand, and having helped her make pancakes several times, I said that I would make breakfast for everyone. Matt looked at me uneasily but joined the others in front of the TV in the living room.

Still in my pink nightgown, I dragged a chair across the floor until it was next to the stove, then climbed on it so I could reach the baking ingredients in the upper cupboards. I lifted a half-open bag of flour from over my head, and a white cloud puffed into the air as I set it down on the countertop. I took out a pink-and-white sack of sugar and quickly gathered up the cooking oil and eggs. Because we were out of milk, I thought water would be a good substitute. I poured some from the faucet into the mixing bowl while I stared out the kitchen window at the nearby trailers, all of them filled with strangers.

I stirred everything together to make a thick, white liquid that roughly resembled lumpy pancake batter. Once I had lit the stove and heated the frying pan, I began to cook the little disks of batter. I stood over the burner with my spatula and listened to Luke repeatedly crash into the floor while my siblings watched a *Tom and Jerry* cartoon. I felt like a surrogate mom with Matt as the dad, both of us yelling at Luke and Aaron all day.

"Hey, Lukey, settle down or I'm gonna have to turn the TV off, 'kay?" I hollered, after I heard him bellow from the couch. The noise subsided. Meanwhile, my pancakes looked perfect, golden brown with a delicious, toasted smell. I carefully set two on each plate, smeared them with peanut butter and syrup just as Mom did, and delivered them to my TV-watching brothers, who gratefully grabbed their stacks. I settled into the recliner with my own plate and a self-satisfied smile.

"These are gross," Matt said matter-of-factly, and tossed his plate of half-raw pancakes onto the carpet. I watched for dissenting opinions from the others, but Aaron's face just twisted into a frown and Luke spit out his first bite. I gathered up the plates and returned to the kitchen. My recipe needed tinkering.

After adjusting a few ingredients, I came up with a round of pancakes that somehow managed to be both burned and raw. Several batches later, I finally produced something doughy but edible, and my brothers reluctantly chomped their way through a few scorched disks. That was the final straw. We *had* to go to Safeway for more groceries.

Luke and Aaron were still in front of cartoons when Matt and I stepped out into the early-afternoon sunlight and a blue, cloudless sky. Walking along a busy, paved road in the middle of a Texas summer was like walking on the edges of red-hot burners on an electric stovetop. By the time we'd walked the quarter mile to the Safeway parking lot, our blond heads were scorched and our clothes were soaked.

The glass doors parted and ice-cold air rushed at us in a welcoming breeze. I had never been happier to step inside a grocery store. I pulled a cart from the rack and joined the throng of shoppers, my nose at roughly the same height as the cart's red handle. Rolling up the first aisle as if I knew what I was doing, I quickly found myself overwhelmed by the towering walls of colorfully printed packages. Supermarket variety had always amazed me, but Mom's swift trips had made shopping look easy. Luckily, Matt was there to fill the basket with chips, Popsicles, peanut butter, milk, sugar-coated wheat puffs, and a spongy loaf of wheat bread.

We had only made it to the middle of the frozen-foods aisle when Matt stopped short, took the envelope from his pocket, and counted the food stamps. He scanned the basket, concentrated hard, and counted each item under his breath, the back of his neck still fire red from our walk.

"It looks like we have enough to pay for everything with a little bit left over," he said with a shy smile, handing the envelope of food stamps to me. "You go pay for these, and I'll meet you out front."

I looked at him, annoyed. "Why do I have to do it?"

"Because I said so, that's why. See if the lady will exchange one of the food-stamp dollars for quarters, and then you can buy somethin' from the quarter machines on the way out, 'kay?"

I nodded, taking note that the back of Matt's neck wasn't the only thing that had turned red; his cheeks were the exact same shade, and his light freckles barely peeked through. I could tell he was embarrassed, but I couldn't quite understand why. I took the food stamps, waited in line, then handed them over to the cashier. She looked at me kindly enough as she peered down through her reading glasses, but she had a severity to her that made me worry she was about to ask where my mother was. Instead, she licked her index finger and thumb, counted the stamps, and handed me two $1 stamps in change.

I handed one right back. "Can I get four quarters, please?"

The cashier twisted her chin down at me until it doubled. "Sweetheart, I cain't exchange cash for *food stamps,*" she said in her thick Texas accent. "It's against the law."

Something about the way she'd emphasized those two words, *food stamps,* made me feel as if every eye in the store were watching me. My face went hot with shame, and I was suddenly angry at Matt. He knew it would be embarrassing to pay with food stamps. I lowered my head, took the brown-paper sacks of groceries, and walked out of the store as fast as I could.

"They can't give you cash for food stamps," I said, quietly resentful, to Matt.

"Hey, I didn't know that. I promise I didn't." He covered his mouth with his hand but couldn't resist laughing.

I was incensed. "*You* have to pay for the food next time," I said sourly, thrusting the stamps in his face and sulking all the way back to the trailer park.

The TV was off when we got home, and Luke and Aaron were nowhere in sight. I put the groceries away while Matt looked around for them, opening and closing the doors to every room. Then he ran outside.

"Luke and Aaron. It's time to come inside now."

No response.

Matt's calls grew distant as he searched the area farther and farther away from the trailer. I was worried. While Luke had wandered off before, Aaron never had. I folded the paper sacks, laid them on the table, and heard a quiet sound I didn't recognize. I glanced over my shoulder toward the hallway. Nothing was there. I stood frozen in place and listened to the sleepy afternoon air. There it was again—a soft thud, the sound of scampering maybe. I couldn't tell where it was coming from. Not until I left the kitchen for the living room did I hear a giggling under the floor. I darted outside.

"Where are they?" asked Matt frantically. "Did you see them?"

"There." I pointed under the trailer.

Matt and I crept toward a narrow opening in the white skirt of siding under our home and looked at each other wide-eyed. The smell of sulfur was unmistakable.

"Luke and Aaron!" Matt shouted. "We know you're in there. You kids get out from under this trailer. Right now!" He crawled farther, and there they were amid the spiderwebs and patches of weeds and stickers and pieces of trash. Luke wore a silly grin as if he didn't know what was going on. Matt yelled again and again until the two boys slowly began to creep toward us. Luke kept his hand behind his back.

"Luke, let me see what you have in your hand." Matt demanded, his face beet red with irritation. "Were you two playin' with matches under there?"

"No," they both said in unison, each looking at the other as if the other was lying.

"Show me your hand, Luke!" Matt yelled, grabbing Luke's elbow. The box of matches hidden inside his palm rattled while Matt clawed for them. "Luke, give 'em to me. Hurry!" Luke refused and my brothers began to wrestle, falling to the dry lawn and rolling around, blades of yellow grass clinging to their jeans and T-shirts and hair. "You better give 'em to me, Lukey!" A cloud of dust flew up, Luke started to sneeze, and that gave Matt an opening. He snatched the little red box from his brother's hand.

"Are you kids stupid or somethin'?" Matt scolded, wiping the dirt and grass from his jeans. "What the heck is wrong with you?"

Neither replied. Luke wiped his runny nose on his dusty shirtsleeve.

Matt smacked the top of Luke's head, then smacked Aaron. "Don't you know that you could burn this trailer down? *Again?* Just wait till I tell Mom on you guys. You're gonna be in big trouble when she gets home."

Aaron rubbed his eyes with his fists, started to bawl, and walked slowly up the steps and through the open door.

Luke just stood there. "When's Mom comin' back?"

Matt stuffed the matches into his front pocket. "I don't know. Now, get back inside the house. I can't believe you guys."

I followed my brothers up the steps, went into the kitchen, and poured everyone a glass of milk; my hands were shaking. Luke was almost eleven now and still playing with matches, as if he didn't know how dangerous that was. Not long ago he had tried to light a lamp pole on fire in the trailer park. He also had begun wandering farther and farther away from home. Sometimes he found his way back, sometimes we had to get in the Microbus and go look for him. I worried that Matt and I didn't know what we were doing. I wanted Mom to come home.

The phone rang that night and Matt got to it first. I heard Mom's voice on the other end saying they were in Oklahoma and didn't know when they'd be home. Just as I asked Matt to give me the receiver, the line went dead. "Mom didn't have any more change," he explained, his voice so nonchalant I almost burst into tears. I couldn't cry in front of the others, though. It didn't seem right. I just stared at the TV until the feeling passed.

— 21 —

A few days later, on a muggy afternoon, we heard a knock at the door. By then, my brothers and I had spent hours and hours in front of the TV, having only taken brief breaks to sleep, or to retreat to our bedrooms or outside when Luke became so overwrought by a program that his jumping shook the entire trailer to its core. Matt and I were slouched on the orange couch, Aaron in the brown reclining chair, and Luke was lying in his usual spot on the floor. We were all watching *General Hospital,* one of our favorite shows, which, even though Mom would probably have preferred we not absorb the sinful deeds of Luke and Laura, Mom never banned because she loved it as much as we did.

When we heard the rapping sound at the front door, we all jumped. Our eyes darted from the TV to the door, and then to each other. We weren't expecting anyone, and visitors to the trailer were rare even when Mom was home. The knock came a second time, and Matt slowly rose from the couch and opened the door. The living room flooded with light and heat. A man and a woman, both middle-aged, both dark haired, and both well dressed stood on the threshold—he in a shirt and tie, she in a gray suit with stockings and high heels. Each carried brown leather briefcases, and for a moment I thought they might be Jehovah's Witnesses. The Church frequently sent missionaries into our trailer park on Sundays in search of converts. But it wasn't Sunday.

This will not end well, I thought to myself as I turned off the TV, my eyes fixed on the man and the woman. I watched as the two of them scanned the room. Their eyes stopped at the sink piled high with dirty dishes and the old cereal bowls sitting on top of the kitchen table, its surface sticky with spilled milk.

The woman looked at the man with a stunned expression. Then she quickly recovered, forced a smile onto her face, and turned to Matt. "Is your mom at home?" she asked through lips covered in a lavender lipstick and teeth straight and white.

"Um, no, my mom's not here right now, but she's comin' back anytime."

I was impressed by Matt's smooth delivery of the lie. The man asked, as sweetly as the woman, if they might come in. Matt hesitated a moment, then stepped aside and opened the door wide for the pair, who now introduced themselves as representatives of the Department of Social Services.

"One of your neighbors telephoned our agency and said you kids have been alone for a few days," said the woman. "We're just checking in to make sure that isn't true."

None of us said a word, and the couple walked farther into the living room, suddenly fragrant with the clean smell of the woman's perfume. I liked the way she combed her hair: short, feathered back, and held meticulously in place with hair spray.

"Where is your mother?" the woman asked.

"Oklahoma City," Matt replied.

"How long has she been gone?" the man asked.

"A few days."

"Have you had a babysitter?"

Matt shook his head.

"Have any grown-ups checked up on you while your mother has been gone?"

Matt looked at the two of them a moment. "No."

The man eyed the woman, then asked, "Do you mind if we look around?"

"Sure," Matt replied, and soon the pair were in the kitchen, swinging open every one of the cupboard doors and poking their noses in the fridge. Noticing the big, green bowl full of runny batter—my latest failed attempt at pancake making—they asked what we'd been eating. Matt answered truthfully: cereal, popcorn, and peanut-butter-and-jelly sandwiches.

The man tried to make his way to the hallway and bedrooms, but Luke was in the way. "You need to get up, buddy," Matt said, whispering into his brother's ear. "Sit on the couch and get out of the way, 'kay?" Luke reacted as if he'd had water poured on his head during a dream. He scrambled to his feet, his greasy hair matted where he'd been lying on it.

I heard the man's footsteps as he walked down the hall but didn't follow him. I imagined the expression on his face as he discovered my bedroom floor littered with dirty clothes, and I felt a deep sense of shame. Matt was now biting his fingernails and staring at the floor. The same question seemed to run through both our minds—what do we say or not say? We knew enough not to mention anything about polygamy or Mom's being married to Lane, but that was the extent of our coaching in this regard.

"This place is a mess," the man said, startling us as he stepped in from the hallway, his expression almost as fearful as ours, his hands stuffed into his pockets as if he needed to avoid contamination. He reached up to scratch the top of his head and then quickly pocketed his hand again. "There's an open flame under the hot-water heater in the back bedroom. There are plastic bags and clothes sitting all around

it. It's a miracle it hasn't started a fire." He took in a deep breath and
shook his head at the woman. "We have to get ahold of the mother.
And there's no way we can leave them alone."

The woman told us all to sit down. "We need to decide what to
do," she said with a serious glance in our direction. Matt and I sat down
next to Luke on the couch, our shoulders hunched forward and our
elbows on our knees. The woman shooed Aaron off a chair and motioned for him to join us. The man pulled in a chair from the kitchen,
wiped crumbs from the seat, shook his head, and sat down.

The woman popped the gold latches on her briefcase and took out
a pen and pad. "Do you kids have a phone number where we can reach
your mother?" Her voice sounded kindly, like that of the Wicked Witch
just before luring Dorothy into a trap.

"No, we don't," Matt finally answered. "We're not sure exactly
where she is right now. She called us from a pay phone . . . somewhere."

"How long has your mom been gone?" asked the two of them in
unison.

"It's been maybe two days," Matt replied. The woman began scrib-
bling on her pad. "Not that long."

"Has anyone else been here to watch over you or cook for you?"

"No, but we've had something to eat every day." Matt sounded
proud, as though he were solely responsible for this achievement. But
the woman just put down her pen and looked at the man.

"Do you know when your mom will be home?" asked the man.
"We can't leave you here without an adult. You might have to come
with us."

The second he said that, I began to shiver; my Wicked Witch suspicions were right. I expected to feel the Kansas wind stir and to see
her face turn green. The two adults seemed to detect my fear, and I
could feel them struggling to maintain a gentle demeanor.

"Surely you must know a grown-up who lives close by," the woman
said, "someone who can take care of you till your mom gets home."

THE SOUND of GRAVEL

There was a long pause. I heard a car start outside, its motor purring, and felt Aaron fidgeting beside me.

"We do," said Matt. I gave him a puzzled look. "Mom's friend, Gary," he said to me, emphasizing *friend*. We couldn't say he was Lane's brother. That might lead them to ask about Lane. "He has a little grocery store."

After a few minutes of searching in the kitchen, the man found our phone book, and Gary's name inside it. He picked up the receiver, stared at it in hesitation, then dialed the number.

No answer. Matt's face turned red with frustration and fear. The man dialed the number a second time. Nothing. "I think you're going to have to come with us," he said to Matt, then turned to the rest of us. "You kids go ahead and get some clothes for a few days. We'll try calling your mom's friend one more time before we leave."

Matt and Luke left for their room and Aaron and I for ours. Just as I'd feared, the floor was littered with clothes, and I quickly sorted through them, separating the lightly dirty from the filthy. In the closet, a plastic garbage bag filled with clothes was indeed sitting next to an open flame, just as the man had said, and I yanked it out of harm's way. After going through a few dresser drawers, I was finally able to cobble together some outfits for Aaron and me.

"Here." I handed my brother a button-up shirt and pants. "Change your clothes."

"No."

I turned to look at him.

"I don't like buttons," he said calmly.

"That's all we have that's clean."

Aaron looked at me, his arms folded defiantly across his chest. I threw both the shirt and pants at him, but he didn't move. They fell back to the floor where I'd found them.

"Those pants have snaps on them," he said.

That my voice rose surprised both of us. "We don't have time to keep lookin'. Those people are ready to take us *now*!"

"I'm not wearing those clothes." Aaron stamped his foot in the pile of clothes.

"Yes, you are, you little *shit*!" I yelled.

Aaron's mouth fell open with shock. "I'm gonna tell Mom when she comes home you said the S-word," he whispered.

"I don't care what you tell her! Just change your clothes." I noticed my brother look at me with fear for the first time in his life. I grabbed his shoulders and lowered my voice. "Look, do you get what's happenin' here? These people are from the government and they're taking us away from Mom. We have to be good or they won't bring us back." I felt my throat harden and my eyes well up, but I knew I couldn't cry. I picked up Aaron's clothes and shoved them into his folded arms. "Now, put these clothes on. *Right now*."

Afterward it would seem to me that I crossed some sort of threshold that day, that I'd been merely a sister in the morning, but by afternoon I was something else altogether. As Aaron glared at me and then slowly began to exchange his T-shirt for a button-up, all I could think about was the danger we were in. Without another word I helped him button his shirt, then I stuffed some jeans, shirts, and underwear into a brown-paper grocery bag.

We all met back in the living room, and I had the distinct feeling that the man and the woman were dreading what was about to happen as much as we were. They looked at each other forlornly, and the woman walked into the kitchen to try Gary's phone number one last time. I looked down to see my fingers trembling, and then up again when I heard the woman speak.

"Yes, hello?"

Thank goodness. After the woman had apprised Gary of the situation, he agreed to take charge of us while Mom was gone, and a half hour or so later we heard his car pull into the trailer's parking space. He entered without knocking. His dark brown hair had been carefully combed behind his ears. I'd never seen him wear the white, button-up shirt he had on, or those plaid pants or white leather shoes. He looked

as if he'd been playing nine holes at the country club when the social
workers called, but Gary didn't play golf.

He told the social workers that he had already reached Mom by
CB radio, and she was on her way home. Satisfied, the pair gave Gary
their card, told him that Mom should call them right away, and left.

An awkward silence followed. Gary hardly knew us and was as
uncomfortable as we were. "Let's go to the movies," he suggested.

We passed a few hours there, and when we walked out of the theater, it was dark outside. A full moon, golden and forbidding, was in
a periwinkle sky. I stared heavenward during the drive home and then
up at the ceiling for hours once I'd gone to bed. Still, I found myself
comforted by the sound of Gary readjusting his body on the couch in
the living room, and by Aaron's slow breathing on the bunk below.

Eventually, I heard an engine out front. Truck doors opened and
closed, a key turned in the front-door lock, and at last I could hear
Mom's and Lane's muffled voices in the living room. I crawled out
of bed, climbed down the wooden bunk, and made my way down the
hall. There she was, my mother, looking more tired and pale than she
had when she left, with Meri slumped over her shoulder asleep. Mom
paced nervously back and forth between Lane and Gary, who sat on
the couch explaining the situation.

I couldn't help myself; I ran into the living room and threw myself
at her, wrapped myself tightly around her legs, and squeezed them as
much out of despair as relief. Mom patted my head with her palm and
ran her fingers through my messy hair; and as she did, the worry on
her face seemed to dissolve into a smile of relief. In the next moment,
she leaned down, wrapped her free arm all the way around my upper
back, and pulled me tightly against her. She seemed to feel as wretched
as I did.

The next morning, Mom phoned the man and the woman, set up
an appointment, and later that week visited their offices. When she
came home, she said she had been warned by the social workers never
to leave us alone again. To ensure that didn't happen, they had placed

her on probation for the next two years, during which time we would not be allowed to move out of the El Paso area and could expect unannounced visits from the department at any time.

Mom was incensed. "People in this country think they're free, but they're not. The government has their fingers in all our business. I just can't believe this."

Mom was angry, but as a result of her probation we were forced to live in one place for a longer period than we ever had before. I found a new kind of peace in being settled, in not being abruptly taken out of school or being forced to get used to new surroundings every few months. For that, I was grateful to the US government and its tyranny, even if the peace didn't last much beyond the probation.

Later that week, Mom was washing dishes with her back to the TV when the evening news reported that the man known as the Mormon Manson—my uncle Ervil—had died of a heart attack in a Utah prison. Mom spun around, wiped her hands on a kitchen towel, and hurried into the living room. There, she watched with a pale, stunned look on her face as the reporter recounted Ervil's infamous crime spree. Mom counted on her fingers the number of years that had elapsed since my dad died; it had been almost nine years since he'd been executed.

"I can't believe it," Mom mumbled, her face taking on an eerie glow as she searched the screen for further explanation. "After all the heartache that man caused . . . He should have suffered in prison for a lot longer than he did." She took off her glasses, leaned forward over her swollen belly, put her head in her hands, and began to sob. Her shoulders jerked up and down as if the news had shaken loose an old and long-buried sadness.

Given her attitude toward the US government, Mom didn't find the same peace that I did in being forced to stay in El Paso, but she tried to make the best of the situation. She took us on road trips on the weekends and during the holidays. That Christmas, we visited Grandpa and Grandma in Strathmore and took a side excursion to see Audrey at the state hospital. Eventually, doctors diagnosed her with schizophrenia, a disease that had afflicted several members of the LeBaron family, including two of my father's siblings.

That Christmas was the first time I'd seen her since the day Mom had taken her away, and although it had only been a few months, she was a changed person, and not for the better. She was fourteen and heavily medicated, her upper eyelids red and droopy, her cheeks sunken, her personality almost completely unresponsive. She had teeth marks on her pale, bruised arms, and the nurses explained that she had been in a fight with another patient. We weren't surprised when the nurse said that Audrey had started the brawl. The doctors told us that at times they still had to feed Audrey intravenously, and that the drug cocktail they gave her was the only thing that kept her from being violent toward herself and other patients. I thought my sister looked barely alive, although she seemed to remember all of us.

The hospital allowed Audrey to come to our grandparents' house and spend one night with us, although her presence in the outside world only highlighted how she no longer had a place in it. At my grandparents' with Audrey, Mom's face became etched again with its familiar helplessness. She wore that look all day long; right up until the moment she took Audrey back to the hospital.

We returned to El Paso just after New Year's, when it was time once again for Mom to give birth. She had already decided to have the baby at the hospital in Casas. She wanted a natural delivery and couldn't find a doctor in the entire state of Texas who would allow a woman who'd had two past C-sections to deliver naturally. Mom took the trip with Lane in the second week of January. Because we knew Social Services would be checking in on us regularly, Lane asked his wife Alejandra and her family to stay with us in El Paso for the week.

Having overnight guests in our tiny trailer was no small feat, especially as Alejandra brought along seven of her and Lane's ten children. The two youngest were a pair of barely one-year-old twins, Alex and Lane Jr. Seeing them confirmed that Lane's description had been accurate—they looked nothing alike. Alex had brown eyes and his mother's dark hair and complexion, while Junior's skin was olive, his hair sandy blond, his eyes light blue. They were the unlikeliest and the cutest pair of twins I'd ever seen. Alejandra spent most of her time in the trailer on the couch, alternately nursing a blond or a brunet while Meri lay limp on a pillow in the corner.

Given her icy relationship with Mom, I expected Alejandra to treat me harshly, but she didn't. She always smiled at me, and her gold-capped tooth only added to the warm effect. I liked having her around. Most of our communication was nonverbal as she spoke little English, although her children were always ready to step in and translate. They were all perfectly bilingual. Alejandra made her own flour tortillas for the elaborate and delicious Mexican meals she prepared for us three times a day. It was the best food I had ever tasted.

I shared my top bunk with Alejandra's daughter Maria. She was just as kind and friendly as her mother and had a self-assuredness and poise that I had never seen in a woman, much less a girl only two years older than me. I found her fascinating. Maria was a carbon copy of her mother, with long, lustrous hair that she parted in the middle and wore in braids. She loved to sew and spent hours making blankets and dresses for her Barbie dolls. While it was not an unusual hobby for girls in our community, Maria's attitude toward it was.

"I'm gonna be a fashion designer when I grow up," she said to me one day. "What are you going to be, Ruthie?"

The question left me at a loss for words. I was taken aback by the confidence with which she predicted her future life, a life that had no place in our world of marriage and birthing babies. I had no idea that girls had a choice in what they would do with their lives. That Maria thought she could choose her own future seemed like a radical notion to me.

Maria had three brothers who were close to Aaron's age, which meant that our trailer was descended upon by a wild pack of boys who never seemed to tire of running up and down the hallway while Maria and I cleaned up after them. One day after school, Maria had finished her chores while I washed the dishes. As I scrubbed, I became more and more frustrated. I just couldn't take the sound of all the boys playing while I worked. I turned off the faucet, dried my hands, and joined Alejandra and Maria in the living room for an afternoon of Mexican soap operas.

Unfortunately, the pile of dirty dishes was twice as big after dinner. I was sprawled out on the floor with everyone else, watching *The Dukes of Hazzard,* when Maria tapped me on the shoulder. "Ruthie," she whispered, "my mom said that she's not gonna let you go to bed until the dishes are done. She says you're acting spoiled and lazy."

Feeling like Cinderella, I slowly and dramatically rose from the floor with a sour expression that I made sure Alejandra saw. I stomped into the kitchen. Suddenly it seemed to me that Mom had been right not to like Alejandra, and I couldn't wait for Mom to come home. I spent the rest of the evening in the kitchen, scouring it from top to bottom while the Dukes' stock car rumbled in the background. I don't think our kitchen had ever been cleaner. The trailer smelled like Ajax and Pine-Sol for days.

On the fifteenth of January, Mom delivered her fourth boy, and two days later, she and Lane brought home Micah. Newborns always generated excitement, and Micah was no exception. My brothers and I fought for the chance to hold the tiny creature that stared up at us through a bundle of blankets. Micah's dark blue eyes scanned the room with intense curiosity; he had an alertness that I found comforting. His skin was so thin it was almost see-through, but it glowed, as if he were lit from within, the blue button eyes providing the only contrast. I thought he looked like the son of a snowman and half wondered if he might melt away when summer came.

Alejandra and all her kids were packed and ready to go well before we even heard the sound of Lane's truck in the trailer park. Alejandra waited in the kitchen during the excitement of Micah's debut, and she and Mom pointedly ignored each other; their iciness seemed out of place on such a happy day. As soon as the truck was loaded, Lane and Alejandra each lifted a twin to their shoulders and headed straight for the door. *"Gracias,"* Mom said as they walked past, her straight-lipped smile obviously forced. Alejandra, her head hidden behind the blanket of her baby that she held over her shoulder, didn't respond. The door rattled shut behind them.

The sky was overcast, and the air in the trailer cold and damp. Mom took in a deep breath and smiled as Lane's truck pulled out of our driveway as if she was relieved to finally be home. Micah's birth must have been a great confidence booster to her, in part because the natural birth was uneventful, as she had predicted it would be, and in part because the doctors pronounced Micah normal and healthy.

Mom handed the baby over to Aaron, who asked to hold him first. She moved slowly, as if still in pain from the delivery, and her breathing was louder and heavier than normal. She sat next to Aaron on the couch, leaned forward, and placed her forehead in her palm. Meanwhile, my five-year-old brother held Micah in a fragile embrace, as if the baby were made of glass. It wasn't difficult to imagine the two of them a few years down the road—wrestling together on the carpet, playing freeze tag, fighting over what to watch on TV. Aaron grinned from ear to ear, his red cheeks glowing in excitement as he stared at his brother.

Mom scanned the room with tired eyes. "Ruthie, I need you to make spaghetti for dinner," she said as she pulled herself slowly off the couch and limped into the kitchen. "And sweep the floor in here." She picked Micah up from Aaron. "Matt, you wash the dishes and help Ruthie feed Meri." Then Mom retired to her bedroom, now more cramped than ever with the two cribs, one for Micah and one for Meri. We wouldn't see her again until the next afternoon after school. "Ruthie, have you seen Lukey since you got home from school?"

Mom's voice startled me. I'd been lying on my top bunk, engrossed in a teen magazine, trying to hear myself think as Matt's music blared from the next room, vibrating through the thin plywood walls. I looked up at Mom, puzzled.

"Have you seen Luke?"

For a second time I didn't hear the question, distracted by how rested she looked. After just one good night's sleep, Mom seemed back to normal, with her usual pink cheeks and lips. "He ate a peanut-butter-and-jelly sandwich and watched cartoons with us," I said as I sat up and opened the magazine flat on my lap to mark my page. "I didn't see him after we turned off the TV."

Mom pushed her glasses up the bridge of her nose with her fore-finger, silently turned, and loudly asked Matt if he knew where Luke was. He didn't.

She shook her head in disappointment. "You kids need to keep a better eye on him. You know he likes to leave when no one's watchin'." She shook her head again. "How am I supposed to do this all by myself?"

She waited for a bit in silence as if she expected an answer, but I didn't know what to say. A moment later, I heard the front door fly open. Mom stood on the wooden steps and shouted Luke's name. When there was no response, she turned and headed back in the house. The door clanked shut and woke up Micah, who began to cry.

"Both of you get up and go look for him right now," Mom com-manded, rushing down the hall to attend to the baby.

Matt and I didn't feel the least bit worried about Luke. We just put on our shoes, dragged wet combs through our hair, and headed down the street for Safeway. While Luke was wandering off more and more often, he tended to end up in the same places—the grocery store or the bus-stop bench in front of the Dairy Queen. His face always wore the same blank expression when we found him, his tongue sticking straight out of his mouth while his eyes nervously followed traffic.

The dark, forbidding skies of the day before had given way to plump, white clouds and a gentle sun, but I walked lazily with my head down and my shoulders slumped inside my purple jacket. Sure enough, as soon as the sliding glass Safeway doors parted, we saw Luke.

In those days, Luke was obsessed with anything made of paper, especially such things as junk mail, newspapers, and magazines. He carried a stack of papers and colorful pamphlets under his arm and used the hand on his opposite arm to hold up his jeans, hand-me-downs from Matt. They were still too big for his skinny body, and he never remembered to wear a belt.

Looking at him there, seeing him before he saw me, it struck me how much he looked like a normal boy. He wore his baseball cap a little bit crooked, but then boys sometimes wore crooked caps. At least one of his shoes was always untied, but all boys walked around that way from time to time. He barely showed any signs of his disability.

"Hey, Lukey," Matt called across the store. Luke looked up, but not in our direction, as if he'd heard something but didn't know where it was coming from.

"*Luke,*" Matt called out again. This time Luke's eyes darted toward us. He looked surprised to see us. "Bring your papers and let's go home."

Luke reluctantly shuffled our way, but not before he added one more circular to the pile under his arm. His pants inched farther down past his white Hanes underwear with every step. At last he reached back and pulled up his pants.

"What are ya doin' here, Lukey?" Matt asked.

"Huh?" Luke replied, confused. "Yeah, I'n doin' fine." His voice was loud enough for the entire store to hear.

Matt laughed good-naturedly. "No, why are you all the way over here, buddy?"

Luke just shrugged. "I'n not sure." Then he blinked and turned toward the exit.

"We've been lookin' for ya. How come you didn't tell Mom where you were goin'? She's all worried about ya. Let me see those and make sure they're all free." Matt pulled the pile of papers out from under

Luke's arm and quickly rifled through them. Luke could never tell which publications were free and which weren't and had been stopped for shoplifting.

On that day, Luke had only collected free stuff, so Matt handed the papers back to him and we walked home. Luke went straight to his bedroom to study his new stash and to add it to the pile of periodicals, pamphlets, and hundreds of pieces of junk mail he had already collected.

As the years passed, it began to seem as if Luke's mind had been frozen in time. As Matt entered his teens and began teasing us relentlessly, Luke remained the same. As Mom's voice took on a permanently raspy quality and the creases on her forehead grew deeper, Luke remained the same. He even seemed to stay the course as things went from bad to worse for the rest of us. Strangely, his stagnant mental development became a source of comforting constancy.

— 23 —

In late November, not long before Micah turned a year old, Mom found out she was pregnant again. No one was surprised, and life went on as usual until 1983 rolled in with a spate of bad weather that brought us thick, dark rain clouds for weeks. The conditions were particularly awful one Friday afternoon in mid-February as my brothers and I walked home from school. Aaron had started the first grade by then, so the four of us braved the lightning, thunder, and slanted rain that day, the four of us arriving home soaked and weather-beaten.

When we tramped through the door, Mom, with a dazed expression, was on the couch feeding Micah on her lap with a blue plastic baby bottle. I felt like a cold, wet dog and didn't stop to think about what that expression might mean. Instead, I peeled off my drenched jacket and went straight to my bedroom to change my clothes. I was still snapping my jeans when the phone rang.

Mom answered it, there was a pause, and she struggled through a little Spanish. It was the same pattern I heard whenever we received a collect call from LeBaron. I walked into the living room to see her head nodding at the operator's words.

"*Sí,*" she finally said.

I dreaded the phone calls from the colony because they usually portended a visit from Lane. He had already broken the promise he had made during his nonapology, and I never knew when he might appear in my bedroom again. He always came to the edge of my top bunk bed at night before he went to Mom's room. It was always after she had gone to bed. Lane would come into my room to say good-night, but it always turned into a struggle. I'd push his hands away from my private parts, begging him to stop, which only seemed to make him more aggressive. I'd tell him I was going to call for Mom or report to her what he was doing to me, but Lane would promise to give me money and candy or ice cream if I stayed silent. He said that I would hurt Mom's feelings again if I told her, the same way that I had the first time. His visits made me physically sick, and he always left me with a feeling of powerlessness, as if I didn't have a choice. I never knew what to do. I wanted to tell Mom what Lane was doing to me, but what if he was right? What if it made her upset? She was always talking about how much she had to do and how exhausted she was. What if telling her only made everything worse? I felt embarrassed, ashamed, and partly responsible because no matter what I did, I couldn't seem to stop Lane.

The line now having connected, Mom was listening to whatever the caller had to report. Suddenly she took a deep breath. "Oh, no. That *can't* be true," she said as if in shock. She cast her eyes around the room until they met mine. She looked like an animal wounded beyond saving. She whispered for me to come and hold Micah, then turned back to the phone. "I just can't believe it. When? *When?*" Then she took her glasses off and covered both eyes with one hand.

"No wonder he hasn't been coming to see us. He can't even afford to take care of the wives he's got." She drew in an uneven, shaky breath through her nose, and I knew she was stifling a sob. "Why would he go and do that—and not tell us."

Micah was unhappy with his bottle, reached out for Mom to pick him up, then started to cry out when she ignored him. As much as I wanted an explanation from Mom, I knew she'd be furious if I let the baby cry, so I took him out of the room and bounced him on Aaron's bed. Eventually I heard her weak voice utter, "Okay, thanks for letting me know."

As soon as she'd hung up, Mom started to sob. Then she walked straight to her bedroom and slammed the metal-framed door behind her. She lay there for the next half an hour, crying loudly enough for all of us to hear. I wanted to check on her, but I knew it wasn't a good idea until she'd settled down.

I went into the kitchen to refill Micah's milk bottle when Mom's bedroom went silent. An eerie quiet descended upon the house.

Suddenly Mom flung open her door. "You kids get some clothes packed," she commanded. "We're going to LeBaron."

"For how long?" Matt yelled from behind his bedroom door.

"I don't know. Three or four days. Lane got married again without tellin' me—a few months ago—and I need to go home and find out what's goin' on down there."

ONCE WE WERE on the road, Mom explained that her sister wife Susan had called to tell her the news. Wife number two did not like hearing that there was now a wife number four, and especially not from wife number three, even though Mom certainly got along better with Susan than she did with Alejandra.

Apparently, the new bride's name was Marjory. She was a decade older than Lane and a widow with thirteen children, most of whom were already married with children of their own. I felt Mom would have been more accepting of the marriage if Marjory had been a younger woman, of childbearing age. An older wife who could no longer have kids suggested that Lane had a deeper, more painful motivation for what he did—he must have married for either love or sex. Adding to Mom's rage, Lane had violated an unwritten law of polygamy: a man who wants a new wife needs the blessings of the wives he already has.

We stopped at a McDonald's so we'd have something to do while we waited in the hour-long line to cross into Mexico. Mom ordered us a sack full of hamburgers and a milk shake for Meri. Her health had so declined that the only way to feed her was via a two-foot-long tube that we inserted into her throat, past her esophagus, and down into her stomach. The Microbus periodically lurched forward as I tried to carefully place Meri's head on my lap and position her so that the milk shake would slowly melt down her throat without choking her or running out her nose. I inserted my straw into the slushy drink, pulled it out with my thumb over the end, dripped a few drops onto Meri's tongue, and let the rest slide down the tube.

When at last we got to the checkpoint, Mom pulled our paperwork from the glove compartment and handed it to a patrolman. The men wore camouflage pants stuffed into tall, black army boots and olive-green jackets with bright gold buttons, machine guns clipped closely at their sides. They examined the bus from all angles and then pushed their unsmiling faces up against the windows and ogled every one of us. After a bit more posturing, they waved Mom along.

Eventually Meri and I fell asleep, until the bumpy dirt roads of LeBaron brought me back to consciousness. Bleary-eyed, I was shocked to discover that the line of peach trees that had run through the middle of the alfalfa field separating our property from Alejandra's was gone. Now, we could peer straight through to Alejandra's house, which only added insult to Mom's injury.

Mom parked the van and left the headlights on so we could find our way over the rocks and puddles to the front door of our house. The night air felt cool against my arms and neck, and I was comforted by the sound of water in the ditches and the smell of the alfalfa fields and wet earth. I staggered out of the bus with Meri on my shoulder and struggled to balance my heavy sister, whose body now flopped around like a rag doll sewn over a skeleton.

The smell of alfalfa disappeared as soon as Mom opened the door, replaced by the familiar odor of mice droppings. We hadn't been home in ages, but it soon became apparent that someone else had been there. The house had been broken into and ransacked. Drawers were over-turned on the cement floor, boxes of family pictures were upended, and clothes were everywhere. Break-ins like this were common, and Mom always shrugged them off. "The people who took our stuff probably needed it more than we did," she said that night, although, on first glance, it appeared that the burglars hadn't taken anything. Looking around at the chaos, I couldn't help thinking that the thieves had probably created such a big mess in retaliation for our not having any-thing worth stealing. Since we were all exhausted, Mom declared that the cleanup could wait until morning.

The next morning, amid all the clutter, I came across a happy sur-prise. Lane had finally installed a showerhead in the bathroom. I stared awestruck at the gleaming silver pipe that ran up from the cement floor, gently curved around the ceiling, and descended a few more feet before dead-ending into a beautiful, new showerhead, also silver and gleaming. I wanted to run my finger along its length. But as soon as I touched it, a powerful surge of electricity stunned me. I jerked my finger back. I should have known there would be a catch.

Lane, whose do-it-yourself skills had just begun to impress me, would later explain that the electric current was necessary for the pipe to heat water on its way up. The shower was something of a mixed blessing. He warned us not to touch that metal tube, "especially if you're barefoot and wet," two things that were unavoidable in the shower.

But before Lane could explain why we needed electricity in the shower pipe, I reported my experience to Mom. She dismissed the danger with the same shrug with which she had dismissed the thieves and immediately searched her purse for a rubber coin holder. "This'll do till we can find out what's goin' on," she said, wrapping the little blue oval around the shower's metal spigot. On her way out the door, she noticed the hole where the doorknob was still missing and stuffed a mismatched sock into it for privacy.

That day I also learned that I was now old enough to handle one of the most dreaded chores in the house—washing out dirty cloth diapers. I cringed at the thought of how unpleasant my task would be. When Mom saw the resistance written on my face, she laughed. "Oh, don't be so silly, Sis. You have to get used to washing diapers out some-time. You know, for when you have your own kids."

As we tidied up and the house slowly returned to what passed for normal, Mom's preoccupation with Lane's latest exploits reached a fever pitch. Finally, when she couldn't take it anymore, she grabbed her purse and rushed out the door.

"I'm going down to talk to Susan," she said breathlessly. "Ruthie, you and Matt are in charge."

No doubt Mom would rather have gone directly to Lane, but that would have been taboo. Searching for a husband at another sister wife's home was considered an intrusion on the other woman's allotted time or, worse, spying.

I bolted for the shower as soon as Mom pulled out of the driveway, eager to try out the new contraption, in spite of its hazards. The water was frigid at first, but slowly it became warm, or rather lukewarm. It induced goose bumps, but still I reveled in the luxury of showering in primitive LeBaron. Maybe it was my surroundings, but it seemed like the most elegant shower in the world. For a moment, I could live like a princess—as long as I didn't touch that silver pipe.

MOM RETURNED FROM Susan's in the early evening but relayed noth-ing of what she'd learned. She just walked to Lane's shop silently to grind up wheat kernels. She then made six of her signature cylindrical loaves of bread, whose smell filled the house. She took the leftover dough and made what she called scones by separating the raw, sticky mixture into handful-size pieces, rolling each portion into a ball between her palms, and flattening them one by one with her fingertips. She then fried the pieces, placed them on a platter over a paper towel, and got them ready to serve for dinner by spreading butter and honey on top or sprinkling cinnamon and sugar over them.

Matt was out milking the brown cow in the corral when the bottom of the kitchen door scraped against the cement floor and Lane's leather-soled boots stomped inside. Mom appeared to have practiced for this moment. She continued her work without acknowledging him.

"Hey there," he said to us, his eyes wide. "Your mom didn't tell me you were comin'. I'm surprised to see ya." He tried to put his arm around Mom's shoulder and kissed her cheek, but she threw it off.

Micah, still wearing the blue pajamas with the plastic feet that he'd been wearing the night before, shuffled into the kitchen, his bottle in hand. He had started walking at nine months, and Lane smiled widely as he watched his young son's steady footsteps. Lane took a seat at the table, scooped up the toddler, and bounced him on his knee. The heel of my stepfather's boot tapped hard against the floor. The sight of Mom, obviously angry but still serving Lane's dinner first, just as she always did, was something I just couldn't watch.

In that moment, seeing him pick up his scone and happily feed a piece to Micah as if nothing were wrong, I found myself hating Lane more than ever. I stormed out of the kitchen. But when Matt brought in his silver bucket of milk, Mom called us all to the table for dinner. Those were the only words she spoke. She doled out the fried scones in silence.

That night, while I lay on a lumpy mattress on the rickety living-room hide-a-bed, the beams from a full moon streaming through the windows, I heard Mom's quavering voice. She was crying through tears—but her words were unintelligible. I craned my neck in the direction of her bedroom, deeply curious as to how Lane was explaining himself, but the adobe walls were too thick. I fell asleep trying to decipher their muddled argument.

— 24 —

Mom's eyes were still swollen the next day. Things with Lane otherwise seemed to have returned to normal. They readied themselves for church and left Matt and me in charge of our siblings. On their way out, Mom told me she needed some alone time with her husband and reminded me that the diapers still needed to be washed.

I had already learned to put off that chore as long as possible, but by late morning I began to fear Mom would soon be home, so I took the diaper bucket outside and placed it on the damp patch of tall grass next to the faucet just outside the kitchen door. I opened the lid just a crack and quickly turned on the hose, hoping to drown out the smell before it reached my nose. But the stench of day-old dirty diapers whooshed up at me anyway and I gagged.

I was still a bit woozy when I heard the sound of footsteps sloshing through mud in the distance. I looked up to see a girl in a yellow, long-sleeved dress with white tights and black patent-leather shoes with silver buckles, my stepsister Sally. She was about to jump over the ditch at the edge of our driveway.

Sally was Susan's daughter from her marriage prior to Lane. Sally was a year older than me, and she had her mother's thick, dark brown hair, which always made me jealous. She wore it in barrettes and ponytails or curled and left loose around her shoulders. As she smiled and walked across the long, muddy yard toward me, I noticed her full, light pink lips, and also the red birthmark above her upper lip that I always thought looked like a strawberry stain from heaven.

Excited to see her, I slammed shut the diaper bucket and silently prayed that the smell would dissipate before she reached me. I stood up, dried my hands on my jeans, and smiled back.

"Do you want to spend the night at my house tonight, Ruthie?" she asked after we exchanged greetings.

"Don't you have school in the morning?"

"My mom said you might be able to spend the day with me at school, if the teacher says you can. We could go to school together in the morning and ask her."

"But what if she says no?"

Sally went to Primaria Miguel Hidalgo, the same school across the highway where I had started the first grade a few years earlier. Going back there for a day sounded like fun, but if the teacher said no, I would have to walk back home by myself.

"Sometimes my teacher lets us bring our friends even if they don't go to our school—but just for one day," Sally reassured me.

"Well, sure. But I have to finish my chores and ask my mom when she comes home from church."

"Do you want me to help you?"

I thought about the smelly diapers, and the idea of washing them in front of her embarrassed me. I said no thank you and that I would walk to her house if Mom said yes.

As soon as Sally walked off our property, I finished washing out the diapers as quickly as I could and hung them out to dry with wooden clothespins on the clothesline beside our house. I knew I'd never be able to go if my chores weren't done. I held the empty diaper bucket with both hands when I heard Mom's Microbus sputtering up the road and ran toward the driveway as the bus came into view, turned the corner, and splashed through the wide, shallow section of the ditch. I ran along Mom's side of the van and pleaded my request before it sputtered to a complete stop just outside the kitchen door. She didn't hesitate to say yes. Mom had returned alone, as that night would be another wife's turn to host Lane. For a moment, I froze, worrying that Lane would be at Susan's. Luckily he wasn't.

THAT NIGHT I shared a bed with Sally and Cynthia, one of Sally's sisters. Their house was close to the highway, and the next morning we all walked the short distance to school together. Before class started, Brenda and Natalia greeted us in the schoolyard. I felt as comfortable and familiar with them as I had back in first grade, and the happy feeling of being at home lasted all day long. I was elated to find that recess still meant hopscotch, and our playing continued where we'd left off years before.

I didn't want the fun to end, so Sally and I decided to play at her house after school. We chatted happily about Barbies on the way there, but then discovered that no one was home. Not thinking anything of it, we went on to my house. When we were about halfway there, I heard the screen door swing open at Sally's grandmother's house. Grandma Rhoda, as she was known, waved and asked us to stop by. Her disposition was always as sweet as the homemade baked goods and candy she offered whenever she saw us, as warm and inviting as the fresh-baked bread in her kitchen.

But that day, she had a serious, sad, weary look on her face, and it stopped me in my tracks. She was carrying a large mason jar of homemade vegetable soup, which she handed to me. "Ruthie, give this to your mother and tell her to let me know if there's anything else I can do for her."

The jar felt warm against my hands, and I eyed the soup hungrily, wishing Grandma Rhoda had included some of her homemade cinnamon rolls.

"How's your mom doing?"

"She's fine."

Grandma Rhoda's eyes dimmed and her mouth fell open.

"Is my mom sick?" I asked, not understanding the melancholy mood.

"You haven't heard?"

"Heard what?".

"I'm so sorry to be the one to have to tell you this." Grandma Rhoda embraced me suddenly, stroking my hair. Reluctantly I rested my head against her belly.

"Meri died this morning."

My body grew stiff. I didn't believe it and thought that maybe someone had made a mistake, that Meri might just be acting like her usual unresponsive self. I had worried my whole life that Mom would be taken away from me, but I never for a second suspected that Meri would be—in spite of her disabilities. Meri was too young. I thought that she would continue to grow and grow, and that we'd all respond accordingly, pushing her around in bigger and bigger strollers and feeding her through bigger and bigger tubes.

When we arrived at my front door, I stood there for a moment, paralyzed by the knot of guilt that had formed in my stomach. Sally looked at me with a worried expression. I had complained too many times about how hard it was to help take care of her and how much I hated washing out her diapers and feeding her through a tube. *Please, God, let Meri somehow not be dead and let this all be a big mistake,* I prayed silently. *I promise I won't ever complain about taking care of her again.*

The doorknob whined in my hands as I turned it. I saw Matt sitting in the rocking chair in the living room, his head down, his body shaking as he cried. He looked up at me, his swollen, red eyes turning their attention to the other side of the room. There, on the couch, lay Meri's body, her head propped up on a pillow just as it always was during feeding time.

She wore a white cotton dress with ruffles around her neck, shoulders, and knees, white tights, and white Mary Janes with silver buckles. I'd never seen those clothes before and couldn't imagine where Mom had gotten them. I took one step toward the couch, then heard footsteps entering from the kitchen. Mom's hair was matted on one side, as if she'd just woken up. I looked in her eyes and felt them bore into mine. Then, without a word, she lunged for me and wrapped her arms around me so tightly it hurt. My face rested in her trembling bosom.

"We lost our little girl," she said quietly. Mom's body felt weak, and as she held me tighter, I realized that Mom was no longer holding me to console me, but that she needed me to comfort her.

When I finally got close enough to see Meri's face, I noticed that her skin had turned purple and her lips a shade of light blue. Still not sure she was dead, I leaned in close to see if she was breathing, and I noticed that her right eye was slightly open, a heartbreaking sight. But I didn't cry. Instead, I calmly lifted my index finger to her face, brushed her eyelashes with it, and gently pulled the eyelid closed. I let go, and the lid popped open again.

I heard the sound of Lane's pickup, and then its door slamming shut. "Matt, come help me," he called out, and after another minute the two of them carried a tiny, white coffin inside, Lane's face heavy and expressionless. He and Matt placed the small box on the living-room carpet and opened it, revealing a white satin interior with ruffles. I stepped away from my sister's body so they could lift her from the couch and place her inside. Meri's head rested in death as it had in life, on a pillow, and they folded her arms across her chest.

Mom broke out in heaving sobs as Matt and Lane closed the casket and tamped down its wooden lid. Meri's coffin was placed in the back of Lane's pickup, so it could be transported to the graveyard in a neighboring town. We couldn't afford to have Meri embalmed, so we needed to bury her that night.

A line of cars followed our Microbus, their headlights helping light our path down the dark, dusty roads to the graveyard. The moon was full, and its light shone on white tombstones of every size, many covered in bundles of faded plastic and fabric flowers. Wreaths hung from wooden and stone crosses with small, faded ceramic statues of Jesus wearing his thorny crown, the blood dripping down his face. Tumbleweeds blew across the gravel in the light, cool breeze.

When we arrived, Meri's coffin had already been set next to the grave that Matt and two of my stepbrothers had dug, its lid now removed so that mourners could see Meri in her white satin bed, her eye still open. Doors slammed as more and more cars pulled up, and soon dozens of people—some from Lane's family whom I hardly knew—had created a circle around Meri. No one from Mom's extended family could come; there wasn't time for them to travel from the States.

Someone said a blessing, and then mourners were invited to speak on Meri's and the family's behalf while we all stood in a circle around my sister. Linda, one of my Mom's friends, stepped forward to give a long eulogy. She told the crowd that God had sent Meri to our family as a gift to teach us unconditional love and generosity, even as we struggled to take care of the little girl who, in her few short years on earth, never learned to take care of herself.

Much more followed, but I heard nothing further. That one word—love—opened up something in me. Suddenly, and for the first time that day, I began to cry, and then I began to sob. The circle of faces turned to watch me; I buried my face in Mom's pant leg, continued wailing, and felt her hand gently pat the top of my head. I had loved my sister, I told myself. Even though I had resented the heavy burden of taking care of her, I'd *loved* her. The secret anger I'd bore about it all suddenly had nothing to attach itself to. Meri was gone.

The graveside service didn't last long, and when it was over, a long line of well-meaning people formed beside me. They hugged me and told me how sorry they were. Over their shoulders I saw Matt and my stepbrothers shoveling dirt, heard the sound of it hitting Meri's coffin as they slowly covered it. Clouds of dust rose out of the hole and floated away in the moonlight.

— 25 —

Just two days after Meri's funeral, we returned to El Paso. The trip was quiet and uneventful. Wispy, pewter rain clouds hung heavily above us and magnified my sense of loss. I rolled around in the back of the van, uncomfortable with having so much of the space there to myself. I fought the urge to reach into the diaper bag for Meri's plastic feeding tube even though I knew she wasn't there. Taking care of her wouldn't be my job anymore. Being unoccupied left me feeling disoriented and uncertain, as if my place and purpose in the family had shifted. I didn't know how I belonged anymore. Only after her death did I realize how strong the bond between my sister and me had been.

Although I continued to grieve for Meri for a long time after we got back to El Paso, my brothers seemed to settle back into life as it had always been. Throughout the spring, Matt teased and wrestled with Luke as much as he always had. Luke continued to wander off farther and farther from the trailer park when no one was watching him, and on a few occasions the police found him and brought him home. Meanwhile, Aaron became even pickier about what he would and wouldn't wear and argued with Mom over his outfits almost every morning before school. Lane rarely came to visit us in El Paso anymore. Mom said that he was having a yearlong honeymoon with his new wife, Marjory. She didn't have a bunch of little kids crying at home, Mom said, and she offered him a break from his family responsibilities. I was happiest when Lane wasn't around. He still visited my bedside when he had the chance, and I still hadn't told Mom. She seemed so tired and unhappy and spent a lot of time in bed with migraines. Then, at the beginning of the summer, Mom brought home a new baby.

She'd chosen to have another natural childbirth, so Mom and Lane went back to LeBaron the last week of June, returning with a little girl in the first week of July. They chose a Spanish name, Elena. I found the name kind of funny for a little platinum-blond doll of a child with big, almond-shaped eyes and a pointy chin. She was instantly adored by all of us, in part because, like Micah, she was a normal baby. Elena and I had little bonding time in the beginning. When a new baby entered our home, protocol dictated that the baby who no longer needed to be nursed and burped was handed off to me. So, Micah became my new responsibility, and thus began my love affair with my youngest brother.

Micah was a happy, curious toddler with a perpetual smile and a habit of using short words and phrases incorrectly, which made everyone laugh. He followed Aaron all over the single-wide with the rubber nipple from his blue bottle latched between his teeth, wanting to do everything his big brother did.

The woman from Social Services who had paid that first surprise visit was still checking in on us. She always wore slacks or a skirt and a nicely matching blouse, with perfectly placed makeup and clean-smelling perfume. She would ask my brothers and me how we were doing, but always with kind eyes and a gentle manner. I no longer saw her as the Wicked Witch. Instead, she came to seem personable and comforting—to all of us, except Mom, who grew more nervous and cagey with each visit. I was surprised to see Mom suddenly struggle with her performance, knowing she used to be able to lie with a perfectly straight face. I didn't know what to think of the change in her. She answered the caseworker's questions like a guilty defendant at a trial, constantly adjusting her glasses and chewing her fingernails.

The first time the caseworker appeared after Meri's death, I was afraid Mom might have a nervous breakdown. She talked louder and faster than ever before and tripped over her words while attempting to explain that she'd buried Meri in Mexico, that we couldn't afford a funeral in the States or the autopsy that would have been required. I had a hard time understanding why Mom stumbled as she told the woman these things, all of which were true. With a shaky hand, Mom produced the death certificate, all of it in Spanish, and explained that she didn't know why Meri died, just as the doctors had never known the cause of Meri's illness.

The caseworker showed up again not long after Elena was born, on a weekday late in the afternoon when the sun burned through the windows and made the trailer feel like a sauna. The fans blowing in every room hardly made a difference. The woman admired the new baby for a few moments and then asked who and where the father was. Mom appeared genuinely shocked, as if she'd never expected that question. Then she looked down and stared angrily at the carpet as if she'd just noticed a stain and couldn't wait to discover which of her children had spilled something.

"I'm not sure," Mom said quietly after a moment. "I've been seeing a few men."

My body became rigid with discomfort at the awkward line of questioning, not to mention the thought that the pristine caseworker now had even less respect for Mom than the little she'd had before. Suddenly I feared that the woman would turn her attention to me, demand to know who the fathers of Mom's babies were, and discover I was an even worse liar than Mom. But the woman surprised me, surprised all of us.

"Well, Kathy, I don't think we have any reason to keep up with our visits. Your children seem safe in your care," she said, sounding not entirely convinced, "and you haven't given me any reason to believe otherwise."

Without another word, she pulled a stapled packet of paperwork from her briefcase, clicked her pen open, and scratched a few things on the first page.

When she looked up again, the caseworker considered Mom's expression for a moment. Mom's mouth had dropped open, and she'd been left speechless by the new development. The woman offered Mom a few things to sign, then rose and began making her way to the door.

"Good luck," the caseworker said. She scanned Mom's face one more time, then looked at me and smiled sadly. In a moment she was gone.

"Ruthie, I'll never let myself get into that kind of trouble again." Mom jumped from her seat as soon as the woman pulled out of the driveway. The worry vanished from her face, immediately replaced by a gaiety that seemed to promise nothing but better days ahead. Soon, she opened the freezer and pulled out a carton of pecan-praline ice cream, one of her favorite treats, scooping it out with a tablespoon into pastel-colored cones.

That same week, Mom neatly tore a check from a checkbook, placed it in an envelope, licked the envelope shut, closed her eyes, and sighed deeply. She'd finally paid back her parents for loaning her and Lane the money to buy the trailer. Mom beamed for days, and we all basked in the light of her warm glow.

Being off probation emboldened Mom. She demonstrated a new confidence, which had its downsides, as I learned a few weeks later. "We're moving back to LeBaron, this time for good!" she announced. "We don't need doctors for Meri anymore, do we?" She said this as if it were a wholly positive development. "The government's not gonna control me. I don't want to be livin' in Babylon when it collapses." She shook her head. "And it'll be good for you kids to be near your dad.

Lane can make us some money renting out this trailer"—she clearly loved her plan—"and I can still get Social Security for Luke."

Mom's enthusiasm was powerful. It swiftly carried us back to our adobe house in Mexico, where her merriment continued.

Right after we moved back, Lane showed up unexpectedly. "Well, hello there," Mom said, her eyes shining when she heard the scrape of the kitchen door that always announced Lane's arrival, the same scrape that sent me fleeing the kitchen.

From down the hall I heard him say, "I need some help takin' Mexican workmen into the States." The tone of his deep voice didn't match Mom's lighthearted greeting. "Some people I know need some workers to help on construction sites in New Mexico."

"We just moved back here," Mom said, her merriment gone.

"Well, I know, but you and the kids can stay with me in Albuquerque, and the kids can work too. Susan and Alejandra are already there with their kids. Ever'body's workin' to help the family."

We'd been in LeBaron for less than a week and would be back in Babylon before the month was out.

26

For Lane, taking Mexicans to the States meant ripping out the built-in seating areas in the camper and placing boards over the hole, creating a small cavity underneath. Mom's assignment was to somehow construct a comfortable bed for her children to lie over the boards. We would cross the border at night, when my siblings and I were asleep, and with three Mexicans hidden beneath us.

We planned to pick up our stowaways in Casas, and my first thought when I saw them was that they'd never fit in Lane's hidden compartment. Two were tall and lanky, but a third was stout with a large belly. They were standing against an adobe wall when our headlights first illuminated them. They squinted in our direction, waved, and took last drags from their cigarettes. Lane told them they could sit in the back till we reached the border. He and Mom were squished together in the front cab with Elena and Micah. Matt, Luke, Aaron, and I lay in the top bed over the cab.

Somehow we all fell asleep on that tiny mattress. A screech of tires woke me up. Then, the truck began to fishtail, throwing me first against

Aaron and then the wall. I had almost pulled myself to a seated position when the truck hit something large that generated a tremendous thud. The tires squealed again and I crashed forward into the window. It didn't break, but we heard the sound of something shattering underneath us, then the truck came to a sudden stop.

In the eerie silence that followed, I looked up to see my brothers piled together against a window. Below, I watched one of the Mexicans jump out of the camper door onto the highway and the other two quickly follow. My brothers and I jumped out next and ran toward the passenger's side of the truck, finding Mom standing outside and leaning through the passenger window with a crying Elena in one arm. With the other, Mom scooped up Micah, and I was relieved to discover that all three were fine.

"What happened?" I yelled.

"I think we hit a horse," Mom replied quietly and calmly. She sat Micah on the ground and shook glass from the plastic feet of his pajamas.

I stepped back to see that the truck was parked sideways in the middle of the two-lane road, its windshield completely shattered. A huge gash was in the left front fender, and a headlight had been torn from its casing. Lane's boots crunched over broken glass as he came into view. In the beam of the one good headlight, the road ahead looked completely red, covered in blood. I saw Mom's jaw drop open and then followed her gaze to the road and the headless body of a white horse, its hooves black and legs lifeless. The horse's head lay on the other side of the highway, its eyes still wide with a look of shock.

It took Lane and all three of the Mexicans to drag the horse by its legs to the side of the road. Then one of the men lifted the head and placed it next to the body. Lane wiped blood from his hands with a greasy towel he found behind his truck seat, brushed glass out of the seats, and told everyone to get back in the truck.

Eventually, we made it to an auto parts store in Juárez, slept in the camper until the establishment opened the next morning, and then stood around most of the day waiting for the new windshield to be installed. By nighttime, we were in line for the border crossing.

Predictably, the line moved slowly, and with every inch we crawled forward, the breathing of the men below me grew heavier, and the smell of their sweat stronger. I could tell that what we were doing was serious business and that the whole family would be in trouble if we were caught. I didn't know exactly what would happen if the border police found the men at the bottom of the truck, but I was sure my siblings and I would be taken away from Mom.

I felt confused. Through the camper window, I stared at the back of Mom's head in the front seat, watching it come in and out of the light as we inched forward, and I remembered her promise not to get us all in trouble again. I realized then that I couldn't count on her promises and began to wonder why she didn't seem able to protect my siblings and me. I just couldn't understand it.

A cold fluorescent light shone through our camper's dark windows when we reached the border. Faces of patrol officers appeared, and I felt my heart race and my body shake. The border men circled the camper and approached from behind. A few seconds later, they flung open the camper door, and their voices went silent as they peered inside. I watched the beam of a flashlight dance from Matt's face to Aaron's, to Luke's. I closed my eyes tightly just before the beam reached my own face.

"What nationality are all these kids?" said a deep, thickly accented voice.

"American," replied Lane.

"Are you carrying any goods with you purchased in Mexico?" the deep voice continued.

"We only bought a few souvenirs for some family, that's all."

There was an interminable pause.

"All right. Looks good," said the voice, and he shut the camper door.

After a few more exchanges between Lane and the patrolmen, I heard the engine rev and felt the camper accelerate, and soon we were in El Paso. That next morning we dropped off Lane and three exhausted and dazed Mexicans at a job site, and then Mom drove us to meet up with her sister wives in Albuquerque, New Mexico.

27

This can be your contribution to the family income," Lane said to
my stepsister and me. Maria and I looked down at the table filled with
pine nuts, our eyes barely disguising our contempt. I don't know what
I had expected when I'd overheard Lane say "the kids can work too,"
but it definitely wasn't selling pine nuts on the side of the road in Albuquerque.

Polygamists from LeBaron had a long history with pine nuts. Each
fall, families would pack up their kids, make their way to the border,
pick up a few Mexicans, and drive to one of the dense mountain for-
ests in New Mexico, Nevada, or California. There, they would pick
pinecones, separate the *piñones* from the cones, then sell the *piñones*
to stores or to restaurants in the area. The money they made from this
was usually enough for a family to pay for a year in Mexico. Now Lane
had decided we would be doing it too.

Lane unloaded the camper onto a cement slab that sat next to a
mobile home he had rented. With one bedroom and one bathroom,
the single-wide was roughly half the size of the one we'd had in El Paso.

Still, this one was newer looking and hadn't been in a fire, so I was satisfied—until I realized that Alejandra's family, not mine, would live there. Polygamy protocol dictated that first wives always had first pick of living quarters, and Alejandra had reasonably chosen the single-wide. Mom and the six of us would be staying in the camper for the rest of the summer.

I slept with Mom and Elena on the top bed that jutted over the cab of the truck, except every third night, when it was Mom's turn with Lane. On those nights, I was demoted to the mattress in the camper's lower level and a restless night with four brothers in one bed. I was eleven years old, old enough to realize that our situation was ridiculous and humiliating. I also realized that things could have been worse: Susan and her family were staying in an even smaller dwelling nearby. The conditions there were so cramped—Susan and all her children slept on a single foam mattress surrounded by enormous brown bags of *piñones*—I actually found myself grateful that Lane had married Mom second.

Marjory, Lane's new fourth wife, didn't come to New Mexico with us. Lane had been spending less and less time with her, which seemed to make Mom happy. Mom said Marjory was busy visiting her adult children who lived in California. Of the three families living in Albuquerque, Alejandra's had the nicest living situation, but I quickly realized that her privilege was a mixed blessing. Yes, she had a bathroom and shower, but she had to share both with two other families, who could use her facilities at any time. And hers was the only full size kitchen too. The atmosphere while the three women tried to prepare meals for all their families in that tiny space at the same time was always tense. Waiting for dinner meant huddling among three sets of siblings, suffocating and sweltering, in front of a TV, especially with three women cooking in a hot kitchen.

One of the worst aspects of the pine-nuts experience was the food. We could rarely afford meat and certainly weren't allowed to eat the nuts we were selling. So we ate beans and rice, always, at every meal.

Anything seemed preferable to sitting in a crowded camper and eating a bowl of beans and rice—even selling pine nuts on the side of the road.

I came to see something liberating in Maria's and my pine-nut stand at the far corner of the Safeway parking lot, a spot we had chosen for its being near a busy intersection. People coming from any direction could see our card table, as well as our signs, the words PINE NUTS written large enough that drivers wouldn't confuse us with a lemonade stand. We sat for hours on end under a tattered green umbrella waiting for cars or the odd Safeway shopper to stop by. Sometimes, when the boredom overwhelmed us, Maria and I would fill plastic bags with pine nuts, one pound in each, measuring them out with the help of an old, rusty, white scale from a grocery store. We also poured pine nuts into Dixie cups, which we sold for fifty cents apiece. We never had many customers, although people often stopped by to ask what those odd-shaped, little nuggets were, as if they'd never seen them in their lives. I would launch into a long and detailed description of what pine nuts were, where they came from, and how they were picked and sorted. Anyone who stood there and patiently waited through my pitch was rewarded with a single nut as a free sample.

Lane dropped us off with our card table each morning, and he drove by to check on us once a day too. And at the end of every day, Lane collected what little money we had made from our sales. He continually reminded us to give him each and every penny of our proceeds, but soon enough Maria and I learned to skim off the top. We were just pocketing what we felt we were due, nothing more than the allowances other kids would get, or so we told ourselves. As soon as we were sure Lane was gone, we would slip off to a nearby McDonald's and blow a few dollars on cheeseburgers, ice-cold Cokes, and ice-cream sundaes.

One day, I noticed Maria hiding more money than she usually spent on lunch and asked her about it.

"You can cut open old Polaroids, put the money behind the picture, and then tape it up so no one will notice." She smiled proudly.

"What are you doing that for?"

"I'm saving up money."

"Why?"

"So I can run away from home."

This took me by surprise. Maria hadn't complained about her home life before. I wondered if she wanted to run away because Lane was abusing her the way he'd been abusing me. Maria was thirteen and had already developed a woman's body. She wore her long, dark brown hair in two braids that went down the length of her back. Her flirtatious, almond-shaped, brown eyes were already earning her a great deal of attention, as were her full, perfectly shaped breasts that bounced under tight cotton T-shirts, and her pear-shaped bottom. Whenever she walked across the street to McDonald's or walked anywhere in public, men whistled and called out to her.

Like Maria's, my breasts were growing and my body was changing. Over the past several months—ever since Elena had been born—it seemed as if Lane had been seeking me out more and more. I tried to avoid all contact with him, but he was always asking me to accompany him on errands or to help him with tasks around town. Then he'd take me for a ride to a place where no one could find us: a barren parking lot, under a bridge, or into a dark alley that reeked of garbage.

"What are you doing all the way over there?" he'd ask in his high-pitched, nice-man voice, a voice I never heard him use with anyone else or in any other situation. "Come sit closer to me. I'm not gonna hurt ya." He'd pull me onto his lap, his grimy hands reaching under my blouse for my developing breasts, which felt so tender and painful in his hands that I wanted to scream. I'd feel his penis stiffen beneath me, and then he'd grind his lap violently against the seat of my jeans. I felt so humiliated and powerless that I couldn't even recognize how much worse it would have been if Lane had unzipped his pants.

Hearing that Maria wanted to run away, and thinking it was because of Lane, I began to feel disgusted. I started thinking about what he might be doing to my beautiful stepsister. What awful experiences would lead a thirteen-year-old girl to stuff dollar bills behind family photos and run away into a world of strangers?

"Why . . . do you want to run away?" I asked Maria reluctantly.

Maria noticed my serious tone, looked at me with concern, then smiled.

"If I stay here or in LeBaron, I'll never get to do what I want to do." She sighed. "I'll just do what every other girl does: get married at fifteen. I don't want to do that, and I don't want to be somebody's third wife. I'd be too jealous to share like that. You know?"

I nodded silently.

"I don't want to suffer the way my mom did when my dad took his other wives. Does your mom like it?"

"No," I said quietly. "She cries all the time."

"Mine does too. I don't want that!"

I watched her stuff the last of the dollar bills in her jeans and worked up the courage to ask her the question that had been plaguing me. "Maria, does your dad ever kiss you on the mouth when you're alone with him?"

She looked up at me alarmed, as if she thought I was crazy. "He's my dad! Why would he ever do something like that?"

"I dunno," I replied as quickly as possible.

"Well, does he ever kiss *you*?"

"No," I replied without a moment's hesitation. "Of course not."

"Then why'd you ask me?"

"I dunno."

As much as it would have hurt to hear that Lane had been subjecting Maria to the same indignities he'd been inflicting on me, it hurt more to know that he hadn't. Why had he only chosen me? I was consumed with a new and powerful desire: I wanted to run away too. But first I'd have to save up my money.

— 28 —

We lived in Albuquerque selling pine nuts for two months. Lane didn't have many jobs hauling loads during that time, and he pursued me as if he had missed me. He found every excuse possible to take me on errands: to sell pine nuts to local markets, to pick up additional loads of nuts, to look for parts to fix his truck or the single-wide, and to find more supplies for our stand. I did everything I could to avoid him, but in our three families' cramped space, there was no place to hide. Mom was distracted with the baby and my younger siblings and didn't even notice the extra attention our stepfather paid to me. Each morning I'd wake up and vow that today would be the day I'd tell Mom what Lane was doing to me, but each day I'd find a reason why I couldn't share my secret: Mom was too tired, the babies had been up all night. Every time I came close to saying something, a small voice in my head would tell me to keep silent, that it would only make things worse if I told the truth, and what if Mom didn't believe me?

But I was starting to feel desperate. Whenever Lane touched me, I felt he left fingerprints that stained my skin. His marks were everywhere, on my arms and chest and legs and private parts, and to see myself naked was to see a body covered from head to toe with these welts. I stopped looking at myself in the mirror, even when I was fully clothed, a strategy that helped me live with my shame, for a while at least. When the mirror was unavoidable, I would become so nauseated I had to look away. I could hardly keep from retching every time I combed my hair, so vivid were the stains of my stepfather's desire.

As I hid from mirrors, I hid from Lane too. I slept with the covers over my head and hoped against hope that a blanket could protect me. I thanked God for my brothers, who had been forced by circumstance to sleep sandwiched next to me in the same bed, which made Lane's nighttime advances impossible.

I began to take refuge in a world of fantasies. I imagined slicing my wrists open and watching my soul escape through my wounds, floating up to heaven as my arms were bathed in blood. When I was seven years old, a half brother of mine—one of my father's sons with one of his other wives—had committed suicide. I had vivid memories of attending the funeral and watching so many people mourn the death of such a young, troubled soul. A few months after that half brother died, another of my father's children followed suit, hanging herself with her husband's belt. It came to seem that suicide ran in my family, and by the time we were living in New Mexico, I had become fixated on how I might be able to follow in my half siblings' footsteps. I fantasized about slicing up my skin, cutting myself in all the places where Lane had touched me.

I felt that my skin had betrayed me. Something on it must have been different that invited Lane's touches, something that indicated I wanted him, regardless of whatever I said otherwise. I had goodness and virtue in me, but it was wrapped in a skin that was evil. Because my skin was all the world knew of me, it gained the upper hand. The tug of suicide grew stronger each day, and as it did, I started thinking about what might be waiting for me in the afterlife.

The afterlife, as had been explained to me in Sunday school and by my mother, was run by men who had been polygamous on earth, men like my father and Lane. "As man is, God once was; as God is, man may become," the church elders would remind us. Women who had been faithful and loyal wives would become goddesses—heavenly servants to the men who ruled over them. But no one had ever explained what would become of girls like me. When I asked Mom what would happen to dead girls who hadn't been anyone's wife, she said my soul was sealed to my father, and if I died before I married, I would go to my dad's kingdom, not Lane's.

This should have been comforting, and for a while it was, though gradually I began to doubt Mom's certitude. After all, I had already been born into my dad's kingdom, but that hadn't protected me from slipping into another one. How did I know that the same thing wouldn't happen in heaven? That I wouldn't slip into Lane's kingdom again and be stuck there for all of eternity? Or perhaps I would end up in hell. The thought of spending all eternity with Satan terrified me almost as much as the prospect of spending it with my stepfather.

The more I thought about all this, the more terrifying Lane seemed. One afternoon, as I sat in the back of his pickup with Susan's daughters Sally and Cynthia, I watched as Lane parked the truck and walked into a convenience store with his crooked step. From behind, I could see dirty pink hands at the end of forearms filthy from grease stains. When he got to the door and turned briefly to smile back at me, deep crow's-feet stretched from his eyes, intersecting the wrinkles etched across his brows and cheeks, making his face look as if it were formed of globs of clay. I met his smile with an angry glare.

Once Lane was gone, I wrapped my lightly freckled arms around my legs, pulled my knees up close to my chest, and moved away from the gunnysack of pine nuts I'd been sitting up against.

"Are you okay, Ruthie?" Sally asked.

I slowly turned to face her. She wore her hair in short bangs that lay flat over her dark eyebrows and milky-white forehead, with a straight part down the middle and brown barrettes on either side. Then I glanced at Cynthia, who, despite being my age, wore her hair in exactly the same style as her sister, right down to the brown barrettes. From there, my gaze floated down to Cynthia's face. She stared at me with a frightened look in her eyes. For a moment I thought that the angry look I'd given Lane had scared her. But it wasn't a face of fear, I realized; it was a face beyond fear, a face like mine.

I turned to her older sister. "Sally, does Lane ever kiss you on the mouth when you're alone with him?" I felt the hot sun beating down on us, and the smell of toasted pine nuts filled the air. Sally's eyes widened; so did Cynthia's. They turned to look at each other, then back at me, their expressions blank. Then tears began to form at the corners of Cynthia's eyes. She turned her head down, pulled her legs to her chest, held her face in her palms, and began to sob. Sally too began to cry, her twelve-year-old body trembling as the truth struggled its way out of her, and she looked at me with an expression I had seen before, in the mirror.

"All right, then. Thanks, have a good day," said a deep, dreaded voice in the distance.

Our eyes darted up. Lane stood in the door of the store, looking back at the manager. My stepsisters and I straightened our backs against the hard metal cab and pulled ourselves together. I sniffled and pinched my runny nose with my fingertips and wiped my hands on my jeans as Lane appeared beside the truck and poured the pine nuts from a Dixie cup back into the bag beside me.

"Anyone want to ride home up front with me?" he asked in his nice-man voice. We shook our heads and said no thanks. We didn't look at him. He climbed back into the truck and drove us home.

My stomach twisted as I sat on the thin living-room carpet in Alejandra's trailer that night with an untouched bean-and-cheese burrito on a paper plate over my lap. Sally, Cynthia, and I had gone for a walk around the trailer-park loop trail once Lane had parked the truck, where I'd discovered that their experiences had been almost identical to mine.

Like me, each had thought she was the only one who'd been harmed, but unlike me, they had never told their mother. My stepsisters and I were afraid that our moms wouldn't believe us, or that we might be punished. Then again, it would be a lot harder for our mothers to doubt all three of us, so we vowed to go together to tell them the truth that night. My stomach balled up and the skin on my face felt hot. I was no longer alone in my suffering, but still I dreaded the night's confrontation.

It was Alejandra's turn with Lane that night, and as we walked back to the camper, I asked Mom if I could talk to her in private. It felt crazy to be asking this of a woman who was carrying one baby in her arms and felt another tugging at her pants, but Mom said sure, we could talk before she put the little ones to bed.

We hadn't been inside the camper two minutes when we heard a light tapping at the door. As I opened the door, Micah climbed up onto a seat near where Mom had laid Elena.

"Mind if we come on in?" said Susan sweetly. Sally and Cynthia were just behind her. The two seemed as nervous as I was, with tight faces and closed, straight lips. I made room for them all as they stepped down the narrow space between the stove and the tiny fridge and sat at the table.

Mom put a pink baby blanket over her shoulder, covered her nursing breast, and lifted her blouse beneath it so that Elena, still just a month old, could nurse. The camper grew completely silent except for the sound of the baby's sucking.

"What's goin' on, girls?" Mom finally said. Susan stood in the narrow hall with her forearms folded between her pregnant belly and her chest. She nodded as if she'd been about to ask the same question.

My stepsisters and I looked at each other as if wondering who should speak first. I decided it would be me.

"Mom, do you remember what happened with Lane in El Paso?" I said, my pulse pounding in my neck and my eyes boring holes into the tabletop. I looked up at her. She nodded. "He never stopped." I fought as hard as I could to keep from crying.

"Are you sure?"

I looked up, surprised to hear the deep skepticism in her voice. She was squinting from the glare of the bare lightbulb over her head, but I no longer felt intimidated. I told Mom and Susan everything, describing all the times Lane had pulled me onto his lap and put his hands on me when he had asked me to run errands with him. Then Sally and Cynthia explained that he had done the exact same things to them.

Susan looked wide-eyed, obviously stunned, and turned to Mom, who appeared shocked and perturbed.

"Well, how come you girls haven't said anything before?" Susan asked.

"He said that if we told anyone," Sally answered, "it would make you mad and you'd feel bad." She put her elbows on the table next to mine, drew in the stifling air, and held her chin in her hands. Mom and Susan looked at each other again, their faces unchanged.

Elena had stopped nursing, and not until Mom looked down as if she'd completely forgotten a baby was there did I realize I'd gotten through to her. She put Elena on her shoulder and patted her back, the rubber sole of her shoe tapping at the same time. For a while I thought she might be at a loss for words, but then came the torrent of questions.

"Are you sure you're not just saying this about Lane because you girls don't like him?"—"When did all this happen?"—"If this really did happen, why didn't you come to us with it sooner?"

I corroborated Sally's story in a tired voice, sounding like a teacher who's told her student something a hundred times.

"Lane told us not to tell you because he said we would hurt your feelings, and we thought we'd get in trouble and he'd whip us with his belt." My stepsisters nodded in agreement.

"We were embarrassed," Sally added. "We were afraid that you wouldn't believe us. But now there's three of us . . ."

As her voice trailed off, I watched Mom closely, afraid that she thought we were lying. Finally she put her hand over her mouth, bowed her head, and caught a few tears on her fingertips as they fell down her cheeks. As hard as I tried to be calm and grown-up, the sight of Mom crying was too much for me; my eyes welled up and my throat tightened.

"I don't believe this is happening," Mom sobbed. "What are we going to do?"

"I have no idea." Susan's arms were still folded over her round belly. "I guess we should talk to Lane about this together so he knows all three girls came forward."

"Let's get the kids in bed," Mom said, after the two had stared at each other a moment. "We should talk to him tonight while all the kids are asleep."

"Alejandra won't like it if we bother him on her night," Susan added.

"I don't care about that." Mom sounded partly angry and partly desperate to find out what Lane had to say. She sniffled and wiped her nose. "We need to get to the bottom of all this tonight."

Late that evening Mom finally returned to our camper from her meeting with Lane and Susan, but I was still wide-awake, waiting to hear what had happened. Instead, Mom walked right past me, a dark figure whose face I couldn't make out, and went to bed.

LANE USUALLY CAME to get me and take me to go sell pine nuts each morning. But the morning after Sally, Cynthia, and I told our moms about what had happened, he didn't come. Mom said Lane had asked one of Maria's younger brothers to go with her to the Safeway parking lot.

"Why isn't Ruthie going to work today?" demanded Matt, who was forever watching to make sure I did my part.

"She's stayin' home with me today," Mom replied. "I need to go grocery shoppin' and need some help cleanin' up. You go on and mind your own business." Once he and everyone else had left the house for jobs or play, Mom sat me down across from her at the table. Elena was in her arms, nursing again.

"Ruthie, Susan and I talked to Lane for a long time last night." Mom's eyes were closed and her head was turned away. "And he said he's very sorry for what he did to you girls." She took in a deep breath, leaned back against the foam seat, and rested her head against the window. "He even cried real hard when we talked about it."

Mom opened her eyes to check on Elena's nursing, still without looking at me. "He promises he'll never do anything like that again." I watched her draw in a breath and blow it out slowly. "And I believe him. I know in my heart that he's ready to repent, and"—at last she looked at me with watery eyes, her lips lowered at the corners—"I think he deserves another chance."

She broke out in sobs but collected herself when she registered the shock and fury on my face. "I know that's not what you want to hear, but, Ruthie, I want you to listen to me real well because you need to understand that Lane is a good man. He has some problems, but God can help him get over them. Jesus talks so much about forgiveness in the Bible. He says that we should forgive seventy times seven times, and your dad always talked about how important it is to give people another chance."

She continued for a bit longer, but I had drifted away, realizing that my earlier suspicions had been correct: Mom seemed perfectly willing to sacrifice me for Lane. *This can't be,* I told myself. *I must be misunderstanding.*

"I'm not going to forgive him, Mom. I don't want to live with him anymore."

"I know you don't, Sis, but it's not in God's plan for women to be single." I looked at her quizzically. "I want what God wants, and I know this is the right thing to do." Elena had fallen asleep. Mom laid her onto the blanket beside her. "He was crying, Ruthie."

I wondered how it didn't occur to Mom that I'd cried too, countless times over the years—tears of pain, tears of anger, tears of shame. But that morning, I couldn't cry. I was beyond tears. Finally realizing that Mom couldn't protect me from my stepfather made me feel too sad to cry. It was as though something in me just closed up.

"I want you to know, Ruthie, that if it happens again—if it *ever* happens again—you tell me right away, and I will leave him for sure."

Mom tapped her forefinger hard on the tabletop as she spoke those last words, and I knew that they were no more sincere or true than the nonapology Lane had given me so many years ago in El Paso, when he had promised he would never touch me that way again. Apparently my mom could lie to her own daughter with as much ease and confidence as she had when she lied to the social workers and border patrolmen. The only difference was that this time, it seemed as if she had actually convinced herself that she was telling the truth.

"For now, Susan and I are gonna pack our things and go back to LeBaron for the rest of the summer, so you girls can have a break before school starts again. Lane will stay here with Alejandra and keep workin'." She looked at me as if she expected an expression of gratitude.

Now it was my turn to avoid her gaze.

"Life is gonna get better, it'll all work out for the best," she continued weakly before she broke into tears again. "This is one of those times when we have to show God we have the power to forgive." Her sobbing increased until her words were almost unintelligible. "Just like Jesus taught us in the Bible."

She folded her arms on the table and buried her head in them. That night, as she and I raced to ready the camper for the trip back to LeBaron, I caught her occasionally wiping her eyes and sniffling. She shed many tears that day, but I didn't think a single one of them was for me.

PART IV

BREAKING

Elena and Micah in front of our house in LeBaron, 1986.

— 29 —

Over the next few months, I did what I could to avoid Lane during his rare visits home. In the fall, Alejandra's family returned to LeBaron, and Mom enrolled me in fifth grade and Aaron in third at Alma Dayer LeBaron, a low-cost private school named after LeBaron's founder, my grandfather. The school, across the street from my dad's church and boasting the same white stucco walls, had been built while we were living in California and El Paso. Because their families didn't have the extra welfare money we did, Sally and Maria went to the Mexican public school across the highway, and I found myself missing our time in New Mexico as I entered a classroom where I didn't know any of the other children. But all the classes at Alma Dayer were taught by mothers from the church, which made the situation much easier. Sally, Maria, and I spent time together whenever we didn't have to babysit or attend church services.

On Friday nights, we dressed in our Sunday best and took square-dance lessons at the church from Lane's mother. We shuffled awkwardly through the Virginia reel, the fox-trot, the two-step, and the waltz. My half sisters Natalia and Brenda would join us for this weekly ritual of watching and laughing at the boys, who hadn't yet grown into their Wrangler jeans and cowboy hats. On weekends we went to rodeos our relatives held at different ranches on the outskirts of town and rode borrowed horses along the dirt roads through vast, dry landscapes of mesquite and cacti.

While I kept myself distracted from my troubled home life, Matt was experiencing a very different kind of struggle. Even though I hated how much he teased my siblings and me, I had to admit that my oldest brother was smart. He had always performed exceptionally well in school. He had learned to read and write early, excelled in math, and had been on the honor roll consistently since first grade. While some parents might have seen Matt's grades as a reason to nurture his intelligence and keep him in good schools, for Mom and Lane this meant that by the time Matt was twelve, he'd acquired all the skills he needed. They took him out of school before he finished the sixth grade, and he never went back. Lane said it was more important that Matt—and several of his stepbrothers—pick and sell pine nuts all over the western United States to help provide for the family.

But there was more to Matt's troubles—much more, as I learned one Saturday afternoon in the middle of winter. The bitter bite of a frosty, wet cold snap had washed away the autumn leaves, and once again the barrel heater was working overtime in the corner of our living room. The smell of burning wood mingled with the scent of roasted red chili peppers and warm corn tortillas. Mom had made enchiladas for lunch, which meant spicy red sauce and homemade white cheese layered between corn tortillas and topped with a fried egg.

The rest of us having eaten and her nursing of Elena complete, Mom finally had time to eat herself. She handed me the baby to burp and sat down to a quiet meal alone. Mom hadn't even taken a bite when Matt charged through the kitchen door, bringing with him a whining gust of winter wind. Mom's hand stopped before the fork reached her mouth, her eyes following her son as he paced frantically in front of the table, his wet rubber-soled tennis shoes squeaking over the cement floor.

Matt's face was bright red from the cold. The acne on his chin and forehead had a purplish hue, and his expression so twisted in anger it looked as if he were wearing a scary Halloween mask. For the first time in my life my brother frightened me. He put his hands on the plastic chair opposite Mom and leaned hard onto it.

"I'm not working for Lane anymore," he said, his voice even but powerful. Mom's eyes widened and her chin doubled as her head drew back. "He never pays me for my work, and I'm sleeping in a camper in the back of a truck in the middle of winter!" Matt paused to take a breath and Mom just stared at him. "I'm going to San Diego to work with my brothers," he said defiantly.

Mom placed her fork on her plate, cleared her throat, and replied calmly, "Look, Matt, you know that those government checks are barely enough money to feed us. This family depends on you now." I was surprised by the indifference in Mom's voice, as if she was deaf to any criticism of Lane. "You're doing a real good job," she said quietly. "Don't you turn your back on us now."

Matt threw off his jacket, scraped a chair across the floor, and sat down, tapping his toes on the cement floor. His eyes scanned the kitchen nervously and he chewed his fingernails as he considered his options.

"Besides," said Mom, her voice rising, "I wouldn't dream of letting you go off into a big city on your own. You're *fourteen*! There are temptations out there you don't even understand."

"On my *own*?!" he shouted. "Mom, Lane leaves me alone in the States all the time. He left me and Hugo in Santa Fe for two weeks. We slept in the bed of the camper with nothin' to keep us warm but two sleepin' bags. I almost froze my butt off! Nothin' to cook, no water, no way to wash ourselves *or* our clothes. We looked like a couple of damn *cochinos*!"

"Don't you cuss in front of me," Mom said angrily, leaning forward and meeting his stare with her own. "I'm your mother."

"Okay, fine."

"You show me some respect, I don't care how mad you are." She shoved her plate to the middle of the table.

"But, Mom, he didn't leave us one cent. Not one cent, Mom." Matt was on the verge of tears and my heart bled for him. "If we hadn't sold a few pine nuts every day, we would have starved."

"Oh, stop it!" she snapped. "You weren't going to *starve*. Stop exaggeratin'. You should be countin' your blessings. We don't have lots, but we have *never starved*."

Matt bowed his head and began to weep. "Mom, I can't stand it anymore. I hate Lane. I *hate* him." Matt's shaggy hair shook with his body each time he let out a sob. I wanted to cry with him, but even more I wanted our mother to take him in her arms and say she was sorry for the ordeal she had put him through.

"Loren said he'd pay me twenty-five dollars a day while he teaches me drywall," Matt said. "He told me I could live with him, sleep on the couch in his apartment." Loren was one of my dad's sons, a few years older than Matt. He and several other half brothers had left LeBaron a few years earlier to work construction in Southern California, and my brother wanted to follow in their footsteps.

Matt rested his elbows on the table, rubbed his swollen eyes with his palms, and continued to cry. The more he did, the more Mom kept her eyes fixed on the table.

"Mom, don't you see—if I'm actually getting paid for the work I do, I can help out more with the family," he murmured. "The dollar goes a lot further down here. And all my brothers are there. It's not like I'm going to be on my own. You know?"

My mother raised her head and leaned back in the chair. "Let's talk to Lane about it tomorrow. Tomorrow night is my night."

"I'm not talkin' to Lane about nothin'. I don't care one tiny bit about what that man wants me to do." Matt stared at Mom and she stared right back. After a few long minutes of silence, it seemed that something had been communicated that I didn't quite understand. "Loren said they need me right away. I can take a bus to the San Diego border tonight." Matt lifted his jacket from the back of his chair and headed down the hall to the kids' room.

I watched as Mom slowly pulled the cold plate of enchiladas back in front of her. "Take a shower and I'll give you a haircut before you leave, so you don't look like an orphan when you get there."

The rest of the evening passed in a blur. I remember Mom separating Matt's wet hair into clumps, the snips of the scissors, and the wavy clips of hair floating to the cement floor. Soon, her mint-green suitcase was packed and standing at Matt's side in front of the door, and then we were saying good-bye to my brother, encircling him as he stood with his hand on the doorknob.

"Hey, Matt," Luke said, big eyed and stoic. "Where ya goin' this time?"

The wind blew through the barrel heater's rusty cylinder chimney and filled the living room with a hollow, ghostly whimper. Matt put his arm around our brother and gave him a sideways hug. "I'm goin' to San Diego," Matt said with a close-lipped smile. "California."

"That's where I'ze born, right, Matt? I'ze born there, right?"

"That's right, Brother, that's where you were born." A proud smile spread across Luke's face.

Matt reached down to give me a hug. My throat hardened and my eyelids stung. I so wanted him to take me with him.

He hugged the others, then lifted up on his soles and embraced Mom tightly. With his head buried in her neck, I heard him promise he'd call and be back at the holidays.

"Yes," said Mom when they separated. She put her hands on his shoulders and spoke in a faraway voice. "Make sure you call Maudy's collect as soon as you get there so we know you made it."

Matt adjusted the visor on his hat and just looked at her. They seemed to be having another private exchange. "Well, I better get going or I'll miss my bus."

He gripped Mom's suitcase and walked out the door. Luke, Aaron, Micah, and I ran to the window and watched as his figure grew smaller and smaller. A steady wind blew over the tall, dry weeds in the yard as Matt walked through them, their tips bent to the muddy ground as if they were bowing. I breathed heavily on the glass and fogged the pane. By the time it had cleared, Matt was gone.

Later we learned that it had taken all night for his bus to reach Tijuana. Matt walked his fourteen-year-old self to the border crossing alone. But as soon as he entered California, there was Loren, just as promised, waiting to greet him. Our half brother picked Matt up on the side of the road, the two drove straight to a construction site, and Matt started work that very day.

— 30 —

After Matt left, life became ever more chaotic and crazy, so much so that I found myself wishing that my older brother, who had teased me relentlessly for most of my childhood, were still around to help me deal with the insanity. I barely went to school. We were either traveling with Lane to work in the States, or Mom took Elena and went with him while I stayed home to watch my other siblings. When I did go to class, I was confused by the lessons and completely clueless about what was expected of me. I avoided Lane, and initially he left me alone. Almost every night, I'd dream of Matt's coming back to take me with him to California. But as day would break, I'd awake and know such dreams were beyond hope. My only options, it seemed, were to get married or convince Mom to leave Lane. The first was unsavory and the second impossible. Still, I had to try.

The spring I turned twelve, I found myself a passenger in Lane's truck during one of our many drives from Albuquerque to LeBaron. Lane's old, white pickup had been replaced by a small, black Datsun with a gash in the driver's door so deep it made the whole truck look

like a crushed tin can. We were driving a load of old items Lane had
bought or scavenged—car parts, washing-machine parts, old heaters,
used toilet bowls, broken appliances of all kinds. Mom was in the
Microbus, just behind us, carrying another load of worn-out miscel-
lany. Lane always planned to resell everything once he'd fixed it up in
his shop, but I knew the bulk of it would end up in the growing pile
of rusted metal behind our house. Lane had a knack for taking something broken and turning it into junk. The air in the small cab smelled
of blackening banana peel and stale automotive grease. I had barely
fallen asleep, with my hands folded across my stomach and my knees
pressed up against the passenger-side door, when I felt something between my legs. I was trapped. Lane had reached his large, swollen hand
over the brake lever and placed the heel of it on the crotch of my jeans.
As he began rubbing his hand back and forth, I decided that this time
I'd do something different. This time, I didn't push him away. I had
a trap of my own. I pretended to sleep, as angry as it made me, letting him touch me there until my stomach was full of knots and my
underwear wet and sticky. I thought that every second he touched me
would offer further proof to Mom that Lane was a filthy liar. I thought
about showing Mom my soiled underwear, forcing her to see what Lane
had done to me. I was sure that she wouldn't be able to turn away from
this fresh evidence. She would have to leave him, and we would have
to move our family to San Diego and live with Matt.

*Suffering through this right now is how I'll get what I want in the
long term,* I told myself. Mom won't be able to stay with him if I can
prove to her what he's been doing to me.

Mom must have flashed her headlights because it wasn't long before we were pulling over at a rest area. I found Mom in the ladies'
room.

"Can I ride with you?" I asked.

My voice was serious, and Mom stopped washing her hands the
second she saw my face in the mirror. I hesitated, suddenly afraid of

confronting her the way I'd imagined. I wasn't sure I could talk to her about this one more time; I didn't want to tell her again that she'd been wrong about her husband.

"Mom—"

"You can ride with me."

I didn't have to say anything. She knew.

THAT TRIP BACK to LeBaron was the last we would ever take in the Volkswagen Microbus. Just after we arrived home, it finally broke down for good, and Mom parked it behind the house alongside all the other rusted metal we had accumulated back there. Not long afterward, its mottled-white rooftop began to disintegrate, its tires grew flat, and the van started to look as if it were melting into the tall weed patch around it. We repurposed it as a place to store old clothes.

The Microbus was replaced by a two-door Chevy Chevette, the first in a long line of battered cars Mom would drive until they were broken beyond repair. A subcompact car wasn't exactly a substitute for a van, but that didn't keep us from taking our usual trips to and from the States. The whole family just packed itself into the Chevette, clown-car-style. The tiny vehicle served another purpose: serious, private conversations could be held there away from the noise and ears of a large family—small, serious gatherings I came to call the Chevette Tribunals.

A few weeks after the Microbus's last Albuquerque trip, Mom called a meeting in the Chevette to discuss Lane's actions. Lane and Mom sat in the front seat, while I sat behind them. Mom announced that the subject of the meeting would not be that she and Lane were splitting up—they couldn't, the children needed a dad—but how we needed to move on from this unfortunate patch as a family.

"Open and honest communication is the key to healing," Mom announced over her shoulder as Lane, in the driver's seat, peered at me through the rearview mirror. I averted my eyes, staring at my step-father's plaid cowboy shirt, his belly bulging into the steering wheel of the small car.

"I really don't see why you're making such a big deal out of this," he said with a smile.

I couldn't believe he could be so dismissive. I sighed deeply and rested my head against the back of the seat.

"It's not like I went to bed with you, Ruthie. And you know I never put nothin' inside you. All I did was touch you right here and here once in a while." I waited for Mom to be outraged for me, for her to feel the way I did, completely betrayed and violated. Instead, she watched as Lane put his hand over his chest and crotch and shrugged his shoulders. "I really do believe all you girls are overreacting. In fact, Ruthie"—out of the corner of my eye I saw his head swivel around in my direction—"you liked me touchin' you. You enjoyed it."

"*I did not,*" I yelled.

"Then why'd you act like you did?" Lane said serenely.

"I *didn't*. I hated it. I tried to stop you every time it happened. I hated it!"

My body sank deeper into the seat with each accusation that my mom—my flesh-and-blood mother sitting not two feet from me—didn't reject. I felt my chest collapsing in on itself; my breathing became heavy, almost impossible. *Please, Mom,* I pleaded silently, *please say something.*

"Lane," Mom said, "it doesn't matter whether or not Ruthie enjoyed you touching her. She's a child, you're an adult. You should have known better."

I felt as if I'd entered some sort of backward universe. "Mom, he's lying. I never said I liked it." I wanted to jump into the front seat and choke the life out of him.

"Okay." He shrugged. "I guess I misread ya. If you don't like it, it won't happen again."

"It won't because I won't ever let you near me again! I hate the sight of you!"

"Well, hey, that kind of negative attitude won't help this family at all." He turned back to me. "Ruthie, hatred will eat ya up inside and take ya straight to hell. Read what the Bible says about hateful people and deal with your hatred. Pray about it. Your mom's gonna stay here and we're going to try and work things out. So you and I need to learn how to get along."

I was furious. How could he be so casual about this? How could *he* be taking this opportunity to preach to *me*?

"Ruthie," Mom said, also turning around. *"Ruthie."*

I will not look at you, I said to myself. *I hate you too.*

"I want you to forgive Lane and I want you to get over what he did. Put it in the past where it belongs. I want to keep the family together. Do you want Aaron and Micah and Elena to grow up without a father, like you? You don't have to see him. You can stay away. That way you won't be a temptation anymore."

I finally looked at her. "What about Elena, Mom? Have you thought about what might happen to her?"

Lane whipped around and bared his teeth like an animal, sticking his finger in my face. "Hey! I would *never* do that to any of my *own* kids."

"But it's okay to do it to me because I'm *not* your kid?!"

"No," Mom said angrily. "It's not okay for him to do that to *any* kids and he knows that, and he's promised to stop. And he *will,* Ruthie, especially now that he knows that it bothers you so much. And as for Elena, I really don't think Lane would be attracted to his own children the way he is to his pretty stepdaughters. That's not something we have to worry about."

I looked up at last, just in time to see Lane shake his head, his lips pursed as if he couldn't believe he was letting himself be subjected to this.

"All right?" asked Mom, catching my glance.

"I don't want to talk about it anymore," I said wearily. "Can you let me out?"

After a tense second I heard the passenger door click open. Mom pulled the seat-back lever, and I pushed the seat forward to crawl out of the Chevette. I couldn't wiggle my body out from behind her fast enough.

That was not the last of the awkward Chevette Tribunals. The entire summer before I started sixth grade, I was repeatedly summoned to the backseat of the car and lectured by Mom about how my inability to let bygones be bygones was preventing the family from moving forward. Typically, the conversations started with her sharing a piece of inspirational wisdom or reading a passage she'd found in the Book of Mormon or the Bible. She would talk about how God tests our powers of forgiveness and then call for me to be more Christlike. And at the end of these conversations, I would bolt out of the Chevette, shrugging my shoulders and staring at the ground.

When Mom wasn't traveling with Lane—and when I hadn't been left in charge of my younger siblings—I was free to hang out with my friends and explore the countryside. Sally, Cynthia, and I spent a lot of time hiking over hot rocks on the *L,* swimming at the giant reservoir in our front yard, going to rodeos, and borrowing our brothers' horses to go horseback riding. But I still had trouble looking my stepsisters in the eye when I talked to them. Our mothers' decision to stay with

Lane had been heartbreaking. I was sure they felt the same way. We never spoke to one another about Lane again; it was just too painful. Better to pretend it had never happened—that it wasn't still happening—to any of us.

I was so angry with Mom that summer that I ran away. We were supposed to take another trip to El Paso with Lane one morning and I did not want to go. The night before we were supposed to leave, I got into the hide-a-bed in the living room fully dressed. I lay awake until I heard everyone in their bedrooms snoring. Then, as quietly as I could and with the slow-motion movements necessary for an unde-tected escape, I slipped my feet out of the bed and into the pair of shoes I'd placed next to it. I took one soundless step, then another, then a third, until I reached the rickety door. The house remained quiet as I took my first step outside under the dark purple sky. I had told a cousin of mine that I wanted to run away, and without asking why, she said I could sleep at her house until I figured out where I was going to go. My plan was to take the bus to San Diego and to find Matt. I ran from Mom's house to my cousin's under the dim light of a half-moon, pray-ing no one from the colony could see me.

Once I got in bed at my cousin's house, I lay awake for a few hours imagining what Mom's face would look like in the morning when she'd wake and find the hide-a-bed empty. Then the thought made me feel guilty. My stomach grew tight with knots. I felt justified in my actions, but I didn't want Mom to worry. I was angry with her, but also desper-ate for her approval. I stared at the wooden ceiling until I was finally able to fall asleep.

After a fitful night, I woke up with a tight neck and shoulders. I lifted my heavy head off the pillow and peered out the bedroom window to a clear blue sky. Then I saw Mom's Chevette parked on the side of the road outside the barbed-wire fence that surrounded my cousin's yard. Someone had seen me running the night before and had told Mom where to find me.

I slowly rose out of bed, turned the knob on the bedroom door with a heavy, reluctant hand, and dragged myself into the living room, where Mom was standing, her navy-blue purse over her shoulder. She glared at me with the angriest pair of eyes I'd ever seen, then spun around and walked off.

"Bye, Ruthie," I heard my cousin say as I walked out of the house. I rolled my eyes, nodded, and made my way to the car. I caught up to Mom but she didn't say a single word until I'd clicked the door closed.

"What the heck were you thinking?!" she screamed, her voice so loud I thought the windows would shatter. "Is your head in the toilet? I've been looking all over the colony for you. What if a criminal had picked you up on the streets last night? *What's wrong with you?!"* I slouched forward in the seat and stared at my white tennis shoes, stained permanently from my midnight run. I wanted to crawl into a hole and escape the tirade. I wished she'd said those last four words to Lane instead of me.

As we sped down the dirt road, I felt Mom's eyes boring into the side of my head. "What Lane did to you wouldn't seem so bad if some old Mexican man got ahold of you," she ranted.

I couldn't even muster a reply. We rode the rest of the way without speaking.

The silence continued after we arrived home. Lane had left for El Paso, and my siblings had been deposited at Susan's house before Mom had gone looking for me. The house was empty. I had followed Mom through the kitchen door. She threw her keys onto the table and walked toward her bedroom.

Suddenly I heard a tremendous voice screaming. It took me a second to realize that the noise was coming from my own throat.

"WHY WON'T YOU LEAVE HIM!" I heard myself yell with a burning rage that made my skin hot. Mom turned and faced me with the look of a determined bull staring at a matador's red flag. The force of it had made me step back through the threshold and into the living room. But I couldn't stop that part of me that was crying out, that part of me that no one had listened to. "Lane has never done anything

for this family! He doesn't even support us." I stared right back into Mom's angry glare. "He hardly ever comes home! Why do you keep having babies with him?! He is nothing but a worthless . . . *asshole*!"

Seeing the look on Mom's face—the shock, the anger, the humiliation—I immediately wished I could suck the word back inside me. I had to look away and my body began to tremble. I turned back to apologize just in time to see her hand fly at me. She slapped my cheek so hard I had almost lost my balance. I caught a glimpse of myself in the mirror as I fell backward, my body cowering and my eyes wild. I looked like an animal on the side of the road that'd barely escaped being flattened by a truck.

"Don't you dare speak to me like that." She looked at me for a long time. "It's none of your business why I stay with him." She turned and hurried toward her room. "I am still your mother, and I deserve respect."

ONE DAY A few weeks later, as the summer began its transition to the cool desert winds of fall, there was a knock at the door. The man behind it wore a white straw cowboy hat, a thick, dark mustache, and glasses with bottle-thick lenses. He greeted us somberly, which is perhaps why I didn't immediately recognize him as a church elder.

Mom invited him in, but as soon as he saw the multitude of faces behind her, he asked if he could have a word with her in private outside. I watched them through the foggy film of my breath on the living-room window, the two of them leaning up against his green Ford pickup. The man spoke slowly, gestured gently, with long pauses between his sentences. Mom nodded and cast her eyes at something in the distance. She didn't say a word and never looked directly at the visitor.

Finally, Mom came back inside. She told me that the church had decided to hold meetings about some gossip they'd heard about Lane. The allegations that he'd been inappropriately touching girls in the colony had made their way to the church elders, and they wanted to separate fact from fiction. Mom, Lane, and all his wives were being summoned to a series of hearings. If the rumors were even partly true, the man said, they would need to take swift action against my stepfather.

Weeks earlier, Sally and Cynthia had told me that they'd discovered that Lane had abused another of their sisters. Rumors of his abuse—of several of us—had slowly spread throughout the colony. I didn't know how that had happened, as Mom had been determined to keep our problems within the family, and I was never approached or questioned by a soul. Then again, given that Lane had molested at least four of us, it was a wonder that the news hadn't spread sooner.

Thus began a community tribunal about Lane, and one I thought would be much fairer than our family conversations in the Chevette, although neither my stepsisters nor I were ever called to testify. We stayed home and babysat. I spent those nights playing cards with my siblings, doing anything I could to keep my mind off what was being said in the meetings. I'd lie awake in bed, embarrassed at the thought of what Lane might be saying to the church elders, who were also my family. It nauseated me to think that he was telling them that his stepdaughters had enjoyed his advances. I thought about asking to attend a meeting myself to tell the other side of the story, but I doubted anyone would listen to me. What chance did I have of being heard by the leaders of a church who believed its men were training to be gods? Plus, I was too embarrassed and ashamed to discuss the details of what had happened in front of all of them.

Mom was alone when she returned from the first meeting. In a tired voice, she explained that everyone present had been questioned as in a court. Lane sat in front of twelve judges—all male church leaders—and called witnesses, in this case his wives. She said that the church leaders had read passages from the Book of Mormon and the Bible so that the women could understand what child abuse was and how to handle it. Still, Mom seemed to have been more affected by Lane's repentance than the church's warnings. She described his slumped posture, the sad sincerity of his public apology, and of course his tears. Did I have any idea, she wondered, how hard it was for him to cry in front of that group of men, his lifelong friends and fellow church elders?

The meetings went on for weeks before the elders finally announced that they'd made their decision. The night of the verdict, I had fallen asleep in Mom's bed when I heard the sound of the kitchen door opening. I heard two sets of shoes on the cement floor. The light in the bedroom suddenly came on, so bright that it hurt my eyes, and I peered over the blanket. Mom's eyes looked tired, red, and swollen, while Lane's looked angry. He took his clothes from the pipe where they'd been hanging, folded them, and stuffed them into a black plastic bag. Mom sat on the bed and watched him, her expression forlorn. Neither acknowledged me.

Lane swiftly exited the bedroom with his bag of clothes, Mom trailing behind him. "Aren't you going to even say good-bye to me?" she pleaded through her tears. "Lane, why won't you say good-bye to me?" He silently strolled through the kitchen and out the door. "Good-bye," she said as he started his truck. "Good-bye," she called out as he drove away.

The church leaders had decided to ban Lane from the colony for two years, after which they would reconvene to decide whether he should be allowed to return to his families. Mom sobbed as she recounted the events of the evening. "In the meantime, the wives have to take turns visiting him out of town or in the States, so you'll have to be here to watch your brothers and sister." She said it as if she wanted me to respond sympathetically. She buried her face in her palms. "Oh, Ruthie, what am I going to do? God, how am I going to handle all of this? Why couldn't we just keep this within our own family? Why does the whole town have to know about it?" The weight of her questions felt heavy on me as I sank deeper into the mattress and tried to think of something to say.

———

OVER THE NEXT few months, Lane's wives took turns going to care for him. I babysat for days or weeks at a time during Mom's stints with her husband. I didn't enjoy all the chores and housework that fell to me, but I was so relieved to have Lane gone that I did everything Mom asked of me without complaint or protest.

Only a couple of months after he'd left, Mom arrived home from a visit with him carrying a gallon jar of peanut butter. While my siblings fought each other for the chance to make themselves sandwiches on Mom's stale homemade bread, she took me to her bedroom so we could talk privately.

Her face was relaxed and smiling, and I felt myself relaxing too. She hadn't seemed that happy in a long time.

"Listen, Ruthie"—she put her arm around me as we sat together at the bottom edge of her bed—"before I left for El Paso, my sister wives and I went to the council and asked if they'd let Lane come home."

I felt the blood rushing out of my face. I looked down and shook my head.

"Taking care of the farm is too hard without his help, and we feel like this family needs a man around to lead us and to discipline the kids. They need to see their dad once in a while." She sounded calm and almost excited as she spoke, as if she hadn't even considered how I might feel. "And it's unrealistic to make him stay at all these hotels and make us go out of town to see him. We miss him, and he's lonely without his families. He needs us as much as we need him."

My gaze fell to my bare feet. I tried to focus on them to keep from crying.

"Also, Susan and I just found out we're both pregnant."

I nodded and rolled my eyes. I felt sick at the thought of their still wanting to have sex with Lane after what he'd done to their daughters.

"I have to . . . go." I stood on my legs weakly. "Is that it?"

"Well, no." Mom adjusted her glasses. "The council thinks Lane
has suffered enough for what he did—all the public embarrassment
and shame. And he *has,* Ruthie, more than you can imagine." I pulled
my arm away just as she was about to reach for it. "So the council decided to let him come back."

I nodded to myself, walked through the door and down the hall,
hoping I'd be out of the house before she spoke again, but she called
out to me, "I want you to know that you don't have to see him or be
around him anymore. You can leave and spend the night at Sally's or
Maria's houses whenever it's his turn to sleep here."

By then I was walking out the door of the house. I could still hear
Mom, but her voice sounded distant and small, as thin as the promises that fell from her lips.

"I swear to you, Ruthie, if anything happens again, I'll be the first
to take him to the authorities."

— 32 —

Just like that, we were "a family again," as Mom put it, which in our case meant spending the next two years in a whirlwind of moving from one place to another. Mom would say it was too hard to survive in LeBaron with the newly devalued peso, and suddenly we would head for Albuquerque or El Paso. We'd follow Lane around for months, living in campers and trailers as he failed again and again to make money hauling loads in his semi. I avoided him, and mostly he left me alone. We even lived in San Diego with Matt for a few months. Then, just as predictably, Mom would grow tired of moving around or become preoccupied with Babylon's bankrupt morality, and she would move us back home to LeBaron.

In the midst of all this ping-ponging back and forth between two countries, we added a new member to the family. Leah was born in the summer of 1985, when I was thirteen years old. Mom named her after Grandpa because, she said, the baby was as stubborn as her father, Leo. Leah looked just like Micah had when he was a baby, another snow-man child with invisible lashes and brows.

The following year, we finally settled back in LeBaron "for good," according to Mom. Matt, then seventeen, was still living in California, but he would come down to visit every now and then. I was fourteen but no longer in school—Mom insisted that it was more important for me to be around to help her take care of the house and the kids.

Aaron was nine years old and in the third grade. Micah, kind and quiet, followed Aaron around constantly, trying to do everything his older brother did. Elena had grown into an adorable and intelligent three-year-old. At a year old, Leah was the baby in the family. She had started walking before she was even a year old and was a curious child. She'd follow me from room to room, desperate to know what I was doing and wanting to explore everything she could. Even though he was allowed to live in LeBaron again, Lane continued to work odd jobs in the States. With her seven children more or less settled wherever we were—Matt in California, Audrey in the state hospital, and the rest of us on the farm—Mom started accompanying Lane on more of his trips. She'd leave home for a long weekend and put me in charge.

Luke, at sixteen, was still wandering off and getting lost in the Mexican countryside or going with brothers or cousins to work with them on their farms. Despite his handicaps, he was the strongest and most athletic of all Mom's children. He became a helpful worker on my relatives' farms, where he loaded hay or cleaned corrals for a few pesos a day. He couldn't drive because he'd begun having light seizures that caused his body to tremble and his hands to lose control of whatever they were holding. He also lacked the hand-eye coordination needed to pop a clutch and shift gears, or to brake while keeping the steering wheel straight. But he was gentle and loving. He adored animals, so much so that he refused to eat meat. His eyes would fill with tears whenever anyone talked about butchering cattle or when Mom killed a chicken for supper. Her few attempts at getting Luke to eat meat failed. He would retch and spit it back onto his plate.

Most days, Luke would find his way home after work, but if I hadn't seen him by sunset, I'd go looking for him. One Saturday evening in

June, when Mom and Leah were in El Paso visiting Lane, and it was late and Luke hadn't yet come home, I fired up Lane's Datsun pickup, a beat-up, old truck he left on the farm as its bed was often stacked with bales of hay. I couldn't drive on the highway—the truck didn't have a front windshield and I didn't have a license—but that didn't stop me from searching every dirt road in the colony. I drove off the farm to go look for my brother. The sky was ablaze in spectacular shades of orange, red, and plum, and the warm wind blew in my face. I spotted Luke on the gravel road that led to our house, and when I stopped to let him in, he wore a goofy smile as if he were the happiest boy on the planet. His messy hair was peppered with dry, yellow hay, he had dirt underneath his fingernails and embedded in his cuticles, and fresh mud was on the bottoms of his tennis shoes. I wanted to tell him to brush himself off before getting in the truck, but then I realized the truck was even filthier than he was.

The sherbet sky faded into darkness as my tires splashed through the wide, shallow ditch at the foot of our long driveway. The lights in the house were already on, and the door to the kitchen was wide-open, allowing the light from inside to illuminate a nighttime game of marbles outside in the dirt. I parked a few feet from three little figures huddled over a crooked circle with their faces close to the ground. I watched Aaron flick a marble at Micah's with his thumb. Elena was only three years old and didn't have any of her own marbles, but she knelt next to four-year-old Micah anyway, not being the sort to let those details stand in the way of her participation. Their eyes followed Aaron's marble as it struck the last marble and knocked it outside the circle. I turned off my headlights as Micah squeezed his eyes closed and threw his head back. "Oh, mannnnn," he sighed with a shy smile, "that was my last marble."

"Time to get inside," I said as I shut the rickety truck door. Micah followed Aaron through the kitchen threshold with his head lowered and his hands buried deep inside his empty pockets. Micah was the quietest child in our whole brood, also the most tenderhearted and sensitive, a lot like the way Grandma had described Mom as a little girl. Both were the background figures, the unsqueaky wheels in their families.

In a family where meekness was discouraged in males, my heart went out to Micah, and I found myself being overprotective of him in a way I hadn't been with my other siblings. Luke, Audrey, and Meri all had crosses to bear, but Micah seemed fragile in a different way. I would watch him through the window while he rode his little blue bike or wrap him in a towel after his bath to keep him from touching the electrified water pipe. It made me nervous when he and his siblings went swimming in the ditches and springs near our house, even though I knew that his older brothers usually watched out for him.

But my number one worry was Luke. The other children listened and remembered when I told them not to touch something. He didn't, and he was always getting shocked, and not just in the shower. Our property was a minefield, with clusters of bare wires visible everywhere, some even sprouting up from the ground like flower stems without blossoms. Once my bare foot was shocked when I was hanging laundry on the clothesline in our side yard, just outside the kitchen door. I stopped walking barefoot outside from that moment forward.

On those weekends I was left in charge, I'd put dinner on the table and sit with my siblings as they ate. Once I was sure that no one had shocked him- or herself in the shower, I'd sometimes go out for the evening, putting Aaron in charge. I was fourteen years old and wanted nights out with my friends. Like Mom, I often felt the need to escape motherhood's heavy responsibilities and uncertainties.

Most of my friends were related to me in some way. I hung out with my half siblings, stepsisters, and cousins, and I even had aunts and uncles who were my age. I had a few local Mexican friends too. Most of us went to church on Sunday mornings, but on weekends, when we didn't have a wedding or a rodeo to attend, we went dancing at discothèques in Casas. Because we were fundamentalists and had grown up in the church, our parents trusted us. We also had a lot of freedom because our parents were often working or traveling in the States. There were always so many young kids in the colony; by the time we were teenagers, no one was watching us closely.

Drinking alcohol was a big part of the Mexican culture that surrounded the colony, and it seeped its way into our nightlife. Some members of our church never drank alcohol, but others served it at their weddings and parties. Mom always taught my siblings and me that Dad wasn't a fanatic. He felt his followers and his children would find joy in making righteous choices the way he always did and thought they should be allowed to make choices for themselves. Mom and Lane never drank, but that didn't stop me. I was drawn to other teenagers who went out a lot and drank alcohol. It was easy to buy, inexpensive, and I was never carded. Mom would have had a fit if she had known my friends and I were drinking, but it was easy to hide from her.

On nights I was out with friends, I was always the designated driver, which didn't mean that I didn't drink; it just meant that I was the one with the truck. I'd drive all over the colony and pick up friends along the way, as many teens as the cab and bed would hold. We'd listen to Don Henley's "The Boys of Summer" on my handheld cassette player while making our way to a dried-up riverbed about a mile outside LeBaron. To most of the colony, the riverbed was a dumping ground, a place to unload garbage, park rusted, broken-down cars, and leave old tires. For my friends and me, it was a place without limitations, where a fourteen-year-old girl could do doughnuts in a pickup truck while she and her friends drank cheap Presidente brandy with Coke and a wedge of lime.

My friends and I took turns behind the wheel, practicing peeling out and driving on and off the roads, creating clouds of dust when we spun our wheels. We'd turn our headlights off and speed through the dark under the crescent moonlight, tempting fate on the rugged terrain—once or twice barely escaping serious accidents because of the huge holes in the ground that were big enough to swallow up the small truck.

Then, we'd park the truck at the riverbed and finish off the bottle of Presidente with lukewarm Cokes. My friends and I would drink and talk late into the night about our crushes and love interests. From there, the conversation often turned to who would get married next—some of my friends were already engaged to their teenage sweethearts and planning weddings—and our opinions on polygamy. We knew that it was a cornerstone of church doctrine, something that our parents believed in fervently, but most of us rejected it. A few young girls happily anticipated their futures as polygamist wives to older men, but they were the exception. Most of my friends thought it repellent that the boys we had crushes on would end up marrying us *and* someone else. We wanted lives more like those we saw on TV, which had made its way to us despite our parents' best efforts to shield us from the influence of pop culture. But our rebellion against polygamy came from another source too: nearly all of us had witnessed our mothers' jealous fits and conflicts with sister wives, which had done nothing to improve our opinion of the practice.

After an evening of such cathartic discussion, I would drive everyone home and then return to my own house, still half-drunk. My siblings would be in bed, asleep in their clothes, their feet and hands dusty from playing outside all day.

One night, as my tired, drunken head hit the cold pillow, my brothers and sister breathing slowly, snoring or talking in their sleep in the next room, I heard the roar of thunder in the distance and became consumed by the thought of how vulnerable my siblings were with me in charge; of how vulnerable we all were in a house where bent nails were what protected us from a stranger's invasion, where, if we experienced any sort of emergency, the nearest telephone was a mile away. I tried to quiet my mind with a silent prayer for protection.

A lightning bolt lit up the room and I shrieked. Driving rain began to pelt our tar and gravel roof, and I heard the usual dripping sound in the kitchen. A puddle had already developed on the kitchen floor by the time I put the milk bucket under the hole in the ceiling.

I felt cold drops land on my arm, then felt my own tears on my cheeks. I stood there a moment, listening to myself whimper, and then I heard something else—the sound of bare feet in the hall. Micah's face appeared in the doorway. He stared at me wordlessly, shivering.

"What are you doing out of bed?" I asked.

"I-I-I-I . . ."

"What is it?"

"I-I-I'm scared of the dark," said the little-boy voice, and not for the first time. Nights like this in the past, stormy nights, had sent Micah running into Mom's room and climbing into her bed. She always swiftly sent him back to his room. Letting a child sleep with you, she said, would spoil him. Still, whenever Mom said no and Micah appealed to me, I defied her. I couldn't stand to see him scared, couldn't bear to see the part of me that was in him seeking comfort.

Thunder roared through the sky again that night and rain dripped from the kitchen ceiling. Micah ran to me, threw his arms around my legs, and almost knocked me down. "P-P-please."

"Come on." I scooped Micah up and carried him into Mom's bed with me. "I'm scared too."

As I pulled the covers up and let Micah settle in next to me, I heard Mom's voice in my ears: *Children need to get used to being in the dark.* She'd repeated that countless times throughout my childhood.

No, I thought, *they don't.*

B_y the end of the summer, Mom was spending more time with us. I wondered if she and Lane had been fighting or, better yet, contemplating a breakup. Susan, Sally and Cynthia's mom, had decided to divorce him—despite having given birth to three of his children—although he did not let go of the marriage easily. Mom noted that Lane spent more time fixing up Susan's house and working on her car in the days after their separation than before, as though he was trying to prove his worth.

But Susan had had enough. Not only had he abused her daughters, she said he couldn't support her family, just as he hadn't been able to support us. I hoped that Mom might follow Susan's lead. But in early July, Mom announced she was pregnant again—and I realized she was never going to leave Lane.

Midsummer signaled the return of LeBaron's social season, which included bridal showers, weddings, and baby showers. It was customary for mothers and daughters to attend these events together, and in spite of our differences Mom and I enjoyed going to celebrate with our friends and family. This festive time was full of family reunions, camp-outs, and rodeos at ranches on the outskirts of the colony. To my astonishment, Mom made good on her promise to keep Lane at a distance from me, and for a brief period I felt a cloud of darkness clear from my life. I began to relish some of my family duties, such as baking cakes for all the birthdays in our house. I also spent a lot more time with my friends, traveling to dance halls and discothèques in larger towns farther away. We never came home until the first signs of morning light appeared in the sky. Mom was either oblivious to my nocturnal activities or chose not to ask; she and I didn't ask each other about much of anything anymore.

July 9 was my father's birthday, and the church held its annual conferences in commemoration. Firstborners made pilgrimages to the colony from all over the United States. For one weekend, the potholed gravel roads of LeBaron would swarm with new-model American trucks and healthy and happy young men who'd driven down to Chihuahua to court girlfriends and visit their families.

As our family grew, so did the others in the colony, and by that summer the colony was crawling with teenagers, which meant more weddings and parties. I found myself more excited than I had been in years past, if only because I was finally old enough to be invited to all of the celebratory events. The weekend of the annual church conference, Mom and I walked to the morning church service together, then attended a barbecue lunch at a home nearby. That night, a dance was held back at the church. The black benches had been pushed against the walls, and a *norteño* band—a drummer, two guitarists, a keyboardist, and an accordionist—set up under the large photo of my father on the wall. As soon as they started playing ranchera music, the whole room began to dance.

On the periphery, I noticed a young man in a brand-new black cowboy hat and tight Wrangler jeans, his leather cowboy boots freshly shined, his shoulders square, and his back straight. He spun around, almost as if he'd realized he was being watched, and motioned for me to come over. It was my brother Matt; he'd come straight to the dance from San Diego without even calling Maudy's ahead of time. I couldn't believe the transformation in him. Though he was only seventeen years old, he had established himself as a hardworking kid at construction sites all over Southern California. By all accounts, he seemed poised to become an American success story. I hurried toward him, but then I saw something that stopped me in my tracks. Matt was standing next to a young woman—and the two of them were holding hands. She wore a tight-fitting red dress and black high heels, a banana comb elegantly sweeping up her hair, and long, thick strands of loose curls fell around her bare shoulders. It was Maria.

I couldn't help but stare. Why was she holding Matt's hand? Was my brother courting my stepsister? Was the world passing me by?

Before I could go over and ask Matt what was going on, someone grabbed me by the arm. Anthony, one of my half brothers, who was three months younger than me, was my regular dance partner at these types of events. Anthony had been born just a few days before our dad died. His mother was in the hospital when she heard the news that her husband had been murdered. I wanted to talk to Matt and thought about shrugging Anthony off, but I knew that would be rude. Besides, he was a fun, aggressive dancer who loved being on the floor as much as I did.

Before I could blink, Anthony's arm was behind my back, my hand was behind his neck, and our free arms were raised straight over our heads. The fast waltz sent us swirling and spinning, knocking into a few annoyed couples and stepping on a multitude of toes. It was like being in your own Tilt-A-Whirl, and just as much fun. When the song ended, I was out of breath and ready for a break. I also needed to adjust my too-tight acid-washed jean skirt.

I stood there a moment, noticing that Mom was sitting alone, watching something intently. I followed her gaze reluctantly, sure she would be peering at Lane, who was present, but mercifully off-limits to her, as it wasn't Mom's night. But she was eyeing Matt and Maria.

My jaw dropped open. My brother and stepsister were dancing *together*. And not just dancing, *dancing*. I wanted to believe this was something innocent, just a boy having some fun with a girl who sold pine nuts, but the body language said otherwise.

I was annoyed and jealous. We had all grown up together; why was Maria getting the sort of attention I craved from boys? And why was the boy who was giving her that attention Matt? Could it be that Matt and Maria were attracted to *each other*? Maria was our stepsister. Why hadn't I known anything about this before tonight?

Anthony asked me to dance again, but this time I said no thank you, turned, and slowly made my way toward Mom's bench.

"Matt and Maria sure are dancin' close to each other," Mom said, leaning in so I could hear her over the music. "I get the feelin' they like each other."

"What do you mean by *like*?" I asked, not wanting to acknowledge what I myself had seen.

"I mean, I think he wants to go out with her, *like on a date*."

I shrugged. "Maria hasn't said anything to me about liking Matt."

"Well, he better be careful. Maria has a jealous streak just like her mother. He can't marry her, Ruthie." I shook my head as I wondered how Mom had already made such a mental leap. "Can you imagine what she'll do when he tries to take another wife? Good luck trying to pull the reins in on Maria."

I looked at Mom blankly. She put her lips to my ear and cupped her hand over them, leaning in close to say, "Lane's told me that she's a hellion at home and won't do anything her parents tell her to. Never, not even after he whips her."

Meanwhile, Matt and Maria were oblivious to everyone, including me and Mom. They were still dancing with their arms locked, their heads resting on each other's shoulder. I just stared in disbelief.

"Hey, Ruthie. Wanna dance?" Anthony asked again.

"No thanks, Anthony. I'm not feeling very good." I got up and made my way through the crowded church, feeling as if I were in a movie of someone else's life. Maybe it was Matt and Maria's movie, I thought, as the song ended and they slowly, lazily awoke from their dream, walking hand in hand off the floor.

Matt nodded at Mom, who was motioning to him from across the room. He had the good sense to leave Maria behind as he strode across the dance floor, the white tile now heavily scuffed with black boot marks.

I could tell from Mom's expression that she was ready to leave, but before she spoke, the band struck up a Mexican two-step. Matt grabbed Mom's hand and pulled her to the dance floor. She turned giddy, placing her hand delicately on her grown son's shoulder while he put his arm around her midback. Her loose-fitting, fuchsia polyester dress swung back and forth just below her knees as Matt guided her across the floor smoothly, expertly. Mom looked delighted. She missed a step from time to time, not having been raised on Mexican music like her children, but in no time Matt had her on track again.

My brother's skill as a dance partner impressed me—obviously, he'd spent many nights on California dance floors. The entire room seemed to be sighing collectively in appreciation. Mom, feeling the attention, became almost ecstatic. The song grew faster, and so did their twirling. The two of them were soaked in sweat, and Matt, his face now the color of Mom's dress, looked as if he might collapse. But he didn't stop. He seemed to know what the moment meant to her, that she was for once getting a taste, however brief, of the attention and adoration she'd always longed for. I hadn't seen that sort of happy expression on her face in years, and it only added to my melancholy. Would I end up like her, I wondered, shackled to a man who appreciated me so little that the only thing that made me feel loved was attention from my adult son?

The song ended and Mom mopped the sweat from her forehead and said something to Matt, who nodded, pulled his truck keys from his pocket, and handed them to her. He wanted to stay and dance some more with Maria, Mom told me during the drive home. Otherwise, it was a silent trip, which was fine with me. I didn't want to talk about Matt and Maria's love affair. How could they have fallen for each other without my knowing? And how come no one seemed interested in me?

My only prospect so far had been one of the church elders, twenty years my senior, who'd asked Mom's permission to court me. Mom refused, though not because I didn't like him or because she wanted to protect me from a relationship with an older polygamist, but because he was my first cousin and she thought that such a marriage wouldn't be advisable in our family, given our history of producing developmentally disabled children. I felt as if I'd dodged a bullet. I thought about the many LeBaron wives I knew, with their blank, expressionless faces, mindlessly watching after crowds of children. People talked about happiness and love, but I witnessed precious little evidence of it.

I knew that my life would never be happy if all it amounted to was having several children by a shared husband. I couldn't understand how love or adoration could be possible in that kind of arrangement, and I desperately wanted those things. But I also knew that it wasn't enough to want them. You had to know how to get them. Mom couldn't teach me that because she didn't know herself. She couldn't show me how to be happy, only how to barely survive.

— 34 —

I didn't think it would be Christmas before I saw Matt again, much less a white Christmas. For the first time in my childhood, the colony's dormant fields were blanketed in a thin layer of snow—as far as the eye could see—and the peaks of the Blue Mountains were capped in white. Mom put up a fake tree that she'd bought at a yard sale the previous summer, one missing so many limbs it looked like something Charlie Brown might have chosen. Still, we dressed up the dilapidated thing as best we could, with Popsicle sticks and yarn, long ropes of popcorn I strung together with needle and thread, and a few strands of tiny lights that blinked in the living-room window. And of course Mom had picked up a few secondhand re-gifts in El Paso the week before.

Though it was another lean Christmas, something was different about it, something besides the snow. The anger I'd harbored toward Mom began to decline with the temperature. I still couldn't understand how she could remain married to a man such as Lane, but I also began to appreciate and admire her ability to create something out of nothing.

And I worried about her. Just weeks away from delivering her tenth child, the toll of all her previous pregnancies seemed written on her face. She suffered agonizing migraine headaches that would keep her up all night. Some days she stayed in bed until lunchtime and took naps in a feeble attempt to restore her energy. She bore the burden alone, with Lane gone for weeks or even months at a time.

That fall, I had enrolled in secretarial classes offered by a local school, but as the holidays approached, Mom asked me to withdraw. "All Ruthie really needs to know about life she can learn at home and in church," she told the schoolmaster. "A young girl doesn't need more than that to find a good man and raise a family." If that was the case, the schoolmaster replied, then why did you enroll her in the first place? Mom's face and reaction looked as if she'd just bit into a lemon. "I can't take care of my family by myself. I need her help at home," she said as she picked up her purse and left.

I didn't resent Mom's decision. I was far behind in my schoolwork, having already missed several days because of Mom's health, and the shorthand and typing classes were all taught in Spanish by an old lady with a cane who perpetually sneered at me. Even before she realized how little I knew of the language, she would shriek at me, *"Chapucera!"*—cheater—every time I leaned over to ask a classmate what the woman was talking about.

So I returned home to learn more about the domestic arts. Each morning, after telling Aaron to fire up the barrel heater, I prepared the milk for everyone's breakfast by skimming the cream off the top and adding it to a container until I'd collected enough for butter, which I made in the blender. Our home was well run, it seemed to me, and no homework was required.

"Hey, Ruthie, can we go outside and play in the snow?" Micah asked the day before Christmas in his raspy, early-morning voice.

"You guys need to eat breakfast and get ready for the day first." I smiled as I cut thick, round slices of bread on an old wooden cutting board. Spreading raw honey over the top, I plopped a slice into each of five plastic bowls and covered them with milk. Micah scraped a chair against the cold cement floor and took a seat, and the others swiftly followed. I turned a ten-quart saucepan over and placed it on one of the chairs for Leah, who was eighteen months old and proving to indeed be just as stubborn as her namesake, Grandpa Leo. She refused to sit in a high chair or do most anything else I asked of her.

The kids ate quickly and dressed themselves for snow play, all except Leah, of course, whose clothes were in Mom's bedroom. Mom was still asleep, her belly swollen under a wine-red comforter and her head propped crookedly on pillows up against the stucco wall. We tiptoed in.

"Morning," Mom rasped. She had deep, dark circles under her eyes that made her skin look even paler than usual. "Did the kids all get something to eat?"

"Yeah," I said. "They're getting dressed for the snow now." I laid Leah down on the bed, changed her diaper, and wrestled her into a pair of red corduroy pants, a long-sleeved, pink blouse, lace-trimmed socks, and tiny yellow rain boots covered in rubber ducks. As I carried Leah out of the room, I saw a hint of a smile on Mom's face. *Maybe she's feeling better,* I thought.

Back in the kitchen, Micah and Elena were raring to go, having dressed themselves in gloves, jackets, and scarves. "Oh, gosh. Let me wipe your faces," I said to the pair, who both had honey from ear to ear and sleep still firmly crusted in their eyes. I ran a rag under water and mopped their freckled faces.

"Would you . . . Please, that's too hard," Micah said, pulling my hand away.

In addition to a stutter, Micah had an old soul's way of speaking. He was formal and articulate without trying to be, and I couldn't help but laugh when he asked me questions.

"Could we go outside now, please?"

I nodded at them both. A smile spread across their half-clean faces, revealing mouthfuls of corn-kernel-shaped teeth. I ran my fingers through their tangled hair in lieu of combing it, and then they darted past me and out the kitchen door, smiling the whole way. I picked up Leah and followed them outside into the fresh, cold air. The sky was a mass of thick, gray clouds.

The two kids giggled as they crunched happily in the paper-thin layer of snow. With Leah in my arms I watched for a few minutes as Micah explained to Elena how to make a snowball, his voice professorial and authoritative. He then demonstrated by rolling a ball of pebbles and dirt and dried twigs and a few flakes of snow together. Elena seemed impressed, wanted it for herself, and began chasing Micah all over the yard to get it.

In his search for what little snow remained, Micah made his way to the thick piles that rested near one of the fences on the edge of the yard. "Micah, please stay away from the fence," I warned. Those fences had always been a mystery to me. Originally just a way to keep animals in or out, Lane had had the idea to use them to ferry electricity from one part of his farm to another. So, for several years, miles of black rubber tubes encasing electrical wiring ran along the fences. It was typical Lane: ugly but functional. Recently, Lane had decided to bury the tubes beneath the fences, but he hadn't done it for appearance' sake.

"He *had* to bury'em," Mom said when I asked. "One of the wires got exposed somehow and a horse nicked it with his hoof." Later, I discovered that the horse had been electrocuted, its lifeless body discovered near the fence. Lane's electrical skills were so awful, you almost wanted to laugh.

"Matt's here!" Micah and Elena yelled in unison as they ran excitedly to the driveway. My brother emerged from his truck and hugged both of them at the same time, one under each arm.

"Matt! Matt! W-w-what's in the bag," stuttered Micah, seeing the large, black garbage bag his brother was carrying.

"What's inside, Matt?" Elena chirped in echo.

"Not yet." He laughed, giving me a sideways hug. "Mom has to help me wrap the presents first."

"Hello, everybody!" Matt boomed as we entered the quiet house, but a long while passed before we heard the shuffling of house slippers and Mom appeared in the living-room doorway. She looked small and weak, although she was smiling broadly. Matt looked alarmed as he approached her and wrapped her in a tight embrace.

"That tree looks worse than Charlie Brown's," Matt said with a chuckle.

"Oh, come on now." Mom smiled and then winced. Her arm reached for her swollen belly as if she'd felt a sudden stomach pang. "Count your blessin's. At least we have a tree this year." She sat on the corner of the couch and let out a long breath.

The sound of Micah and Elena laughing outside caught Matt's attention, and he pulled out his Kodak 110 camera and went to the window. "Well, look at that," he said. The two kids had built a couple of snowpeople in the front yard, a larger one that wore Elena's pink scarf and a smaller one beside it. "It's Mom with one of her kids."

"I don't think so." She laughed.

"Look, Ruthie," he said.

I saw two figures covered in mud, twigs, and tiny rocks, snow-people in name only, a pair of creatures who looked as if they were having one hell of a day. "That's them all right."

By dinnertime, Mom had perked up a bit and was ready to hear about Matt's love life. "How are things going with Maria?"

I stared down at Leah, who was asleep in my lap.

Matt chewed on his thumbnail. "Good. They're going real good."

Mom was silent for a moment, as if she was thinking carefully. "Matt," she finally said, waiting to continue till he looked at her. "If you marry Maria, you're gonna have a hard time livin' polygamy. She's got a jealous streak just like her mother. She'll give you hell when you try to take another wife."

Matt pretended he hadn't heard Mom and reached inside his back pocket to pull out a Velcro wallet with a photo of him and Maria taken at someone's wedding. "Isn't she the most beautiful girl you've ever seen?"

Mom reluctantly took the wallet and studied the photo a moment. "Maria has always been a striking girl, Matt. But you have to think about the rest of your life, the families you want to bring into this world."

I almost groaned. What about love and happiness? I wondered, as Mom handed me the wallet. I placed it gently on Leah's sleeping body. In the photo, Maria was in a pink, puffy-sleeved, over-the-top, satin bridesmaid's dress, her lipstick, eye shadow, and blush in the exact same shade. Matt was in suit and tie and had his arms around Maria. Her head rested against his chest. Their smiles looked goofy, but they obviously adored each other. I handed the wallet back to Matt and glanced at Mom briefly. I wondered how she felt seeing that loving embrace, seeing the two of them express the kind of affection I never saw between her and Lane.

"She looks good," I offered. "But then any girl would look good next to you, Matt."

Mom snickered.

Matt smiled and shook his head. "Very funny."

"You are one ugly son of a gun." I laughed. "You know that?"

"It's just 'cause I can't wear all that makeup like you girls." He slipped the wallet back in his pocket.

I thought that humor might set the conversation on a different track. It didn't.

"Matt," Mom went on, "I'm not sayin' that you shouldn't love Maria or that she's not a good person. I just think you should think seriously about whether she's gonna let you live by the laws your dad taught."

"I hear you, Mom." Matt stood up. "I'm just not sure I want to live plural marriage."

"Why would you say that?" Mom seemed shocked. I couldn't believe that it hadn't occurred to her that her own experience with plural marriage might be the reason.

"What?" Matt asked.

" '*I might not want to live plural marriage,*' " Mom mocked with a hint of disbelief and sarcasm. "Matt, what have you been taught your whole life?" She pushed her glasses back on her nose. "Polygamy is one of our Heavenly Father's most important laws. If you don't live His laws and build families in His name, your life on earth will be meaningless."

I looked around the room and back at Mom's tired face, her hair still sticking up from the spot where her head had rested for so many hours. Didn't she see what that life had done to her? I felt devastated for her. She was as trapped by her beliefs as I had been by Lane.

Matt took in a deep breath and exhaled through his response. "Mom, we're not planning on getting married yet. Who knows, she might not even want to marry me." He looked at me.

"That's true," I said, and we both tried to smile.

Mom's migraines finally subsided on Christmas Day, which was the best present she could have received, save one. While she appreciated the new robe, house slippers, and gift set of jellies and jams Matt gave her, her reaction to his card was what really struck me. She cried the first time she read it, then read it a second time aloud, breaking down again. In language simple and honest, Matt thanked her for having been a kind mother, saying that although he knew San Diego had been the right choice for him, he missed her very much and loved her very much, even if he never told her so. Mom's tears that day were joyful, like the tears she cried when we sang "Happy Birthday" to her each year. I cried too, but only much later, when I realized how little she had asked of the world, and how even that had been too much for the world to give.

35

In mid-January, once again Mom went to the hospital in Casas, to deliver her tenth baby. She called a family meeting to discuss what we should name the child. Finding a name we liked that someone in our enormous family hadn't already taken was so difficult that a group effort was required. Ever since I'd first seen the show when we lived in California, I had been a fan of *General Hospital*. Holly was one of my favorite characters so I suggested Mom name the new baby after her. Everyone agreed.

Holly was born on January 20, 1987, twenty years after Mom gave birth to Audrey, her first child. Holly's skin was a translucent white and as smooth as china, her lips a bright red, and her eyes blue, surrounded by long, dark lashes. Everyone agreed that Holly looked just like Meri, and for some weeks I was terrified that the resemblance might be too strong and Holly would be another sickly child. One day, however, while carrying her in my arms, I felt a warm sensation come over me, a feeling of hope. From that moment I knew she would be a healthy baby, and I was right.

I didn't feel that same sense of hope when I saw Mom. She returned home just one day after the birth and, once again, had lost a lot of blood during the delivery. She was weak and felt terrible. Over a few weeks her vigor returned and she agreed to let me travel to San Diego to work with Matt for a little while. He drove us around to different construction sites all over the city. I helped by mixing Spackle with water in five-gallon plastic paint buckets and smearing it with a six-inch putty knife on bare Sheetrock around plastic light sockets. It was hard work, and my body hurt when I woke up early every morning, but he paid me $25 a day, and I liked having the money to spend on the movies and going out for pizza.

Matt lived in Imperial Beach, closer to Tijuana than San Diego. His home was a single-wide in a small trailer park off a busy street. Even though it reminded me of living in El Paso, the place had its advantages. First, it was within walking distance to the beach. Second, it was parked hundreds of miles north of LeBaron. The third perk over-shadowed the other two: living with Matt, I had access to a working telephone.

The first people I wanted to call were Grandpa and Grandma. Mom hadn't taken us to visit her sisters in years. They occasionally wrote her letters, which Mom would read with tears running down her cheeks. My aunts wrote that Mom was doing wrong by staying in polygamy and having so many kids she and Lane couldn't afford to care for. Mom felt hurt by her sisters' disapproval, but she was relieved that Grandma and Grandpa had given up trying to change her mind about her reli-gion. We visited them and Audrey at least once a year, usually during the summer when my younger brothers weren't in school. I hadn't seen my grandparents or talked to them since the previous summer, so one of the first things I wanted to do from San Diego was to surprise them with a phone call. Hearing my voice usually made Grandma excited, but not that night. As soon as she picked up the phone, I knew some-thing was wrong.

"Grandpa passed away about two weeks ago," she said in a quavering voice. "He was sick a long time."

I almost dropped the receiver. "Oh, Grandma, I'm so sorry. Why didn't someone call and tell us?"

"I didn't want your mom to drive all the way up here, on all these icy roads, with all her kids."

"But—" was as far as I got. I had been at the point of saying the family was wrong not to tell us, that everyone had deserved a chance to say good-bye to Grandpa, especially Mom, but Grandma's voice was so shaky and weak, I couldn't.

I hung up, and my heart was filled with sadness and longing for Grandpa. I felt so grateful for the months we'd spent in his home in Strathmore, which were some of the happiest of my life.

Later that evening, I sat staring at Matt's phone for some minutes before dialing Maudy's in LeBaron and leaving a message for Mom to call me back right away. She called back collect. I accepted the charges and delivered the sad news. The phone went silent.

"Mom, are you there?"

"They didn't want us to be there?" She sounded devastated, shocked. I reiterated what Grandma had said, that she'd been thinking of our safety, even though I knew it was a weak defense.

"No one called me, Ruthie. *No one called me to tell me about my daddy dying.*"

The tenor of her voice broke my heart. "I know, Mom. I'm sorry."

"Well, I should go," she whispered. "This call is gonna cost Matt a lot. When are you comin' home?"

"I don't know. I don't think Matt plans on coming down anytime soon."

"Then see if you can get a ride with someone else from the church. Or take the bus. I need your help at home."

Matt took me across the border to Tijuana the next morning; I took the bus back to LeBaron and arrived later that day. Mom and I hardly spoke when I got there, and for some reason she couldn't look me in the eye. All I could think was that hearing the news about Grandpa's death from me had somehow added insult to injury.

I was angry and sad, not to mention exhausted from my travels. But that night, when I went to bed on the foldout sofa in the living room, a bright, harsh moonlight kept me up for some time. Our living-room window didn't have curtains so I lay there tossing and turning in the glare. As I finally started to drift off, I felt a familiar sensation of being watched. Sure enough, I opened my eyes to a figure looming over my bed. I flinched and sprang back, certain that it was Lane. But it was Mom, holding her head in her hands and sobbing.

I sat up and asked what was wrong. After a moment, she stopped sobbing, sniffled, and looked at me. I'd seen the same face all day, though in the moonlight it didn't look as angry as it did desperate.

"What's wrong?" I asked, breathless. "Are the kids okay?"

"Ruthie . . ." I watched Mom bow her head as if she'd lost her nerve, then slowly raise it again. "Ruthie, I need to tell you . . . that I'm *so sorry*." She began to cry hard now and the moonlight made her tears sparkle. "You help me so much with the kids, and I never appreciate it."

"It's okay." That's all I could think to say. I did feel unappreciated, but I didn't want Mom to feel so upset about it.

She took off her glasses and wiped her eyes with a tissue. "And I'm sorry too for everything that you've gone through, for everything—-*everything*—Lane has done to you." She took a deep breath, desperate to calm herself. "I *do* feel like things have gotten better. Don't you think so?"

A thousand responses ran through my head, but none of them were right for the moment. "Well, yeah. At least I don't have to see him anymore."

Mom took my hands in hers. "I didn't know what to do." She started crying heavily, making me wonder how long she'd been holding this in. "I know he is very sorry for what he did. He's very, very sorry." Was she repeating this on purpose? Once for my sake, once for hers?

I felt my arms reach around the top of her shoulders and pull her to me so I could rest my head on her neck. But before I could, she lunged forward and laid her head on my shoulder.

"I love you, Ruthie."

I hadn't heard those words in a long, long time, if ever, and now I was crying too. I couldn't be angry with her any longer. I felt sorry for her and I sensed her fragility. She wasn't some monster, she was just another human being who'd gone looking for her life and somehow ended up on the wrong path.

"I love you too."

Mom pulled away from me and smiled, patting my back and kissing my wet cheek before grasping the bed frame and pushing herself to her feet. She murmured, "Good night," disappeared into the blackness, and left as mysteriously and abruptly as she'd come.

But I didn't mind. I had become used to the dark.

36

Later that spring, Matt and Maria announced that they would marry at the end of the summer. Mom clearly wasn't thrilled by the match and continued to warn Matt that Maria would never accept living polygamy. The wedding plans rekindled my friendship with Maria, and the two of us spent many hours over the next few months clipping wedding ideas from magazines. Whenever Mom wasn't around, we talked about her concerns.

"You know that my mom wants Matt to be a polygamist, right?" I asked.

"Yeah, I know. But he says it's only a fifty-fifty chance that he'll live it, and I'm willing to take that chance. Besides"—Maria winked—"I'm pretty sure I can convince him not to get another wife."

I didn't want to think about the things Maria might do to convince my brother of this, so I changed the subject.

With summer came the usual LeBaron brand of excitement— drinking and dancing in discothèques, cooling off in swimming holes and irrigation ditches, birthday and wedding parties, and anniversary celebrations. Added to the mix that summer were two additional block-buster events: Matt and Maria's wedding and a big party Alejandra was throwing at her parents' house for her twin girls' birthdays. She'd had a second set of twins after Alex and Junior were born and was celebrating their second birthdays.

All of Lane's wives and children were invited, but Mom was the only one who felt obligated to attend, seeing how her son was marry-ing Alejandra's daughter. No matter how hard Lane had tried to win her back, Susan had stuck by her decision to leave him so she didn't hesitate to decline the invitation. Marjory, Lane's fourth wife, was out of town, visiting her family in the States.

Even though Mom had been so upset when Lane married Marjory, I had come to like the last of her sister wives. Marjory thought it im-portant that Lane's wives be civil to one another, so not long after Holly was born Marjory visited our house to talk to Mom and to see the new baby. The moment she stepped through the door, she looked around wide-eyed.

"With all the builders we have in this town, why are you livin' in a place like this?" Marjory wondered aloud. She was the kind of person who would put her hands on her hips for dramatic effect and say, "Kathy, I'm gonna hire some of these young boys to fix this place up," and then do exactly that. Not a week after her visit, Marjory had made brown-and-white-checkered curtains to hang in the windows in the kitchen, had its walls painted bright yellow, and hired a young man to construct a built-in closet out of Sheetrock that Lane had bought for some project long ago abandoned. Mom smiled for weeks every time she walked into her new kitchen. Even though people gossiped that Marjory's kindness was payback for the pain she knew Lane's latest marriage had caused Mom, I didn't believe it. Generosity seemed second nature to Marjory. When she left to visit her family in the States, she promised to come back with more ideas on how to fix up our house.

The day of Alejandra's party, Mom was tweezing her eyebrows in the mirror when she confided that she had gone to the doctor the day before. She'd missed her period. I was stunned. She was thirty-eight. Holly was just five months old.

"Mom, don't you think you should wait until you stop nursing before you get pregnant again?" I said the words as gently as I could, but my irritation was obvious. "We can barely afford to feed everyone in the family now."

She put down the tweezers, gazed at me, and calmly and matter-of-factly said, "Ruthie, you just have to have faith."

No, you don't, I thought. You also need money and a husband who's not a deadbeat. But I didn't say anything.

"When you're doing what God wants you to do, life will always work out for the best. Don't worry. He will always take care of us." She smiled warmly and turned back to her reflection.

I smiled too, politely, as if I were in the presence of a woman whose cockamamy notions were too charming to be challenged.

"God wouldn't send us another baby if we weren't ready to take care of it." She adjusted her hair. "I'm ready. Let's get the kids in the truck."

"*BUENAS TARDES, PÁSENLE,*" Alejandra said with a forced grin when we arrived. She was in the midst of rolling out a tortilla and motioned us in with flour-covered hands.

"*Buenas tardes,*" Mom blared in an exaggeratedly thick American accent, a clear signal to every Spanish speaker within earshot that she was not available for conversation.

With two-year-old Leah on my hip, I scanned the party, already in full swing with ranchera music blaring. The women were decked out in their Sunday best, in nylons and pumps, looking as if they'd all chipped in for a single tube of red lipstick and then just passed it around. Through the window I saw dozens of dark-haired children playing in a tiny backyard enclosed by barbed wire, and my platinum-headed brothers and sister ran outside to join them.

In Spanish, Alejandra told Mom that everyone was waiting for us outside, so we made our way to the backyard, where we found Mexican men and women sitting in white plastic folding chairs. The only non-Mexican was my stepfather, who wore his trademark red polo shirt, tattered jeans, and a gleaming silver belt buckle. Lane stood conversing in Spanish with a few of the guests, his large, protruding stomach making him look as if he were in the last trimester of his own pregnancy. The sight of him made me ill. I considered snatching Mom's keys and making a beeline from the party, but realized that as long as I stuck close to her, I was safe. Whenever more than one wife was around, good manners kept Lane from paying much attention to either of them. "It could cause conflict," he always said.

A star-shaped piñata floated into the yard on the end of a rope held by Matt. Maria, who'd walked out with him, rushed up to me, hugging two bridal magazines close to her chest. "Ruthie, I found the bridesmaids' dress that I want," she yelled over the music, beaming. The color was royal blue and the design included everything from puffy, gathered sleeves to a flower made from the same material as the sash. I was thrilled.

We turned our attention to the piñata. A line of children from shortest to tallest was already forming, which put Elena second. When it was her turn, Maria's aunt blindfolded Elena with a red bandanna, spun her around three times, then let her swing the stick. Matt and another man raised and lowered the piñata to confuse Elena, but she still managed to give it a better whack than a lot of the older kids who followed her. "Did you see me hit it two times?" she yelled to Mom and the rest of her audience.

"I saw it!" Mom smiled back.

Soon it was five-year-old Micah's turn, and then the twins Alex and Junior, who were six. The three had become inseparable, always spending the night at each other's house and riding bikes down gravel roads, Micah still with his training wheels. "Hit it now, Micah!" they yelled as my brother swung wildly, missing the target by a mile. Both of

Alejandra's boys found this hysterical, while poor Micah looked hurt and humiliated.

The stage was set for an older, heavyset boy to properly destroy the papier-mâché creation, and with one swing from him, candy went flying in every direction. Great dust clouds were kicked up by all the kids who rushed in, shoving each other, stepping on the little ones' toes and even grabbing candy from their hands.

Micah stood motionless in the center of the swirl, as if in the eye of a hurricane. He watched the chaos of the children around him with amazement. Whenever he gently reached for a candy he'd spied, another child either got there first or snatched it from him.

I sat Leah on the ground near Mom and Holly and pushed my way through the craziness, picking up dusty candy along the way. "Here, Micah. Put these in your pocket."

He took the candy from me gratefully, saying thank-you in his typically soft and formal voice. Moments later, one of the wilder kids crashed into him, knocking him to the ground. After a moment of silence, he started to cry. Micah was not the sort to draw attention to himself, and his cries were normally so soft they went ignored. But not that afternoon. With a force that suggested he had been saving up those tears, Micah wailed deeply, earsplittingly, as if he'd been wounded.

"Micah, please," I said, my eyes searching for Mom.

The wailing continued, and with each scream, his pain became a bit more my own, until I found it unbearable. I gathered him up and ran with him in my arms to the side of the house, holding him for a long time as I waited for him to calm down and watched for Mom to come console him. I sat him down against the house and noticed we were both trembling. I struggled with shaky hands to unwrap a candy for him, wiped his tears away, and then unwrapped a candy for myself.

"You need to stop crying, Micah," I panted, my heart in my throat.

"Why?" he asked quietly, no longer breathing heavily.

"Why do you need to stop crying?" He nodded. "Because . . . I don't know. Because the other boys will tease you."

"Bu-bu-but that kid pushed me down. *He hurt me.*"

"But it was an *accident,* Micah. That's all." I turned up my blouse so I could wipe his cheeks with the underside of the fabric. "There's just too many kids for that little yard." Micah and I stood together for a long time. Finally he seemed to have calmed down. "Let's go," I said. He came, but slowly. "Come on, you're not hurt that bad."

I reached for his hand and led him back to the party. Before long, raindrops began to fall. Mom wanted to beat the downpour and get home. She whistled for her brood to help load up the truck.

First to arrive after me was Micah, now giggling, his tears a distant memory. "Hey, Mom, can Alex and Junior spend the night at our house?" he asked, breathless from a game of tag. Mom said she didn't mind since we had room in the truck. Lane was staying at Alejandra's that night, and Matt was off somewhere with Maria. So my three sisters piled into the front seat with Mom as the rain began to fall, and I sat in back with the boys.

Above, the sky seemed a deeper black than usual, and by the time we turned off the highway onto the dirt roads of LeBaron, jagged orange and yellow lightning bolts sliced through the sky and lit up the Blue Mountains. The rain was torrential.

I opened up the hide-a-bed in the living room for the three boys before retiring to Mom's room. I tossed and turned to the sound of the storm until I heard all the boys in the living room snoring soundly. I rolled into Mom's side of the bed against her thick back, and at last fell asleep.

37

I woke up the next morning in Mom's bed by myself. Micah, Alex, and Junior were already up and buzzing around the living room. A slice of sunlight shone through the thin curtain over the bedroom window, carrying with it dancing particles of dust.

"Hey, Mom," Micah yelled at the doorway, jolting me out of my haze. He stood at the threshold wearing a swimsuit. I rolled over and pulled the blanket over my head.

"Hey, Mom," Micah repeated in a voice only slightly less ear-piercing. It was too hot for a blanket, even at eight thirty, and I threw it off.

"Don't talk so loud," I heard Mom whisper as she laid Holly down in her crib. "You'll wake up the baby after I just got her back to sleep."

"Hey, um, Mom?" Micah whispered.

"Yes?"

"Can we go swimming outside in the ditch?"

"I don't know. It's pretty early to be outside swimming already."

"Bu-bu-but, Mom?"

"Yes. What, Micah?"

"It's already sunny."

I closed my eyes as tight as possible, wishing for just a few more minutes of sleep.

"Mom!"

My eyes popped open again. It was Aaron.

"Ssh!" she replied.

"I'm going into town to look for my bike. I can't find it anywhere."

"Okay."

He turned, ran down the hallway, and out the kitchen door. My eyes fluttered closed again.

"Moooooooommmmm. Pleeeeease," Micah begged. Alex and Junior had joined him and were dangling off one another. So much for sleep, I thought. I got out of bed and ran my fingers through my tangled hair.

Leah was already awake and standing in her crib wearing nothing but a disposable diaper. She reached for Mom to pick her up. The tiny room with three boys, two babies, and Mom felt stifling and crowded. I tiptoed past them to the bathroom.

"Hey, Mom—"

"Before you go outside, put your dishes in the sink," she said to Micah. Then: "And you need to get up, Ruthie."

I stopped as I opened the bathroom door and leaned my head against it heavily. "I'm . . . up. I just walked past you."

"Oh, you're up, huh?" Mom said sarcastically as she walked down the hall in her royal-blue bathrobe with Leah in her arms. She glanced at me as she passed. "Then help me clean up this kitchen."

"Oh, shit," I muttered under my breath.

"I heard that."

I walked into the kitchen without looking at her and took my place next to the stove. Mom silently left the room to get ready for the day. She had already begun heating a pan of water for me to use to wash the dishes, and the sight of it filled me with dread. Flies buzzed around my ears, and I turned to find the kitchen door wide-open behind me, which meant that I would spend the rest of the day swatting flies. I closed the door, then picked up a wet washcloth from the sink and began to wipe up droplets of honey, scraps of bread, cereal grains, and spilled milk.

The water on the stove started to boil, so I pulled out a clean dish-rag from the shelf, lifted the pan of hot water off the stovetop, poured it into the sink and mixed it with cold water from the faucet. Preoccupied by my thoughts about the upcoming weekend, I washed the dishes to the sound of the boys splashing in the ditch outside. It was conference time again, and the yearly festivities were in full swing. I wished I had a phone so I could call my friends to find out what the plans would be.

I heard the first few squeaks of a cry from Holly in the bedroom, and then Mom preparing to nurse her as I looked over my shoulder at Micah's bright blond head in the front window, the sunshine making him appear almost fluorescent. Shirtless and untroubled was the world of boys, I thought. I stood there with my hands in the murky hot water and longed for the freedom to play like a carefree child. I wondered what had happened to my ditch-splashing years, which seemed so far behind me now that I was fifteen.

I rinsed the last plate, set it in the dish drainer, wiped my hands dry, and walked outside. The splashing I'd heard outside the kitchen window stopped as the boys left the ditch to shuffle off to Alejandra's house.

I went back inside and tried to lose myself in tasks—sweeping the hallway, gathering up the kitchen garbage and setting it in a bag by the door, checking in on Mom. I peeked around her doorway silently, finding her propped up in bed reading a romance novel while she nursed Holly. She wore a thin, pink-and-blue-plaid cotton blouse and polyester pants. Elena and Leah lay on their bellies at her bare feet, coloring in the same coloring book. Mom's face was a picture of contentment.

The whole house was quiet as I tiptoed back down the hall to the kitchen. Suddenly I heard splashing in the ditch again, the sound of a child running quickly through the water, and then a single set of bare footsteps running up the gravel driveway. My eyes darted to the kitchen window, where I saw a dark-skinned figure racing toward the house. It was Alex, who, not a second after I spotted him, threw open the kitchen door. His chest, hands, and face were covered in mud. He gasped, almost too out of breath to speak.

"Micah—"

"What is it, Alex?"

"Micah and Junior are in trouble," Alex panted. He looked down at his hands, rubbed his muddy palms together, and nervously shuffled from leg to leg.

Trouble. The boys were in trouble. The word suggested something annoying but harmless, that Micah and his friends had been caught picking our neighbor's unripe pecans. I felt myself rehearsing my well-worn scolding speech, but Alex stopped me.

"We were havin' a mud fight in the road, and I was throwin' mud at them, and they ran away from me and tried to cross the fence into the alfalfa field to get away, and—"

"Ruthie," Mom called, having overheard us in the bedroom. "Go outside and see what's goin' on with those boys."

I stepped outside the open door onto the square cement slab. The morning sun stung my eyes, and I shaded them with the flat of my hand as I scanned the road and neighboring orchards and fields. I saw nothing. But my gut felt uneasy. Something was really wrong.

I turned back to Alex, who was still standing just inside the kitchen door, watching me, his muddy face desperate and confused.

"I can't see the boys. What happened? Show me where they are."

He stepped outside the door, stood next to me, and pointed to the road, at a spot between our homes. "They're over there, behind those big bushes."

I looked in that direction but could only see a cluster of giant tumbleweeds caught on the fence.

"Ruthie, I think Junior and Micah"—Alex let out a heavy breath—*"are getting shocked,"* he whispered, his eyes filled with dread.

"Shocked?" I had no idea what he was talking about and wasn't sure that he did. But as soon I heard the word, I broke into a sprint down the driveway, with pebbles and spiky weeds poking the soft soles of my feet. I ran the fifty yards to the driveway's edge where the ditch ran parallel to the barbed-wire fence and the road. I jumped over the ditch, and clods of earth crumbled into the water under my footsteps. I rushed through the open gate and turned right onto the road toward the tumbleweeds. I ran another fifty yards, my pulse pounding in my throat.

Panicking now, I ran, scanning the ditch and the land beyond the fence, but I saw only fields and trees and giant, dry tumbleweeds. But then I smelled something strange, a burning, pungent odor. My legs went weak and I tripped over them, hurrying to the tumbleweeds, so thick with brambles that I didn't see the boys until I was a few feet away.

Micah! His muddy, wet body hung motionless from the barbed-wire fence. His eyes and mouth were wide-open, his head and neck arched as if he'd thrown them back in laughter. His chest, shorts, and pale legs were stuck fast to the fence. Both hands grasped the middle wire as if he'd been trying to pull himself through it when suddenly he'd been frozen in position. One foot was off the ground midstep, dirty and dangling. His other foot was planted on something shiny and silver in the dirt, a piece of metal, the tip of an electrical wire.

I was frozen and couldn't look away. It was my little brother Micah, but drained of his glow, his softness, his tears, and his stutter. I didn't understand what was happening. *Was he still alive?* And there not two feet away was . . . Junior. *He was stuck against the very same fence.* His body was hanging too, as if propelled onto the fence or sucked onto it. His eyes were open and both hands clutched the barbed wire exactly like Micah's. Both boys—electrocuted.

I fell to the ground heaving, my arms folded across my stomach. "Mom," I gasped. "Mom!" I staggered up to pull Micah from the fence and then stopped. I leaned in first to look more closely at his freckled face and his chapped lips to see if he was still breathing. I lifted a finger to touch his forehead, felt a violent jolt, and fell backward.

I looked in the direction of the house, and the distance seemed incredible. "Mom!" I yelled. "Mom . . . help me!" I needed to scream the loudest I'd ever screamed, yet my voice seemed caught deep inside me. I jumped up, and when I did, I suddenly felt my energy return. *"Mom, help me! I think Micah is* dead!*"*

I watched for a few seconds but the kitchen door did not open. I searched both sides of the road for something, a stick or a piece of wood that might help me free Micah from the wires. I turned back toward home. *"Mom—"* I wanted to turn off the electricity, but that meant running all the way to Lane's shop on the other side of the house. It was more than a football field away, and I couldn't risk leaving the boys on the fence that long. *Mom will know what to do,* I thought.

Suddenly, the kitchen door burst open. Mom came running down the driveway, Alex, Elena, and Leah trailing behind. My mother leaped over the ditch, stumbling when she landed, causing her glasses to pop off the bridge of her nose and fall somewhere in the wet earth below her. She looked down briefly but couldn't see them and continued running. Closer and closer she ran in awkward footsteps, her eyes squinting as if she couldn't exactly see where I was. I ran to meet her, and when she reached me, she stood with her face directly in front of me to see me clearly.

"What is it?! What's happened?!" she shrieked.

"Mom." I looked straight into her tired, squinting eyes. "Mom. Micah's electrocuted on the fence. I think he's dead."

Her lips quivered as she sucked in a breath. "What do you mean? This fence doesn't have electricity running through it. Where is he?"

She looked past my shoulder and searched the length of the fence but couldn't see the boys behind the cluster of tumbleweeds. Alex, Elena, and Leah were still running to try to catch up. I was afraid they'd fall into the fence or touch it. "Don't touch the fence!" I yelled, then turned to Mom, who had hurried past me. "Mom, don't touch the fence."

Leah, ever defiant, lifted her index finger and started to reach for the bottom wire. I hurried toward her and scooped her up, grabbed Elena's hand, and took Alex and my sisters to the other side of the road. "Why can't we touch the fence?" Elena whined. I turned to try to help Mom, who looked completely disoriented without her glasses and was wandering down the edge of the road. She still hadn't reached the other side of the cluster and couldn't see my brother.

"Where's my son? Micah?" she called in the most painful voice. "Micah? Where are you, Micah?" He was just inches from her and still she couldn't see him.

She approached the tumbleweed quickly but awkwardly. I took a deep breath and hurried to the other side of the road toward her. "Mom, don't touch the fence," I warned. Just as I said it, she lost her footing where the road's shoulder dipped down into a muddy pothole and tilted toward the fence. As if to steady her body and keep herself from falling, she reached for its top wire with both hands.

"Mom! No!" I screamed.

I raised my arms to grab for her but only caught the air. In a moment, her body collapsed forward onto the barbed wire, then went completely silent and still.

"Mom, wait!" I yelled, as if there were still time to warn her. I ran up behind her, sucked in the dry air, and waited a second to see if she might respond. But then I saw her head was tilted forward, her forehead impaled on a barb, her eyes wide-open.

Save her, said a voice inside me, and a second later I knew what to do. The tail of Mom's blouse hung untucked from her polyester slacks. I touched it lightly and felt no shock, so I grabbed the tail with both hands and pulled. Her body did not budge; the electrical current was holding her to the fence. I gripped her shirttail tighter, planted my back foot, and pulled again. But Mom still didn't move. I grabbed it one more time, this time pulling so hard the seams of her blouse ripped all the way up to the armpits, and finally I felt her body move. With one more tug she fell back against my left shoulder. I wrapped my arms around her to hold her up, but didn't have the strength. She fell backward out of my arms and her head slammed into the middle of the dirt road.

I knelt beside Mom's limp body. Jagged streaks of blood from the wound on her forehead coursed down the right side of her face and into her hair. Her eyes were open, and I could see just a sliver of her hazel irises at the top of her lids as her eyes rolled upward. A moan erupted from deep within her—she was still breathing. Suddenly, two pairs of little-girl shoes appeared next to Mom's head. I looked up. Elena and Leah stood there, shaking, horrified and confused.

"You girls go back inside the house. Now!" I jumped to my feet and reached for Alex, who was standing in front of the boys' bodies, staring at his brothers. "Take the girls back to the house so they don't touch the fence! And check on the baby!"

The children ran to the house, and I turned my attention back to Mom. The moaning continued. I needed to get her to a hospital. I scanned the horizon. There were trees and alfalfa fields, a few houses in the distance, and beyond that, only the mountains. I needed a telephone to call an ambulance. Then I realized, in rapid succession, that the nearest telephone was a mile away, that even if I'd had one, no ambulance would come because there was no ambulance, and that even if there had been one, it would have had to drive forty miles to reach the nearest hospital.

We were stranded. There was nothing I could do and no one was around. I jumped up and down in the middle of the road—it was all I could do—and waved my arms screaming wildly.

I knelt beside Mom again, my throat sore from shouting. I leaned over, put my ear to her mouth, and felt a warm, shallow breath, so I decided to try mouth-to-mouth resuscitation. I put my mouth over her open lips, pinched her nose closed, and forced my breath into her. But all I'd learned about CPR had come from movies, and I soon gave up, fearing I was doing more harm than good.

I jumped up, screamed again, and immediately heard the distant sound of a motor and tires over gravel. A white pickup suddenly appeared up the road. Heeding my call, it sped up, leaving huge dust clouds in its wake. It screeched to a halt right in front of us, and two Mexican men jumped out of the cab.

"*Ayuda mi mamá,*" I pleaded in my broken Spanish, "*y mis hermanitos.*" I saw the men look over to the boys suspended from the fence. They gasped, their hands involuntarily flying to their mouths. "*She's still alive, though,*" I called out, bringing their attention back to Mom. One of the men approached her, touched her forehead, and lifted her chin. He took off his hat and leaned his ear in close to her mouth and then scanned her body as if giving her a checkup. Looking over his shoulder at his companion, he said something in Spanish I didn't understand. The other man rushed around the front of the truck and opened the passenger door. Together, they carried Mom to the truck and gently laid her in the cab, her head dangling to one side, her mouth and eyes now wide-open.

One man got behind the wheel, and I jumped into the passenger's side, lifted Mom's head, and rested it on my lap. Before the second man could get in, I slammed the door shut, rolled the window down and told him that little children were in the house. I asked if he could stay. He nodded yes and then darted toward the house.

As the truck sped forward, I heard my voice screaming out the window at anyone who might hear me, "*Micah and Junior are dead! Don't touch the fence!*" I sucked the summer air into my lungs in giant gulps while I prayed and cried. The truck shook violently as it bounded over the dirt road toward the highway. The wind stung my eyes, forcing me to close them, and when they opened again, I noticed we were approaching Susan's driveway. In it a car was parked with its hood up, covering my stepfather's head as he bent forward underneath it.

"Para! Para!" I yelled. A quiet moan came from Mom's throat, and I opened the door before the truck had even stopped. My knees immediately buckled underneath me and my body hit the dirt road. "Lane, help me!" I cried, and pushed myself back to my feet. His head shot up from under the hood, his face stunned and confused. I rushed to him, sobbing. "Lane, my mom was shocked. I think she's dying!"

He looked at me a half second, dropped his tools to the ground, and without saying a word ran past me to the truck. I saw Mom's messy brown hair as Lane lifted her head onto his lap and slammed the door. The driver sped away, and the tailgate disappeared into a cloud of dust as the truck rushed toward the paved highway. Within seconds, it was heading south.

38

I fell to my knees once more, alone and shaking in the road. A wooden screen door opened and then slammed behind me, and I looked up to see Susan and her youngest son running toward me. I was surprised to see Aaron following close behind.

"Micah and Junior are dead," I said, feeling shocked and disoriented, standing straight up without even looking at them. Aaron cried out and began running toward the house.

"Aaron!" Susan yelled. "You kids wait here until we find out what's really going on." He stopped, turned around, and ran back to us, panting. Susan grabbed my shoulders to keep me from falling again.

"We need to get back to the house. *We need to turn off the electricity!*" I screamed. "Micah is dead! He's still stuck to the fence! We have to turn the power off!"

"Come on now," Susan said calmly, patting me on the back as if I were crazy. For some reason I've never understood, her first instinct was to think I was delusional. "You must be confused. Now tell me what happened." I broke away from her and walked ahead up the road toward home, Susan trailing behind. A moment later a speeding car hammered on its brakes.

"I heard someone screaming. Is everything okay?" asked a woman, one of Lane's sisters I didn't know well.

"Apparently, there's been some kind of accident with the electricity at Kathy's house," Susan explained as she and I got into the four-door sedan. I asked Lane's sister to take us to the far corner of our property where her brother's shop was. We seemed to arrive within seconds. Susan and I jumped out of the car, ran into the shop's dark and dilapidated interior, and pulled the light string above our heads. "Show me where it is," Susan said, still calm.

We made our way through the minefield of scattered tractor and car parts, as well as Lane's multitude of half-finished, abandoned projects, until we'd reached a metal box on the wall in a far corner. Susan wiped away spiderwebs and dust with a freckled hand, opened the box, and flipped the switch I'd pointed to. The shop light went off, and an image flashed through my head, that of two boys plunging to the ground. I doubled over with grief.

"Come on, Ruthie," said Susan gently as she ushered me out of the shop. "Let's go find Micah and Junior. They're okay, Ruthie."

"Micah's dead," I mumbled over and over. "I saw him on the fence."

"You listen to me, Ruthie." Susan put her hands on my shoulders, stopping me. "Look at me!" she commanded. "Micah . . . is *not dead*. Now settle yourself down. Your mom will be back from the hospital soon."

We walked together in silence toward the spot where I'd last seen the boys. A green truck was now parked there. The late-morning sun blinded me as we crossed the shallow end of the ditch, but as Susan and I approached the tumbleweeds on the fence, I could see two men standing there, staring at something on the ground.

One of them looked up at us and shook his head. "Don't bring her over here," his deep voice warned. Susan grabbed my wrist, pulling me back. Micah's and Junior's lifeless arms jutted out from behind the tumbleweed, and Susan gasped. She stood there winded for a moment, then gripped my shirt tightly, pulled me around, and began walking me back to the house.

She tried desperately to calm herself as the reality of the nightmare began to set in. "Well," she said, breathing heavily and patting the back of my hand while her own shook like a leaf, "at least we know your mama's gonna be okay. The good Lord knows what He's doing. You just have to have faith." She drew in a deep breath. "He has a plan."

As we walked the length of our long, dry yard, another car drove up, and then another, then five or six, all filled with friends or relatives and neighbors, people I'd known my whole life but who'd never once visited the house. Car doors slammed and Susan answered all their questions. "We don't know what happened," she said, her voice saccharine and soothing. "The fence had electricity running through it. We don't know why. . . . One of Kathy's boys and one of Alejandra's boys tried to cross the fence. . . . They didn't make it. Kathy's with Lane in the hospital."

Susan and I walked into the living room. Aaron had come back to the house with Susan's son, but no one had any idea how to get in touch with my older brothers. Luke was probably wandering the roads, while Matt and Maria and the rest of Alejandra's family had been in Casas since the party. Susan graciously thanked the man who'd watched the little ones, but he insisted on staying and helping until his friend came back with Mom.

A soft whimper came from the bedroom. I had forgotten about Holly. She was still in the crib where Mom had left her before she ran out. I rushed into the room to find her lying down, kicking her chubby legs and smiling. I gathered her up in my arms and brought her out into the living room. There we sat, all of us, on the floor, the couch, the rocking chair, the piano bench. Waiting. I could hear sounds of women sweeping and straightening up the kitchen. The house was so hot I could barely breathe.

"Mommy's gonna be fine. Don't worry," Aaron told Elena while he patted the top of her head. "She's gonna be home in a few minutes."

About an hour later, we heard a sound outside. The man who'd helped me with Mom got up, lifted his hat, and said that he thought his ride was here. I went to the window with Holly on my hip. The white pickup from before was in the driveway. Soon I was joined at the window by others who were sitting vigil in the living room. All of us watched as Lane got out of the passenger seat, said a few words to the man and his friend in Spanish, and then stood there as they drove off. He gave them a wave and then turned toward the house.

Another truck drove up with Micah's and Junior's bodies in the back. Lane gripped the tailgate for a moment and put his face in his hands. "Let me through," I said to the others behind me at the window, no longer able to watch. Soon, we heard Lane's crooked steps approach the house and the kitchen door open. My siblings followed me from the living room. Lane stepped inside without saying a word, closed the door, and confronted the crowd somberly, his hand still on the knob. There didn't seem to be a drop of blood in his face.

"Lane, is Kathy going to be okay?" asked Susan.

"Kathy—" He paused and scanned the kitchen, looking at everyone but me, everyone completely silent. "Kathy didn't make it." He took in a deep breath and looked away from the eyes that watched him. "We took her to that first-aid center in Lagunitas, but they didn't have what they needed to save her." Now his voice was barely audible and he stared at the doorknob. "She died right after we laid her on the stretcher."

Died. As I heard Lane say it, the word felt like a sharp needle scratching over the record of my mind, stuck repeating the same thought over and over: *Wait a minute. Wait a minute. Wait a minute.* I wanted to go back, start the record over again to see if it might play out differently. This wasn't the way it was supposed to end. I was sure of it. I looked around the room at my brother and sisters, who all stood completely still around the kitchen table, their mouths agape and eyes dart-ing between Lane and me as if they weren't quite sure what to do. I started to feel dizzy until I realized I'd stopped breathing, then I sucked in a big gulp of air.

The rest of the morning felt as if I were living in a series of photographs. I saw only flashes of stunned faces, people watching me with mouths and eyes open wide, waiting for me to react. I walked slowly to the kids' bedroom, stopping at the sink in the bathroom to splash cold water on my face. I packed clothes for my siblings, stuffing them into garbage bags, not knowing where we would go. I accidentally packed a bag for Micah, then closed my eyes to make it all go away. Voices swirled all around me.

"The kids can stay with me for now." "Ruthie, let me hold the baby." "I'll go to Casas and pick out the coffins." "We need to find clothes to bury the bodies in." "Did anyone find Luke and Matt?" "You have to understand, Ruthie. Your mom is in a better place, away from all the suffering and hell on earth." "Where are the baby's diapers?" "Is Leah potty-trained?" "Can't Holly take a bottle?" "All the kids can fit in my car."

An hour later, I found myself in the front seat of a four-door sedan with my five-month-old sister sitting on my lap. I don't remember who was driving; I only remember the feeling of Holly bouncing on my lap as if this were any other day. I felt the car dodge many muddy potholes and hit many more as I turned my head to look back in the seat. Aaron, Elena, and Leah sat behind me in silence, all of them numb. Behind them, off in the distance, our house—our home—was getting smaller and smaller in the rear windshield. The kitchen door was wide-open, the adobe bricks peeking through jagged pieces of cement that barely clung to the walls. The house looked empty and broken—as if it too had touched a buried wire and been electrocuted, as if its heart had also stopped beating.

Alex, Micah, and Junior.

39

The funeral was scheduled for the next afternoon. I passed a long, fitful night in an oversize wooden rocking chair with Holly, trying to train her to accept her first rubber nipple. Earlier that evening, Lane's sister Lisa and I had driven from house to house in the colony, desperately searching for a woman who might be able to nurse Holly. Even when we found someone willing to help, Holly refused to latch on and suckle. She kicked her chubby legs at every nursing mother we presented, clenching her fists and screaming each time one of them tried to feed her. She would cry uncontrollably until put back in my arms. I was the only one who could calm her.

Every time I offered her the rubber nipple, Holly jerked her tiny head back and forth, stubbornly resisting it. My hands began to shake when I thought about how helpless I was. I couldn't help my Mom when she lay dying at my feet, and I couldn't help my sister, even when she hadn't eaten in hours. But just as I was at the point of giving up, a tiny drop of liquid dripped onto Holly's tongue. Either she no longer found the taste of formula offensive or she was too hungry to care.

Soon, she was sucking with abandon, closing her eyes and relaxing her body. I sighed as my sister's warmth began to flow into my arms. It was as if she were melting into me.

Lisa came into the living room and congratulated me on my achievement. I thanked her for her help, carried Holly to a bed in a back room, and lay beside her, my mind replaying every detail of the day. Micah's and Mom's deaths might not have happened if I'd prevented any one of the dozens of bad coincidences that occurred within seconds of each other. If I had been able to stop Mom, to say the exact right thing to keep her from touching the fence, or if I'd been watching the boys play—if even one small detail had played out differently, their lives would have been spared. Why couldn't I have saved them? Why had electricity been running through that fence?

Holly's stomach gurgled and she soon woke up and started to cry. I put her on my shoulder to burp her and almost immediately felt her little body convulse and vomit chalky-white formula all over my nightshirt. I hardly reacted, so minor did this seem in the grand scheme of things. I calmly cleaned us both up, fed her another bottle, and watched her fall asleep again, by which time roosters were crowing outside and a cool blue glow began to wash over the room.

As the sun rose, its harsh light piercing my eyes like tiny shards of glass, I handed Holly off to Lisa and left the house in search of Mom and Micah, whose bodies were being prepared for burial in another nearby house. Just as with Meri, there was no money to pay for a proper embalming so the burials would need to happen quickly. As I walked to the makeshift morgue, feeling the July sun burn into the dry Mexican earth with every step, I had a sick feeling about what I would find. Still, I had to be certain that they were being given the best possible care, that whoever had dressed Mom had put her in the outfit I'd picked out for her, that they'd curled her hair as I had requested, that they'd used the right kind of makeup.

I opened a wooden screen door directly into a square living room. It was dark and empty except for the three bodies lying on long, portable tables. Mom, Micah, and Junior were all dressed in burial clothes. Box fans whirred in each corner of the room, circulating warm, damp air that only seemed to speed up the decomposition. The breeze made the pleats in the boys' dark slacks tremble, and I noticed that they'd been dressed identically, in stiff white shirts and navy-blue ties. Micah's and Junior's hands had been placed at their sides and their hair slicked back like two proper Mormon boys. Micah's face was still freckled and sunburned, and a straight black line ran across each of his palms where they'd made contact with the fence. His fingers looked as if they'd been burned from the inside out.

I was more hesitant to approach Mom, whose body was laid out on the opposite side of the room. Even from a distance I saw that the burial preparations hadn't gone well—she wasn't in the dress I had picked out. Instead she wore white, a color Mom never wore. A woman I barely knew walked into the room, approached me, and explained that my mother's body had been too swollen to wear the dress I'd chosen. She needed a larger size in death than she'd worn in life.

The closer I moved to Mom's body, the more confused I felt. Her hair was combed and curled convincingly, parted down the middle and feathered back, but otherwise, she barely looked like herself. Her face was caked with too much foundation. Her swollen, straight lips were overpainted with pearl-pink lipstick, and her eyelashes too thickly coated with brown mascara. She was no longer wearing her ever-present, ever-slipping eyeglasses. Someone had found and retrieved them from the spot where they'd fallen, but like the dress, her glasses were too small for her swollen face.

On the plus side, her palms hadn't been burned during the brief time they'd made contact with the fence. Her fingers looked just as they had before—just like mine, short and chubby with fingernails chewed to the quick. Mom had always told me that I resembled the LeBaron side of the family, but examining her bare legs and feet under her ruffled dress, I saw clearly that I wasn't just my father's daughter. Our calves were the same shape; so were our feet and toes.

The rest of the morning, I busied myself with dressing my sisters for the funeral, as well as preparing a diaper bag with a clean outfit for Holly, diapers, bottles, and formula to make it through the afternoon. People from out of town began to arrive—but for the most part I didn't have the energy to greet them. Finally I looked out the window and saw a fragile figure walking down the road toward the house where we were staying: my grandmother. I ran out to meet her. She made her way awkwardly, her head down, watching the road and stepping around potholes. The surprise and joy of seeing her, not to mention the man who'd driven her down from the airport in El Paso—Matt—brought fresh tears to my eyes.

Trailing Grandma, my brother looked exhausted by the trip. He rubbed bloodshot, swollen eyes as I ran and threw my arms around him, and around Grandma, as if they were the last links between me and the life I'd once known.

"I should have been there," Matt said, sobbing and embracing me, his entire body shaking. "I'm so sorry. I should have helped with Mom. I should have protected her, protected Micah. What are we gonna do without them?"

"I don't know." I was incapable of any words of consolation. "I don't know what we're gonna do."

All the while, Grandma just stood there, her head lowered, crying yet speechless. It was the first time I'd ever seen her without Grandpa, and the first time she'd been to the colony in over a decade. We walked inside the house, and for a while the three of us found ourselves in a square living room in a round house surrounded by cement walls with rounded corners, trapped in an uncomfortable, heavy silence. Grandma kept her head bowed and her shoulders hunched forward in a navy-blue polyester suit that looked too big on her. She had become so thin and frail.

I watched her raise her solemn, stunned face to adjust her wire-framed glasses and massage her temples. Finally she looked at Matt and me and said, "Well, I guess we'll talk more about the younger kids after the funeral."

"Yeah. We should probably get goin'." Matt wiped his swollen eyes. "Are they all ready to go, Ruthie?"

I nodded. "They're in the backyard. I'll get them and the diaper bag."

It was afternoon and the heat was intense by the time we'd all walked a few blocks to the public viewing of the bodies. Grandma moved slowly and unsteadily down the dirt road, but also scornfully, as if each pothole confirmed her assessment of LeBaron as a mistake, a place far too harsh for her daughter and grandchildren to live. I walked with Holly on my hip and Elena and Leah at my side, both in their wrinkled Sunday dresses, both staring wide-eyed at all the strangers. Next came Luke and Aaron and Matt, each wearing his own version of a lost look. All of us, a caravan of wounded souls, were drenched in sweat by the time we'd reached the house.

On the other side of the screen door was a living room full of people gathered around the bodies, which had now all been placed in white wooden coffins. Mostly the crowd was quiet, except for Alejandra, whom I'd already heard crying from a distance. She sobbed, *"Mi hijo, mi hijo . . . ,"* endlessly as we stepped over the threshold and into the room, our noses suddenly overwhelmed by a smell so putrid, a stench so overwhelming, I almost fainted. Just as I'd feared, the bodies were decomposing rapidly. I felt myself retch uncontrollably. Through a noxious fog I watched Junior's grandmother hold the boy's head to her bosom and repeatedly kiss his forehead as she stood over his coffin. Maria was crying on the other side of the room, and Matt went to her, sobbing again as he wrapped his arms around her.

My one wish had been to see my mother and brother one last time, although I regretted it as soon as I laid eyes on Mom's casket. Over the hours, her head had taken on the cast of a wax figure, one that was melting into her white satin bedding. Her mascara was bleeding, her lipstick caked. The body before me didn't look at all familiar, and I had to look away.

I wasn't sure I wanted to see Micah, but I'd brought along something that I wanted him to have: my most treasured stuffed animal, a Rainbow Brite Care Bear. Just as it had once done for me, I hoped the bear would help Micah get used to the dark. As I made my way to the little coffin, I saw that his arms had sprung up and returned to the position they'd been in on the fence, and from a distance he looked as if he were climbing out of the coffin, his arms reaching toward heaven. I forced myself forward. His head was arched back too, as it had been on the fence. I placed the bear on his chest and quickly walked away.

My nose burned from the stench, and the crowd of people made me so claustrophobic I began to have trouble breathing. But just as I felt I would pass out, I heard my grandmother's voice behind me. "Would someone please close the coffins?" she said weakly, shaking her head and turning toward the door. "Do the kids need to see bodies disintegrating?"

My siblings and I quickly followed her outside, and together we walked the short distance to the church. We took the rickety black bench up front, with Leah and Elena on either side of me and Holly on my lap with a bottle that she was thankfully suckling. Lane sat on the bench behind us. I was furious with him. He had been responsible for the electric wiring on the farm, he was complicit in Mom's, Micah's, and Junior's deaths. I vowed not to look at him that day or, indeed, ever again. Out of the corner of my eye I saw that he was strangely expressionless as the closed coffins were carried into the church and placed on the cement floor in front of us, directly under the pulpit. The large photo of my father brooded heavily over the three caskets.

As the service began, everyone stood for a prayer that was given first in English and then in Spanish. Still standing, the mourners took out hymnals and sang songs in both languages, songs about going home to our Father in heaven. Everyone but me; I couldn't hold both Holly and a hymnal and didn't have the strength to sing along.

When we finally sat back down, eulogists spoke about Micah and Junior, some in Spanish, some in English. Then one of Lane's many sisters came up to the pulpit to tell Mom's story, saying that she had "lived her life by example," that she continued to bring "God's souls onto this earth" despite difficult pregnancies and the burden of disabled children. Lane's sister reminded us that Mom had been widowed young, but had nevertheless remained faithful to the church's founding principles. As the woman concluded her speech, Elena tapped me on the shoulder and whispered that she needed to go to the bathroom. I handed Holly to Matt and led Elena by hand to the wooden outhouse in front of the church and then for a drink of water from a garden hose.

We made our way back to our seats as Alma LeBaron, my father's older brother, stepped up to the pulpit. I had seen him in town, but we had never spoken. Slender and gray haired, Alma stood tall with proud shoulders as he launched into a story about the colony's founding, the church at its center, my father the prophet, and the importance of his teachings. I waited and waited for him to move on to an appreciation of the prophet's wife and her contributions and sacrifices—Mom had been Alma's sister-in-law, after all—not to mention the young boys who had lost their lives. But his story never evolved; he never mentioned the real reason for our gathering.

After enduring forty minutes of this, Grandma got up and walked outside, once more the sole protester. My uncle spoke for over an hour before finally exiting the pulpit, and while I sat through the entire speech, I was so shocked by his omissions I could feel the skin on my face turning red. I whipped around to glare at Lane, breaking my promise to myself. *Do something,* I pleaded with my eyes. *Redeem yourself in some small way by stopping this spectacle and demanding that he recognize my mother.* But Lane just stared back at me, as impassive as ever, his arms folded over his big belly, not a single tear having been shed. *As much respect in death as he had for her in life,* I thought as I turned back around, scanning the congregation with contempt.

When the service was finally over, trucks carried the coffins to the graveyard, and Grandma, my siblings, and I rode behind them in a big van. I sat in the back with my sisters, while my brothers occupied the gray vinyl bench seat in front of us, along with Lane's sister Lisa.

"Why didn't Alma talk about my mom or my brother?" I asked her.

She looked over her shoulder. "Well, he was here to speak at our conferences today, and we had to cancel all our meetings for this. We always welcome anyone to speak the truth in church, even when it's a funeral."

I took a deep breath and sank heavily into my seat. A long line of vehicles trailed behind us as we slowly made our way toward the graveyard. While waiting for all the mourners to assemble, Matt and I passed the time by looking for Meri's grave, but to no avail. No one had ever marked it.

I stared at the mounds of gravel next to the coffins as prayers were said, more songs were sung, and people took pictures of our families next to the caskets. Eventually, the bodies were lowered into the ground just as the sun sank behind the horizon and the heat finally began to break. People lined up to throw handfuls of earth onto the coffins. I stepped forward to do the same, and as I did, someone took Holly from my hip. The tears came almost immediately, as did a shaking from deep inside me. It rumbled out of my stomach and to the tips of my fingers and toes.

I slowly walked toward my mother's grave. I picked up a large handful of gravel and rolled the hot pieces of stone and sand in my hand, thinking about this place: the dry, dusty Mexican countryside, our small, dilapidated home, the dangers buried underground, my family's violent past, and the tragedy that had just fatefully made its power and presence known. Despite it all, Mom had loved this place, but without her, did I belong here? I stared at her coffin. I could have said so many things to her at that moment, but the only words that came to mind were *I want you to know that I always loved you. Always, Mom.* I was transfixed by the idea that she was contained in that white box. *I'm not mad anymore, Mom.* I looked at the fistful of gravel. *I promise you, I will take care of the girls, Mom. I promise.* I said the words quietly, but I meant them. Then I opened my hand and released the warm earth and rock, the sound of gravel, empty and hollow, echoing up from the hole as it struck my mother's wooden coffin.

40

At eleven o'clock the next morning, the family met to talk about what should happen next. Four-year-old Elena and two-year old Leah sat with their little legs crossed Indian-style, parked neatly on the floor of yet another relative's living room. Aaron sat on one end of a couch biting his fingernails; Luke was beside him staring off into the distance, his head tilted slightly to one side, sticking out his tongue. Matt and Grandma looked as if they hadn't slept, and the morning heat only added to everyone's discomfort. Lane joined us, which only made the situation more tense.

Before we could think about the future, we yearned for some kind of explanation. We were all wondering, How the did this happen? What was Lane thinking when he wired that fence? His pose—dark, tan arms folded over his paunch, his legs in a wide stance—made it clear he had anticipated our questions.

"Now, I had a reason for burying those electrical wires," he began, completely unprompted, as if continuing a discussion he'd been having in his head. "I had to take electricity to Alejandra's house." He rested his arm against a wooden pillar as he tried to gauge who might be receptive to this explanation, his disposition completely casual. "I pulled wires through this black plastic tubing, about an inch in diameter." He made an okay sign with his thumb and forefinger to show the approximate size of the tube. "I knew the tubing would keep the wires covered, but for protection I buried the tubing. I buried it along the fence."

I looked over at Matt, who was rolling his eyes in frustration.

"The first piece of wire wasn't long enough to reach all the way from one house to the other, so I cut the tubing and put another piece of wire through that and attached the wires with electrical tape, and the tubes with electrical tape too." The quality of his craftsmanship might have been suspect, but the voice in which he spoke of it was confident, almost arrogant. "But when we had that thunderstorm the other night, the rain washed away the dirt from the wire and the electrical tape too. Micah's foot just came in contact with that end of the wire."

Matt leaned forward on the sofa, squinted at his stepfather, and said with a short, condescending laugh, "Doesn't it seem like you should have maybe buried the wires deeper?"

"No." Lane shrugged. "It was just a freaky thing, the way it happened. That's all." He leaned back against the pillar.

Grandma raised her eyebrows, as if she wasn't in the least surprised by my stepfather's faulty wiring. For a moment it looked as if she might say as much out loud. Instead, she closed her eyes, shrugged her narrow shoulders, and shook her head. When she opened her eyes, she looked disgusted, as if pleading for Lane to just stop talking. But he wasn't ready to give up the floor.

"Micah's foot touched one of the exposed wires while he was crawling through the fence. He was wet from swimming, so two hundred and twenty volts just shot right through him, and that made the electricity run through the whole fence."

The casual tone in which he described endangering his family by leaving live wires all over his property was almost too much to stomach. I watched Matt's face turn from white to crimson and the pimples on his chin flush a deep violet. He inched his body closer to the edge of the couch.

"It seems like if you had done something about those wires sooner, buried them deeper into the ground, this could have been avoided, don't ya think?"

"Wait a minute, now." Lane straightened his back and cocked his head forward. "I don't think it's right to start pointin' fingers at anybody here. You've been makin' lots of money in the States, and you coulda done somethin' to fix that place up."

"Lane," Matt shot back, "I didn't even know the wires were *under* the damn fence. And I sure as hell didn't know they were *taped* together."

"Hey"—Lane raised his palms as if to indicate the subject was closed—"did you ever think that maybe our Heavenly Father knows what He's doin'? He's the one who chose this time to take your mom and your brothers, not me. Now, do I understand why He did that?" Lane shrugged again. "Well, of course I don't."

God didn't put those wires there. You did, you miserable son of a bitch. I felt the words form in my mouth, but the air necessary to speak them caught in my throat when I remembered that a more pressing issue needed resolution—one that Lane's anger would only further complicate.

"I think the children should come stay with me for the rest of the summer," Grandma said. "It would give them a break and it's perfect timing. They're on summer vacation." Lane gave her a smug look and snorted. "They can come back when school starts." He stared at the floor, indulging her. "Besides, I don't think it would be a good idea for anyone to move back into that old house. Do *you*?"

Lane ran his dirt-filled fingernails through his greasy hair and pretended to think hard about her proposal. "Well, it seems to me like there are plenty of people here in LeBaron to take care of Kathy's kids. They can stay with one of my wives for now."

"Lane, I have a three-bedroom house all to myself. There's plenty of room for everyone, and the kids can keep me company."

He rested his chin in his palm and wrapped the other arm around his stomach. "Look, thanks for the offer, but there's no way I'm letting all of these kids go back to the States with you." He looked her straight in the eye. "I don't trust you to bring them back to LeBaron, and I don't want my kids being raised there, away from all my beliefs and what I want them to learn in life." He moved his hand onto his hip. "And I know Kathy wouldn't have wanted that for the kids either."

Grandma gave him a look of anger such as I'd never seen. It was as if all the big and small stupidities she'd put up with over the years in the name of my father's religion, all the injustices that she'd seen perpetrated against innocent children, all the starvation and suffering and now death—all of it was boiling over in her head. But she held her tongue.

Elena got up from the floor and crawled into Grandma's lap, rested her head against the old woman's neck, and wrapped her arms around her. Grandma ran her fingers through the strands of the child's long hair, their lengthy fingernails getting stuck in Elena's tangles. "Do you think my mommy will *ever* come back home?" Elena asked.

Warm tears streamed down my face as I thought of the years ahead. My head felt so heavy I had to bury my face in my hands and prop by elbows on my knees. Leah stood up and looked at me fearfully, her eyes beginning to water too. I wiped my cheeks and adjusted Holly to make room for Leah on my lap. I took in a deep breath, lowered my head between theirs, and cried as softly as I could.

At long last we arrived at a compromise, though not exactly a happy one. Lane decided that the children could take turns visiting their grandmother one at a time. Aaron would be first, Luke second, and me and the girls third. As for Matt, later that night he confided that he and Maria would elope over the weekend. Maria was just seventeen so the whole thing needed to be kept a secret.

"Please, Matt," I said, crying, "take me and the girls with you."

"We can't, Ruthie. Lane will never let us take the girls. Sit tight. We'll figure somethin' out."

"But I don't even have money for diapers or baby formula," I said in desperation. "What am I supposed to do?"

"Don't look at *me*. I used every last dollar to pay for the whole funeral." His frustration gave way to an idea. "But don't worry. Just charge anything you need at Maudy's store. When I get paid again, I'll wire the money to pay the bill."

"Matt, please. *Please* don't leave us here with him."

"I don't have any choice, Ruthie. If anything happens, call me. I'll get here as fast as I can."

EARLY THE NEXT morning, Aaron threw his bag of clothes and collection of He-Man action figures into the back of Matt's truck. Just ten years old, he had to duck to get inside the short camper shell. He slammed the glass door closed and sat with his back propped up straight on a pillow against the cab, facing us as we stood to watch him leave. Aaron looked away for a moment and tried to appear casual as he leafed through a comic book. But when the motor started, he looked up again, raised his hand, and slowly waved. His lips began to quiver and his tan cheeks turned bright red. Soon, he was crying, his head growing smaller and smaller as the truck kicked up dust on the road.

A few hours later, Lane announced that he was going away for work and taking Luke with him. The rest of us would stay with Alejandra and her family, who were themselves staying with her parents in Casas, as there was still no electricity at their house. Lane dropped us off at the same three-room adobe home we'd visited with Mom just a few days earlier, back when my biggest worry was candy in a piñata.

41

A cool breeze blew in from the window one night while I was sleeping, waking me with the news that autumn had arrived. I was shivering, goose bumps covering my arms and legs, in spite of being surrounded by three warm bodies. I soon realized that the back of my nightshirt was soaked in urine. For a moment I thought that Audrey might be next to me, but then I stood up and looked down at Elena, Leah, and Holly sleeping soundly beneath me. It could have been any one of them, as all three were wearing diapers. I suspected Elena, who, at four years old and already potty-trained, had begun to wet the bed after Mom's death. The baby diapers were too small for a four-year-old. I closed the window over the bed, gingerly stepped over my sisters onto the bare floor, and shuddered when I felt the cold cement beneath my feet.

Two months had passed since Mom and Micah died, and my sisters and I had been shuttled from house to house within the colony. Matt and Maria had made good on their promise to marry and were living in San Diego. Aaron did not come back from California when school started, just as I'd both feared and hoped. Luke was usually away on work trips with Lane, whose absence ensured that we would continue to be nomads in the colony for the foreseeable future.

Most recently we'd been living with Marjory. Hers was the most comfortable of all our temporary shelters. She was the most energetic of Lane's wives and lived in the newest, biggest, and calmest home. All of her children were grown and had already moved out.

We'd ended up there after Marjory had a dream in which God had come to her and proclaimed that she would be the woman to raise Lane's motherless children. Marjory's meager existence was supported by her eldest sons, who, like Matt, worked in the States. The whole situation was incredibly awkward, but at least we had hot running water and electricity, neither of which had been installed by my stepdad.

That fall morning, Marjory left soon after breakfast to go shopping in a neighboring town for a few hours. Not long afterward, Elena, who'd been playing outside, burst into the house, bright eyed and thrilled, exclaiming, "Daddy brought us a goat!" Leah froze in the midst of eating one of Marjory's brownies, her mouth open and surrounded by crumbs. "Hey, Leah, Daddy brought us a goat!" repeated Elena. "Come out and see it!"

The pair looked at me and I nodded. They left the kitchen door open when they ran out, Leah dressed in a T-shirt and terry-cloth sweatpants. I took Holly out of her baby walker, wiped chocolate from her face and hands, and followed the girls outside.

Sure enough, there was Lane with a small, white goat at his side. The passenger door of the truck opened and Luke stepped out. His shaggy hair was greasy and sticking up in the back. I avoided Lane pointedly, running up to Luke and throwing my arms around my brother. He hadn't showered in quite some time and he smelled terrible.

"I'm so happy to see you," I whispered to Luke, who was so surprised and embarrassed by the attention that his face turned red. "How was your trip?"

He just smiled and looked down at his feet. I patted him on the back and told him to go inside and clean up.

"I think goat's milk will be better for Holly's stomach," Lane said in a rare gesture of sympathy toward his daughter, who was still having trouble adjusting to formula. Holly sat on my hip, and he reached over to touch her cheek. She grasped his grease-stained finger and shook it like a rattle. Lane smiled. I looked in the other direction.

"I don't know how to milk a goat," I said under my breath.

Elena reached out to pet the animal, and it dashed away, dragging the rope around its neck behind. "Don't stand behind it," Lane yelled as his daughters gave chase. "It might kick ya with its back legs." He looked at me and gave me one of his stomach-turning smiles. "See if you can get one of the boys in town to milk it for ya."

I stepped sideways onto the sidewalk that ran through the middle of the small front lawn, and his finger separated from Holly's grasp. As difficult as the last few years had been, Mom had at least made good on her promise to keep that revolting man at a distance. But now she was gone, and all barriers had been removed.

Lane took his hand back from Holly's and gave me a questioning look, as if he couldn't understand why I might be uncomfortable.

"I really miss your mom," he said with such sincerity that I nodded in sympathy. "She was so good in bed. She gave herself to me like none of my other wives ever did."

If I hadn't had a child in my arms, I would have slapped him. I whipped around and rushed back toward the house.

"I have to go to El Paso to collect rent on my mobile homes," he called out, referring to his latest business venture. "Not sure how long I'll be gone."

Hallelujah, I mouthed, and walked into the kitchen.

Lane followed close behind. "Make sure Luke's ready when I get back, because he needs to go to work with me in the mountains." I nodded, my eyes downcast, angry as he flopped his filthy hands onto the white tile counter I'd just cleaned. "Oh, and . . . I want to take Elena with me too."

I felt goose bumps prickle on my arms and a knot formed in my stomach. "Why the hell would you want to take a four-year-old girl to help you in the mountains?" I tilted my head and narrowed my eyes.

Lane was surprised at my intensity and took a step back. "Hey, she needs to learn how to work just like everyone else in this family. What's the big deal?"

"Who's going to feed her and watch her while you guys are workin'?"

Lane waved me off. "She can ride on the tractor with me." He grabbed a brownie and bit into it, sending dark crumbs falling to the floor.

"I really don't think it's a good idea for you to take her to work with you right now, not so soon after everything that's happened." I took a deep breath, trying to remain casual.

"Well, she's my daughter, and it's not your choice." He gave a little laugh.

Finally, I could take it no longer. A wave of rage ripped through me. "Well, guess what?" I yelled, shaking. "She's *my* sister. So if you take one of us, you're taking *all of us*. Because *over my dead body* is that little girl going *anywhere* without me to watch her!"

Taken aback by my ferocity, Lane held up his hands and stepped away from me. "Fine, whatever. I'll take her with me to the mountains another time." He opened the refrigerator. "Ya got any milk around here?"

"No, I don't. Your wife's out grocery shopping right now." I made a beeline for the door and opened it for him to leave.

After a second he got the hint, closed the fridge, and shuffled my way. "I'll see you when I get back from El Paso." He smiled, and my stomach turned again.

He left, but the energy he'd unleashed was still in me, and I paced the kitchen for a few minutes, chewing my fingernails. *He is the most repulsive, selfish, awful man in the world,* I thought to myself. I slapped my hands hard onto the kitchen table as I threw myself into a chair.

"What's wrong, Ruthie?"

I smelled the soap first. It was Luke. I'd almost forgotten about him. He took the seat next to me, and I noticed that his hair wasn't matted anymore. It was clean and wet, but still uncombed. *My brother—still like a little boy who has to be reminded to shower, shave, and comb his hair—is more caring and understanding than a man with two wives and twenty-five children,* I thought.

I smiled and shook my head. "I'm fine." I offered him a brownie.

"I fink 'Lena and Leah like the little goat. Right, Ruthie?" he said with his mouth full. He took another bite and smacked.

"I think they love the goat, Lukey. Just like you do, right?"

"Yeah, dat's right. We got him in the mountains."

We sat quietly for a few minutes. The hard plastic wheels on Holly's walker squeaked over the linoleum floor, the goat bleated outside the open window, and my sisters giggled in the backyard. I smiled as Luke finished his brownie and licked crumbs from the corners of his mouth, my anger finally dissipating.

"You like working with Lane in the mountains, Lukey?"

"It's not too bad." He put his elbows on the table. He looked at me confused for a moment, as if at a loss for words, which wasn't uncommon for Luke. But then the moment grew longer and longer.

"What is it you want to say?"

"'Cept . . . um . . . ah . . .'"

"Except for what, Luke?"

"'Cept, I'n not too sure if I trust Lane too much, ya know?" Luke scratched his temple and looked down at the table, his face turning a ghostly color.

My heart stopped. "What do you mean?" I tried to catch his glance but he wouldn't look at me. "Why don't you trust Lane?"

"Ah, I'n not too sure." Luke's head slowly turned back but his eyes remained fixed on the table. "Um, I fink sonetines he touches me at night, when I'n sleepin'. Sonetines with his hands, sonetines with his foot, ya know? It's kinda strange."

I couldn't breathe. I felt as if I were choking. "Where, Luke? *Show me.*"

Slowly, he lowered his arm from the table and patted himself over the zipper of his baggy jeans. My stomach seized with nausea, my throat closed, and my eyelids stung with the beginnings of tears. And then—*No. No tears,* I said to myself. *Not now.*

I felt hot and full of anger. I was overcome by trembling. When it came to my own abuse, I had always felt dejected, powerless, and completely bottled up. But the moment I realized that my gentle, defenseless, disabled brother had suffered the same fate, an unfamiliar impulse came over me, a passion so primitive I couldn't make it go away. I had to act. I had to act *now.*

A sound from outside startled me. Marjory was home.

"Don't tell no one what you told me, 'kay?" I grabbed Luke's shoulder. "Okay?" He nodded. "I'm gonna find someone—"

The door flew open and I sat up straight in my chair.

"Well, hello there," said Marjory, noticing Luke as she cheerfully carried in a wooden crate of groceries. "Welcome back." A light, warm gust of air blew across the room as she closed the door.

You have to calm down, Ruthie, I told myself.

"Everything okay?" Marjory asked.

"Yep." I sucked in air and bit my bottom lip. "Thanks for the brownies. We've been eatin' them all day,"

"Where did Lane go?" She peered at Luke, suspicious of his silence.

"Um . . . I think he went to Alejandra's for tonight," I said. "He said he's going to El Paso tomorrow to collect rent."

"Well, it's about time." Marjory rolled her eyes. "I hope he brings us some money."

"He brought us a goat." It was the only thing to say.

She cringed. "A *goat?*"

I laughed lightly at her reaction, relieved that she was buying my performance. "Yeah, he says the milk might make Holly's stomach feel better. Elena and Leah are playing with it in the backyard."

"Well, sounds like fun," Marjory said with more than a trace of sarcasm.

"Hey." I stood up. "Do you mind if I go to Maudy's store? I think I'll call Matt. I want to see when he's coming back to town."

She looked at me and shrugged. "Well, all right. Be sure to tell him hello for me. And tell him not to worry. You kids are doing great here."

I looked down. My hands were shaking. I stuffed them into my Levi's. "Will do." I almost sprinted to the door.

"What's the hurry? Have your sisters had lunch yet?"

"Not yet," I yelled over my shoulder, and closed the door.

— 42 —

I ran to Maudy's on quiet side roads, avoiding eye contact with anyone who might know Lane, which was everyone. I couldn't stop thinking about all the people who'd urged me to shrug off Lane's behavior: my mom, who said, "We have to show God we have the power to forgive, just like Jesus in the Bible." And Lane's sister Lisa, who, on the day of Mom's funeral, had turned to me in the car and said, "Haven't you already put Lane through enough? He's not botherin' you no more. Come on, Ruthie. You and I both know he coulda done lots worse to you. So why don't you stop bein' such a brat about it? You should act more Christlike, like your dad did. He believed in forgiveness and you should too." Even Lane's own words—"Hatred will eat ya up inside and take ya straight to hell"—gnawed at me. When I thought about what he was now doing to my brother, I felt like retching.

All the words I'd ever heard in church, and at all the conferences and Sunday-school classes, seemed to be taunting me now: *honor thy father, honor thy mother, be like Christ, be good, count your blessings, do what you're told, prophets, men, husbands, gods, visions, dreams, destruction, forgiveness, sacrifice, submission, faith, Babylon, heaven and all the blessed little children . . .*

I realized that all those words, words that had held such power throughout my childhood, words that had characterized our way of life, words that had defined me, my siblings, our mom—they meant nothing to me. All the preaching, all the hours in church memorizing scriptures, how could that mean anything when the community supporting it wouldn't defend the innocence and safety of a child? With a certainty that took my breath away, I decided I had to get away from LeBaron, and I had to bring my siblings with me. I vowed that my siblings would not suffer the way I had.

I swung open the metal-framed glass door at Maudy's. Stucco dust rained down as it slammed against the exterior wall. The wooden phone booth was on the other side of the store—and occupied.

"Buenas tardes," said a young Mexican woman behind the white tile counter.

"I need to make a collect call to the States," I said breathlessly, hoping she wouldn't ask why I hadn't paid our standing bill. She pointed at a plastic chair where I could sit until the phone was free. I passed a nervous few minutes, my white plastic tennis shoes wagging the entire time, until the man was finished.

When at last the phone was free, I jumped up, punched the number, and tried to collect myself for the Mexican operator who would connect the call. After a few mumbled exchanges, I heard the sound of a distant ring. Matt answered after the second one. "Yes, I'll accept the charges."

"Matt?" was all I could say before dissolving into tears.

"Ruthie? Is that you?"

I fell to the booth's stool and slumped forward, the receiver in the crick of my neck, my face in my hands. "Matt."

"What's up, Sis? Tell me what's goin' on."

"Matt," I whispered, "you have to come and get me. You have to come and get *all of us.*"

"Why, Ruthie?" His voice was calm and caring, but had a hint of doubt, as if he thought I might be overreacting about something.

"You. Cannot. Leave. Us. Here. Anymore," I had never spoken more seriously to my brother in my life. And then I began to sob.

He paused for a second, surprised by my tone. "Uh, okay. Well, tell me what's goin' on." His voice was serious but reassuring.

"Luke . . ."

"What? Is he all right, Ruthie?"

At last the words tumbled out. I told him what Lane had done to Luke, and that he planned to take Elena to the mountains.

"That . . . *dirty* . . . *son of a bitch*." The anger in Matt's voice was almost uncontrolled. "That . . . *bastard*. Who else knows about this?"

"Nobody. Luke hasn't told anyone."

"Well, don't let him, and don't you tell anyone either. Where's Lane now?"

"He leaves for El Paso tomorrow morning."

"When's he coming back?"

"He said he doesn't know."

"Okay, listen." Matt's mind was racing. "I just bought you a car, an Oldsmobile station wagon. It's old but it runs good. I was gonna bring it down for you and the girls. But"—he took in a deep breath—"here's what I'll do. I'll take tomorrow off, and Maria and I will bring the station wagon and pick you guys up. We'll be there by tomorrow night."

"Then what?"

"I don't know. We'll figure out the rest once the kids get across the border."

"How are we gonna get across the border? The border guys aren't gonna believe we're old enough to be their parents."

"You're right." We both went silent, thinking. "You'll have to find someone to help us."

"Who?"

"I don't know. *Someone*. Ruthie, someone we can trust."

"But who?

"*Someone.* And go get everybody's birth certificates and Social Security cards."

"That's all still back at the house."

"Then go back to the house, Ruthie."

I gasped. "I haven't been back there—"

"Go back to the house and look in Mom's purse. And look in Mom's dresser."

"Matt, can't we do that when you get here?"

"No, we have to have everything ready by then. *You have to get the birth certificates now.*" His voice was so forceful I hardly recognized him. "We have to have them if we're gonna cross the border." I sat there a moment. "Okay, Ruthie?"

"Okay."

"And make sure Luke doesn't tell anyone about this. Understand? If Lane or his family finds out, there's no way we're gonna get the kids out of Mexico."

I hung up the phone, relieved but frightened. Alejandra's house, where Lane was staying that night, was perilously close to Mom's, so I took a roundabout route, through acres of pecan orchards, past a dozen fences, and over several ditches. Twenty minutes later I was there, at the back fence of Lane's farm, staring across at our tiny home.

I touched the barbed-wire fence lightly, thinking I might get shocked, forgetting that the power had been off since the day Susan and I had flipped the switch. I ran up the pathway, past the alfalfa, past the well, the corral, Lane's shop, Lane's rusting pile of appliances, Lane's rusty tractors, and all the broken-down cars of Mom's that Lane had forever promised to fix.

Then I was at the front door, the veins in my throat throbbing and the blood pounding in my ears. I stepped inside gingerly, like a character in a horror movie. The floor was covered by a thick layer of dust, and the stench from mouse droppings was overwhelming. I peeked at the living room where I'd played the piano, where Luke and Matt had played checkers and cards and wrestled, where Audrey had attacked me, and where we'd heard the news about Mom. I walked through the kitchen where I'd made dozens of birthday cakes for my family, where Lane had taken a belt to Mom, and where Matt had told Mom that he was leaving. I walked down the hallway where I'd watched my younger brothers and sisters take their first steps.

Her bedroom. The bedspread tossed aside, as Mom had done when she ran to see what was happening to Micah. The romance novel still open to the page she'd been reading. The air still smelled of her perfume. I felt dizzy and had to rest on the edge of the bed. All at once I felt compelled to throw myself into the line of dresses hanging in Mom's closet, rifling through them until I found the fuchsia one she'd worn that night she'd danced with Matt. My hands began to shake again as I held the dress to my face and smelled the scent of her skin. I lay it on the bed, put my head into it, and breathed again.

A mouse scampered across the floor and startled me from my reverie. I went to the closet and picked up Mom's old, navy-blue purse. The handle pinched my fingers where the leather was hard and cracked. Digging around for her wallet, I felt the guilt and fear that I had always felt when digging through Mom's things. The wallet fell open when I found it, and two $1 food stamps fell to the floor, as did a stack of blue Social Security cards and a wallet-size family photo from days gone by. In it, Micah was on Mom's lap, chewing on his fist and looking at something other than the camera. Meri was on Lane's lap. He was holding her tightly, but her body still collapsed over his forearms and her head hung lifelessly to one side.

I slipped the food stamps, Social Security cards, and other paperwork into my back pocket with the photo, folded Mom's dress, and put it in a plastic bag. I noticed Mom's watch, her makeup, an old pair of glasses, and some perfume and threw those in too. The sun had begun setting behind a cracked windowpane, and the house was growing dark. Now I would have to work quickly. I searched through all the drawers in all the bedrooms, taking every little thing I thought that Luke, the girls, or I might need. Finally, I left and closed the kitchen door behind me.

A cool breeze blew my hair into my face, and for one last time I heard the water running through the irrigation ditches and the crickets chirping. Then I swung the bag over my shoulder and walked away, never once looking back.

When I returned to Marjory's, she looked at the plastic bag suspiciously. "What's going on?"

For some reason, I hadn't anticipated this confrontation and mumbled through a long-winded nonanswer. She interrupted me and pulled a chair out from under the kitchen table, a sign that we needed to sit down and talk.

"Ruthie, is this about Lane?" I just stared at her across the table. "It is, isn't it?" I looked down, unable to hide. "Listen, I want you to know something, honey." Her hands reached across the table and she held my hands. "I know you and Lane don't get along because of what he put you through, but your mom is gone now, and we all have to learn to get along for your little sisters' sake."

I looked up stunned, and once again at a loss for words

"You know, Ruthie, you can't let what he did ruin your life. You can't carry that around with you forever. You have to get over it. And that means you have to *forgive him*."

Her last two words incensed me. I had finally had enough. I pushed my chair back with a screech, bolted up from the table, and ran down the hall. "Hey, Luke, come in here!" I yelled. He was looking through his leaflets when I stormed through the door of Marjory's back bedroom. "Hey, Lukey, we need to talk." He looked up at me startled, then suddenly stood up as if he knew I was serious.

"What's wrong? Have you lost your mind, Ruthie?" Marjory shrieked.

"Tell her," I commanded Luke. "Tell her what Lane did to you."

Marjory listened to Luke's story, and the shock on her face was so obvious I wanted to get down on my knees and thank God for the reaction. And when I told her that Lane wanted to take Elena with him, Marjory began to cry.

"What do you want to do?" she asked through tears.

"We need to get my brother and sisters out of here. Matt is already on his way to pick us up."

"You're right. You have to get out of here, Ruthie." Marjory sniffled. "And so do I."

Now it was my turn to be shocked. Marjory had been raised in a polygamist family and had lived the principle for most of her life. I had no idea she'd been having her own serious misgivings about LeBaron. She felt that she didn't belong here anymore. She said she wanted to return to the Christian church she'd been part of in the States and to live closer to her children. This was apparently the final push she needed.

The next morning, with Marjory's help, I started getting things ready for the trip. Marjory had decided she'd help me and my siblings get across the border, and then we'd go to my grandmother's house in Strathmore. I was counting the minutes until Matt and Maria arrived. Not until nightfall did I tell Leah and Elena that we were going to visit Aaron and Grandma. The clapping and screaming went on for some time. Luke seemed happy as well. I never told any of them that we wouldn't be coming back.

Late in the evening Matt and Maria rumbled into the driveway in an old, brown Oldsmobile station wagon, and I met them at the door with a tight hug of relief. They both looked exhausted and smelled as if they needed showers, but there wasn't a moment to waste. Lane's trips to El Paso were often short, and he might suddenly walk through the door, especially since it was Marjory's night.

The atmosphere was tense when Marjory and the three of us sat at the kitchen table to organize all our paperwork and come up with a game plan for the border crossing. Marjory would come with us—she had already spoken with her daughter in the States—and we would drop her off there once we'd safely made it into the States. Then, we would drive to Grandma's house.

"Matt, I don't care what we do after that," I said, "as long as we keep Mom's kids together." He looked me in the eye and nodded in agreement.

A few minutes later, while Maria and I loaded all the bags into the back of the station wagon, she whispered that she was pregnant. She seemed disappointed when I didn't act excited. I blamed my reaction on the stress of the day, but I couldn't stop thinking about the little girl who'd once been so set on becoming a designer that she'd cadged money away while selling pine nuts. Part of me felt sad for her.

With the car packed, Matt woke Luke up; I woke the girls and put them all in fresh diapers, having only one size to fit all. Holly's diaper looked enormous, while Elena's was so small I had to use masking tape to keep it together.

"Are we gonna take the goat with us?" Elena asked me, still half-asleep.

"Not this time. It won't fit in the car. But a neighbor's going to take good care of it for us."

"Are they gonna feed it until we come back home?"

"Of course they are. They won't let the goat starve. Okay, come on, *let's go.*" I scooped Holly up and headed for the car. I put the smallest of my sisters between the other two, in the fold-up seat in the very back of the station wagon, then went back inside to mix a fresh bottle of formula.

"You ready yet?" Matt yelled, bursting through the door and startling me. "It's already two o'clock in the morning, Ruthie. We gotta get out of here." He started switching off the lights in the house. I picked up the diaper bag and flipped the kitchen light switch, and Marjory locked the door on our way out. I opened the car door behind the driver's side and threw the diaper bag in between Luke and me.

He looked at me sadly. "We not gonna bring the goat, Ruthie?"

"Don't worry, the neighbors are gonna feed it while we're gone."

"Oh, dat's good." He looked out his window into the moonlit darkness.

Matt started the engine and backed the car slowly out of Marjory's driveway. We didn't want to wake anyone up and arouse suspicion, so he drove at a snail's pace while we were in town. I closed my eyes and felt each pothole and pebble we rolled over during what seemed like the longest few minutes of my life. At last the bouncing and the lurching stopped. Matt turned north onto the highway, and the car began to glide. I opened my eyes to see the back of Matt's shaggy head and the open road beyond.

I turned to look out my window. A full desert moon lit the road ahead and shone brightly on the mountainside with the giant *L.* I couldn't help thinking of all the wonderful moments of my childhood that had happened in those hills: the afternoon hikes with my half sisters and friends, scrambling over hot rocks, stickers and sharp weeds scratching my ankles. The hours we spent sitting around the big white *L,* eating Mom's round, dry peanut-butter-and-jelly sandwiches. I knew I had no choice but to leave. I would not live to inherit my father's town, just as I hadn't inherited his name when he chose not to place LeBaron on my birth certificate.

Holly began fussing in her sleep behind me, rousing me out of my thoughts. I picked her up, pulled her over the back of the seat, took out the bottle of formula, and pushed the nipple between her little, chapped lips. She was bathed in eerie moonlight, pale and so thin you could hold her in one hand, her once-chubby cheeks now sunken by malnourishment.

In the front seat, Matt and Marjory mumbled back and forth, trading ideas about what we should tell the officials when we crossed the border, and what we should say if anyone from the colony crossed our path, which was likely. To avoid any chance of passing Lane on the highway to El Paso, we decided to cross the border into Douglas, Arizona, even though that meant driving an extra hour before reaching the United States. My shoulders tensed with each new set of lights that crept up behind us, and I held my breath till the vehicle passed.

"Are we there yet?" Elena asked, suddenly sitting up behind me. Matt, his nerves thoroughly frayed, whipped his head around.

"Ruthie, those girls have to keep their heads down," he commanded, glaring at me. "Tell them! What if someone we know passes us? Come on, now. I already told you that."

"Hey, I didn't know she was up," I snapped back. "Please lie down, Elena," I said quietly. She gave me a puzzled look and then ducked back down. I caught Maria's tired eyes in the rearview mirror, her head resting on Matt's shoulder. I pressed my head against the cold window glass and gazed at the landscape as it rushed past, the reality of my new life beginning to set in.

A few hours out of LeBaron, my exhaustion caught up with me, and I couldn't keep my eyes open. I drifted into a deep sleep and was awoken hours later by the short, plaintive squeal of brakes. Jolting into consciousness, I realized that we were in line at the border. Dawn had come and a deep blue sky hung over the morning.

"Are they practicing, Ruthie?" asked Matt, his face almost angry. "Make them practice." Practice what? I wondered, and then I remembered how each of the kids needed to say "American" convincingly if and when a border agent flashed a light inside and asked what country they were from.

"If they ask you anything, Elena, just say *American*," I told her.

"'Merican."

"Good enough."

"Leah? *American*."

"Melcon."

"Good enough."

"Remember," Matt told the girls, "Marjory is your mom."

"She is?" said Elena, thoroughly confused.

"What's my address, Ruthie?" Matt went on.

"I know your address," I said impatiently.

"I know you know it, but can you say it naturally so they'll think you already live there?"

"Of course I can!"

A minute or so later, just three cars were ahead of us in line.

"Nobody say anything else from now on," Matt whispered.

I usually trembled when I was nervous, but this time the anxiety was too great. All I could do was stay lock still. I looked down at my hands. We crept forward and stopped, crept forward and stopped.

"Okay, here we go," said Matt, looking at me through the rearview mirror. Both of us rolled down our windows.

A tall woman, her hair pulled beneath her hat, leaned forward and peered in Matt's window. Blue eyes scanned the car. "What's your nationality?" she asked him.

"American."

The border agent moved on to my window, looking at Luke and the rest of us. "What's your nationality?"

"American."

"American."

"'Merican."

"Melcon."

The agent nodded and moved back to Matt's window. "What brought *you* to Mexico?" she asked Marjory.

"Oh, just drove down for the weekend to do some shopping." Marjory looked relaxed and smiled casually. *Wow,* I thought to myself, *she's done this before, just like Mom.*

The agent half smiled in reply, took a step back, and looked at something on the car. Then she waved her hand. At first I didn't know what she meant.

Matt and Marjory both smiled and said thank-you. We were through.

No one said a word as the car crept into Arizona. Even after the border was a dot in the rearview mirror, the silence continued. I think we were stunned, not to mention overwhelmed by the obstacles that lay ahead.

"Can we talk yet?" asked Elena finally.

"Yes, we can talk," I said.

Matt looked at me through the rearview mirror, his eyes full of fear and relief just like mine.

"That's the first step," I said, and took a deep breath.

Epilogue

The sun shines brightly through a window above the oval, full-length mirror in front of me. I see a slimmer face than that of the fifteen-year-old girl I was on the night we left Colonia LeBaron; my round, adolescent cheeks have narrowed. Now I look like my father. The square jaw I used to stare at in his omnipresent black-and-white photograph in church—that's *my* jaw now. But I am not ashamed of it. Experience, time, and life have somehow given me the confidence to confront my own reflection.

There is a knock at the door. "Ruth, how's it goin' in there? Can I come in?"

Elena. Her "Can I come in?" sounds eerily similar to her "Can we talk yet?" from so many years ago. I lift my long dress to keep it from picking up dust from the wood floor and go to the door.

"You're almost ready!" says my twenty-six-year-old sister. Her eyes are as wide and happy as they were the day she first laid eyes on the white goat. "Have you seen my stockings and shoes?" She asks me this because over the past two decades I've been the one who's found things and put them away, slipping them into her dresser drawers. And sure enough, I know where they are this time too.

I can't help but think back to that fall in 1987 when we arrived at Grandma Wariner's house in Strathmore, the joy of seeing my brother Aaron again, the peace that came from escaping my stepfather, and the deep heartache and loneliness that came from leaving so many friends and family members behind. But I've never doubted my decision.

I stare at Elena a moment—a woman who is vibrant, beautiful, smart, and most important *safe*. Strands of her thick blond hair fall around her bare shoulders in loose curls. She smiles sweetly at me, almost in admiration, just as Mom used to when I was a girl, with the same heart-shaped face and slightly crooked jaw.

There is another knock. "Hey, I have the flowers!"

Elena reaches for the door and Leah steps in wearing the same chocolate-brown-and-sage dress as her sister. We compliment Leah on how beautiful it looks against her tan skin, the way her long hair falls perfectly over her shoulders. She carries a box of assorted flowers in coral and bright pink: tulips, roses, ranunculus, and calla lilies.

She gives me the once-over, raises her eyebrows, and cocks her head back. A wide smile spreads across her face. "Awww, Sis, I love your dress," says the twenty-four-year-old, her voice kind and loving, one that sounds just like Mom's. "Look at these. The florist sent us the extra flowers she didn't use for our bouquets. She said you wanted them for our hair?" I nod, and Leah takes out an orange-tipped calla lily, places it behind her head, and stares at herself in the mirror. "Can I have this one? Please?"

For a moment I'm not sure whether to say yes or pick her up in my arms, so much does her begging now sound just as it did all those years ago. I think back to the two-year-old who never gave me a moment's peace, who cried and pounded on the bathroom door until I'd come out and hold her while I refilled Holly's bottles. That was when I was earning my GED, dividing my time between high school home-study courses and taking care of my siblings. More than twenty years have come and gone since we moved into Grandma's house, staying there four years before venturing out on our own. Grandma has not lived to see this day.

I look up at the clock and start to feel anxious. Five p.m. is rapidly approaching. "Where's Holly?"

"The hairdresser is with her in the dining room," Elena replies. "She didn't like how it turned out the first time. She thinks the braid makes her look like an old lady."

Another knock. "Holly?" I call out.

Sure enough. She steps through the door in chocolate-and-sage, as beautiful as her sisters. "The photographer is here," says my twenty-two-year-old sister, her age a constant reminder of how long Mom has been gone. "She wants to take some pictures of us getting ready." Holly stops and smiles, gazing at me. "You're all ready."

"Almost. Elena, will you zip me up?"

She does, then arranges the pearl buttons over the zipper. Holly holds out my veil, but I haven't yet decided where to clip it. She places it at different spots on my head, as self-assured, as loyal, and as helpful as she has always been. She looks at my reflection. "Sis, the dress is perfect, but don't forget the sash."

"Here." Elena hands me the sash and takes a bobby pin from the little, round antique table at our side. "Let me pin the veil in and see if it'll stay." I find myself staring at my sisters in the mirror and not me. Something about the way Elena separates a bobby pin and puts it in her mouth reminds me so much of Mom; something in each of them reminds me of different parts of her.

Now that I have finished college and graduate school and have worked for eight years as a high school teacher, I can't help wishing that my sisters were little girls again. I could give them so much more now than I could when I was a young, struggling student supporting all of us on part-time jobs, welfare, and student loans. It was all so over-whelming. No matter what I did or how hard I worked, there was never enough, never enough to give them what they deserved, never enough to pay our bills on time, never enough to fill the emptiness that any parentless family feels. I was nineteen when we moved out of my grandma's house. I wanted nothing more out of life than I did to keep my family together and make sure they were safe. The memory of those days reminds me of how exhausted I had been, but my siblings gave my life purpose, they were the bridge from pain to healing, from past to future. They are as much the authors of my survival as I am of theirs. My throat tightens and my eyes fill with tears.

"What?" asks Elena, catching me watching her. "You're thinking about Mom, aren't you?"

I nod and wipe my eyes. *Look at your three beautiful girls, Mom. Are they not what God intended? When you died, I had no idea how they'd survive, and yet from that moment to this, they have been safe. Is that not what God intended? Oh, how I wish you'd lived to see this day.*

I look over my shoulder. My sisters are perched on the edge of the bed, watching me expectantly. "Are you ready?" I ask.

"Ready."

I mount the two steps and turn the knob that leads to the living room of the old house we've rented for the wedding party. And there they are. First, I see one of Matt's daughters pinning a coral-and-brown boutonniere to her father's black tuxedo jacket. He has a red Charms lollipop in his mouth and looks at me with a guilty smile.

"Your tongue is gonna be red for the ceremony," I say quietly.

"Aw, no one's gonna notice." He's forty now, still doing that thing where he closes his lips when he smiles. He still prefers sideways hugs too and gives me one. I smile, grateful for all of his help and support over the years, years when he made countless trips between Grandma's house in Strathmore and San Diego, where he and Maria lived, where their own family continued to grow and grow.

"Is Maria here?"

Matt nods. They have come, but not as a couple. After six children and ten years of marriage, Maria finally gave Matt permission to take a second wife. Two years later, their marriage was over. In my head, I hear Mom's prediction all over again: *If you marry Maria, you're gonna have a hard time livin' polygamy.*

I hear a galloping sound and look behind me to see Luke bounding down the stairs from his room on the second floor, black jacket in hand. The brown satin vest is buttoned crookedly over a white shirt only halfway tucked in. Otherwise, the suit fits his slim, athletic figure perfectly. After we arrived in California, Luke went to live with my aunt and uncle not far from Grandma's house, then moved into a supportive group home. These days he is a three-season athlete for the Oregon Special Olympics and rarely talks about anything else. "Could somebody help me put dis on, please?" he asks at the bottom of the steps, holding up his tie.

"I'll help you, Luke," says Aaron, appearing on cue and from out of nowhere. Today, as on most days during his past thirty-two years, he is perfectly dressed and ready to lend a hand, an intelligent young man with a genius for thoughtful conversation. He straightens the buttons on his brother's vest, ties his tie, tucks his shirt in, and pins on his boutonniere. Aaron looks the most like my stepfather, but his personality belies any connection whatsoever.

Lane, of course, is not here. My grandma and Aunt Kim fought him for legal custody, and the day the judge delivered his final ruling, Lane didn't show up to the hearing. He lost custody and all visitation rights and never regained them. The list of children he abused grew longer and longer over the years, and all of his wives eventually— finally—left him. Over two decades after Mom died, Lane was driving the same highway between LeBaron and El Paso, still in a beat-up, old truck. It veered off the shoulder and rolled onto the side of the highway. He'd had a heart attack, and he died there alone. Matt was the only one of my siblings to attend the funeral.

I think of the others who are not here. Audrey, who lives in an adult foster-care home with four other women in California, in a town not far from where Grandma and Grandpa are buried. I have visited her there a few times, not nearly as often as I would like, but she is well cared for, and most important, she is safe. I think of my beautiful baby sister Meri, who loved bath time, and who smiled sweetly in spite of her disabilities. I think of Micah, a little boy crouched over a game of marbles or crying after being knocked over at a party. And I think of Mom, a woman who wanted nothing more than to be loved. A woman who wanted a life of meaning, a life lived in service and devotion to something bigger than herself. *I hope I have made you proud, Mom.*

And I think about Alan, the man I am about to marry. Alan couldn't be more different from my stepfather. He is responsible, loving, attentive, generous, and, of course, he's monogamous. It took years of counseling, prayer, meditation, and self-reflection before I felt worthy of a man with such qualities. I had much to discover and nurture in myself first. On this day, I realize that all the work was worth it.

Someone hands me my bouquet of pink and orange flowers, and a man appears on the periphery. I take a big breath, roll my shoulders back, and smile as I take Matt's arm so he can walk me down the aisle.

"Okay, here we go," I whisper. Together, the two of us cross yet another border, our brothers and sisters following close behind.

Luke, Matt, Aaron, Alan, Ruth, Leah, Elena, and Holly.

ACKNOWLEDGMENTS

Bringing this book to life has been an incredible, heart-wrenching, and healing journey, and I'm beyond grateful to have had the opportunity to travel it. I could never have completed this memoir by myself, especially not without the generous and loving support of my husband, Alan Centofante. While I was writing, Alan and I took long walks in thoughtful conversation. He listened patiently as I talked through my painful childhood memories and the struggles I was experiencing writing about them. I couldn't have asked for a better partner with whom to share my life; he has enriched it in every way, and his diligence and hard work helped make this dream of being a published author come true. Thank you, Alan, for loving me unconditionally and for embracing my brothers and sisters who love you almost as much as I do!

Alan helped my manuscript find its way to Whitney Frick at Flatiron Books, and I have been honored to work with her. Whitney has not only helped make my memoir shine, her thoughtful guidance through the publishing world has been invaluable. Thank you for loving my story and for sharing it with your publisher, Bob Miller. Thank you to everyone at Flatiron Books for taking a chance on my book and me: Elizabeth Keenan, Marlena Bittner, Molly Fonseca, Karen Horton, James Melia, David Lott, Kenneth J. Silver, Steve Boldt, and the many others who shared their enthusiasm for *The Sound of Gravel* with me. I appreciate everything you've all done to help my story find its way in the world.

As I began crafting my story, I worked with Wendy Ruth Walker, an amazing writing coach and developmental editor whose guidance and experience helped me through my first draft and gave me the solid foundation I needed to build a completed book that I am excited about and proud of. Thank you, Wendy!

I also had the opportunity to take memoir writing workshops and classes with Jennifer Lauck, *New York Times* bestselling author of *Blackbird*. I had read her memoir several years before I found out that she lives in Portland and teaches writing classes locally. Jennifer taught me more about writing memoir than any other teacher. Her professionalism, generous feedback, and passion for great writing brought out the best in me.

Before reaching Flatiron Books, Scott Vogel's dedication and passion for this project helped bring my manuscript to a new level. Scott, a talented editor, helped me reshape my story and add scenes from my life that I recalled during conversations with him. Scott asked all the right questions and helped me hone in on the heart of my story. Thank you for caring so much.

It has been an absolute pleasure to work with Don Seckler and Meg Cassidy. Meg, sharing your publicity experience in publishing has made this project so much more comfortable and enjoyable for me.

Don, you are awesome at connecting me to my audience through social media. I am grateful to you both for your hard work and commitment.

To Kent Watson and Steve Leach: Your professional advice and early enthusiasm for my story have inspired me and helped me persevere. Thank you!

I also had several early readers who provided honest feedback that helped bring out the best in me as a new writer. Thanks especially to Teresa Majerus and April Christofferson, who read several drafts and always gave the most helpful and heartfelt comments. Every new author should be so lucky.

A huge thank you to Penny Clark Ianniciello for believing in the power of my story and for tirelessly promoting literacy, authors, and books. Also, special thanks to Roberta Yochim. Your early enthusiasm and genuine love for my story motivated me through the writing process and encouraged me to keep writing when I often felt like giving up. And to all the indie bookstores who supported my book and shared my story, thank you!

Thanks also to my friends at city and regional magazines for helping to spread the word about my story. Your magazines continue to build a better world one community at a time.

I have had a tremendous amount of support not only while writing this book, but through the toughest times of my life. There have been many earthly angels along this path.

My Grandma and Grandpa Wariner were the superheroes of my childhood. It's because of their love and influence that I was able to envision a different life for my adult self.

A very special thank you to my aunt and uncle, Kim and Ron Taylor. You have always cared so much for my siblings and me and you've consistently been there for us through the hardest stretches. Thanks especially for taking care of Luke as if he were your own son. You have been a true blessing to all of us.

Thanks also to my brothers and sisters who have shared so many of their memories with me, have been so supportive of my writing, and who were willing to let me tell our story. I began to write when I finished graduate school, once my sisters were older and had moved out of our apartment. My brothers and sisters, Matt, Luke, Aaron, Elena, Leah, and Holly, have encouraged me every step of the way. They have also read the memoir and provided feedback on the final drafts. I couldn't have survived without my siblings and their love. They know me and understand me like no one else in the world. Thanks for always having my back.

And finally, thank you, Mom, for blessing me with love, strength, and kindness. I miss you every day and would give anything to sit beside you and have a woman-to-woman conversation about this book. I wish I had been able to discuss all of this with you, to understand why you stayed. Now I realize that you did the best you could. My biggest regret has been not being able to say a proper farewell. I love you, Mom. Thank you.

READING GROUP GUIDE

The Sound of Gravel by Ruth Wariner

Ruth Wariner is the thirty-ninth of her father's forty-two children. Growing up on a farm in rural Mexico, where authorities turn a blind eye to the practices of her community, Ruth lives in a ramshackle house without indoor plumbing or electricity. At church, preachers teach that God will punish the wicked by destroying the world and that women can only ascend to Heaven by entering into polygamous marriages and giving birth to as many children as possible. After Ruth's father—the man who had been the founding prophet of the colony—is brutally murdered by his brother in a bid for church power, her mother remarries, becoming the second wife of another faithful congregant.

In need of government assistance and supplemental income, Ruth and her siblings are carted back and forth between Mexico and the United States, where Ruth's mother collects welfare and her stepfather works a variety of odd jobs. Ruth comes to love the time she spends in the States, realizing that perhaps the community into which she was born is not the right one for her. As she begins to doubt her family's beliefs and question her mother's choices, she struggles to balance her fierce love for her siblings with her determination to forge a better life for herself.

Recounted from the innocent and hopeful perspective of a child, *The Sound of Gravel* is the remarkable memoir of one girl's fight for peace and love. This is an intimate, gripping tale of triumph, courage, and resilience.

INTRODUCTION

FLATIRON BOOKS

DISCUSSION QUESTIONS

1. What does the title, *The Sound of Gravel* mean? How many references to it did you find, and what effect did the sound of gravel have on some of the characters?

2. What did you think of Ruth's decision to narrate her story from her childhood perspective? Do you think it would've been a different experience to read about these events if they had been written in an adult's voice? Why or why not?

3. From the very beginning, Ruth's life was dictated by tradition. Traditions can give a child comfort and stability, but for Ruth and her siblings, even the traditions of their religion couldn't instill much stability. How do you decide when a tradition is doing more harm than good? What traditions and familial expectations have shaped your life, and how have you reshaped some of them upon reaching adulthood?

4. Growing up, Ruth was surrounded by women who could be considered to be both strong and weak at the same time. In what ways were the women in Ruth's life strong? In what ways were they weak? How did their role affect family dynamics? How did it affect your opinion of Ruth's mother's choices in particular?

5. Ruth writes of her mom receiving a special Christmas card from Matt: "Mom's tears that day were joyful, like the tears she cried when we sang 'Happy Birthday' to her each year. I cried too, but only much later, when I realized how little she had asked of the world, and how even that had been too much for the world to give." Have you ever felt that way at times in your own life?

6. What characteristics of Ruth's early life gave you glimpses of the young woman she would become? Did you notice signs of strength and survival in her early on? What elements from your own childhood do you still carry within you today?

7. How did Ruth navigate deciding whom she could trust as a child? How important is the ability to trust? How did Ruth's ability to trust evolve as she grew up?

8. Think about a time when you made a decision that was contrary to your family's wishes—as Ruth's mom did when she left California to rejoin Lane in Texas. She seemed blinded by love. Have you ever been in a similar situation where you were blinded by an emotion and made a choice? In hindsight, what would you have done differently?

9. Many people say they would do "anything" for their siblings. Putting yourself in Ruth's shoes, do you think you would have made the same dramatic decision she did, regarding her younger siblings, at the end of the book?

10. Ruth writes of the women of LeBaron: "People talked about happiness and love, but I witnessed precious little evidence of it." How could people speak of love and happiness if they've never known it? After reading this memoir, do you think it's possible for polygamous marriages to produce healthy, happy children and families? Do you think Ruth's perception of love is forever tainted?

11. Ruth's older brother, Matt, ended up living polygamy back at Colonia LeBaron. What do you think changed his mind since he seemed so strongly against it when he first left the Colony?

12. How did this memoir make you reflect on your own life? Were there any parts of it that you were surprised to be able to identify with?

FLATIRON
BOOKS

AUTHOR INTERVIEW

A note from the author

There were a few early readers who finished *The Sound of Gravel* and immediately reached out to me, wanting to ask me questions they still had about my life. I wanted to take the time to address those questions here.

SPOILER ALERT:

Some of my responses discuss events described in *The Sound of Gravel*. I recommend you finish reading the book before reading through this Q&A.

Thank you and please don't hesitate to contact me to share your thoughts or pose further questions. You can find more information on my Web site: **ruthwariner.com**.

1. The Sound of Gravel *ends with you and your siblings making your way to California to live with your grandmother. What happened next?*

Aaron, Leah, Holly, Elena, and I lived with my grandmother for a few weeks. Lane showed up looking for my sisters and me, and at that point, we went to stay with a cousin in southern Oregon where Lane wouldn't be able to find us. We stayed in hiding there for several weeks while my grandmother applied for custody with the state of California.

When my siblings and I returned to live with our grandmother, Lane showed up again and went to the police claiming that my grandmother and I had kidnapped his kids. When the police showed up at the door, we explained the situation. At that point we became wards of the state. My siblings and I testified against Lane in court and Lane's wife Susan had several documents notarized and signed stating that Lane never supported us and that he was a known pedophile in LeBaron. On the day the judge was to issue his ruling on custody, Lane didn't show up to court, so legal custody automatically went to my grandmother and her youngest daughter, my aunt Kim who lived nearby in California.

My brother, Luke, stayed with Kim and her husband, Ron. They had four young children at the time. Aaron, Leah, Holly, Elena, and I stayed with my grandmother most of the time, but we spent a lot of time with Kim and Ron as well. I took home-study courses to help take care of my siblings and earned my GED.

2. *How long did you live with your grand-mother? Did you have help from anyone else?*

We had cousins who I had never met, my mom's cousins, take my siblings and me to Disneyland and to their cabin in Tahoe a few times. We spent a few weeks with them at their homes in different parts of California, too. We also spent summers with my brother Matt, his wife, and their growing family.

During the four-year period we lived with my grand-mother, Kim and Ron moved to Oregon, and because my grandmother's health was failing, we all followed my aunt and uncle to Grants Pass, Oregon. At that point, I was nineteen years old so I moved into a home on my own with my three little sisters and Aaron. I started taking classes to become a teacher at the local community college. When I completed that coursework, I eventually enrolled at Southern Oregon University. I attended college there for my undergrad-

FLATIRON
BOOKS

uate and graduate degrees—all while I was raising my sisters. I got my first job out of college teaching high school Spanish on the outskirts of Portland, Oregon.

3. Did you ever see Audrey again?

When I lived with my grandmother, Audrey was living in a state hospital a few miles from our house in California. I visited her regularly then. When I moved to Oregon and was raising my sisters and going to college, I didn't have the financial means to go and see her as often as I wanted to. I remained in touch with the hospital where she lived, and she was eventually moved into a home for women in that same area, not far from where my grandparents are buried. She has caretakers who watch her closely and she's doing better than ever, on less medication and very healthy. I have visited her there, but the honest answer is that I don't visit as much as I'd like to or as much as I probably should.

4. What was it like to be fifteen years old and to be responsible for your three younger sisters? How did you do it?

I wouldn't have been able to take care of my sisters without my grandmother's, uncle's, and aunt's help. It really does take a village. The situation was heartbreaking beyond words. My grandmother wasn't in good health, and having us all move in with her was very hard on her, even though I stayed home from school to help her. My aunt and uncle had four young children of their own, and it was hard for them, too. We had cousins who had offered to take one child each, but I really didn't want to separate my family. Looking back now, I realize that I actually didn't want them to be separated from me. It was extremely difficult to leave my childhood behind at such a young age. The hardest part was letting go of any kind of social life and moving to a place where I had no friends and really didn't know anyone. For me, it would only have been worth it if I could make sure my mother's children were well cared for.

I moved out on my own with my three sisters when I was nineteen. My brother Aaron moved in with us a year later. He was a teenager at the time and he helped with the babysitting, housecleaning, errand running, etc. My mom's cousins, women I had never met before because our family's religion had been kept a secret from them, offered to take one child each, but I didn't want us to be separated. I was on welfare, I took out student loans, and I worked part-time jobs to support us. Financially, it was a huge struggle, and I ended with a lot of debt after my siblings moved out. It took years, but eventually, I was able to pay off all my loans and I am debt-free now. I'm every bit as close to my family now as I ever was, and for me, my strong bond and my relationships with them were worth the effort.

5. *When did you first start writing this book?*

I started taking memoir and creative nonfiction writing classes not long after I finished graduate school and began teaching Spanish. I started working with specific scenes back then, but didn't really start writing seriously until 2009. I was in my midthirties. Ultimately, it took me about five years to finish writing on a part-time basis.

FLATIRON BOOKS

6. *In the epilogue to* The Sound of Gravel, *you say that your siblings were "the bridge from pain to healing, from past to future." Can you tell us in a little more detail what work you had to do to make peace with your past?*

I learned a lot about myself when I was a single parent. Raising children and wanting a better life for all of us had a way of giving me a sense of purpose. I wanted better for all of us and I had to figure out how to be my best self. That desire to improve, to make my life and myself better was an amazing gift that my sisters gave me.

That might be a long way of saying that I am basically a self-help junkie. I had suffered so much and I wanted more than anything to heal. I knew I needed to let go of so much of the pain from my past. If a book has "forgiveness" or "letting go" in its title, you can bet I've read it and bought the journal or workbook that went along with it and filled up every page.

I've followed many of the spiritual writers who have appeared on *The Oprah Winfrey Show*, and I have really found that their stories of overcoming heartbreak and suffering have helped me to heal. That is part of the reason I decided to write my memoir: in the hopes that my story might help readers in the same way that others' stories have helped me.

My education also really helped me heal. Going to college was something I never, ever imagined myself doing when I was growing up in LeBaron. I started classes at a community college when I was twenty-one, and I took as many philosophy and religious studies and world religion classes that I could. I loved being introduced to new ways of thinking. I recognized goodness and truth in so many different traditions. In a way, understanding that I had a choice about what I believed set me free from the dogmatic and rigid way of thinking from my past. You can't imagine the weight that lifted from my shoulders when I realized that my Creator would love me and I had a chance of going to Heaven even if I didn't live polygamy and have several children. Being able to let go of the belief that I needed to live a life like my mother's really set me free.

When I started my career as a full-time teacher, I also had access to mental health benefits that I was anxious to take advantage of. It took me a few weeks to find the right therapist, and when I finally did, her counseling proved to be an invaluable part of my healing and growth journey. I started one-on-one therapy sessions with her and added on group grief counseling. It was an important time of learning about myself and how my past had affected me. That part of my life was characterized by a lot of personal growth, learning to forgive others, letting go, and ultimately of moving forward.

7. *Do you consider yourself to be religious today? Are you a Mormon?*

As I've said, developing my own spiritual beliefs and practices really helped me to heal. I believe in God and have always been inspired by teachings and traditions that emphasize the importance of having a personal connection to that Divine Spirit within all of us. I start each day with a morning prayer, a quiet meditation, and journaling. It's in these quiet moments that I've experienced the most healing—when I've sat still

AUTHOR INTERVIEW

FLATIRON BOOKS

and let my emotions wash over me. I struggle with organized religion in general, though, and I tend to see religion and God as two completely separate things.

I know a lot of wonderful, kind and loving Mormon people, but I no longer consider myself Mormon— fundamentalist or current day LDS.

8. You also mention your wedding and your husband, Alan. How did you two meet? How did you tell him about your upbringing? What was his reaction?

Alan and I met on the top floor of the U.S. Bancorp Tour building in downtown Portland, Oregon, at a fund-raising event for *Portland Monthly*, our local city magazine. I attended with a group of friends, and we met Alan and two of his friends while waiting in a very long line for a glass of wine. I left the party early but ended up running into Alan again in my own neighborhood, which was nowhere near downtown. It turned out that he lived right up the street from my apartment. Initially, we started meeting up just as friends for local happy hours because we were both single and didn't like cooking at home by ourselves. Once we got to know each other better, we both had so much respect for each other and the paths we'd chosen for our lives and the care of our families. That's when I started telling him about raising my sisters, and every time I told him more of my story, the more his face would light up. He was always inspired by my life. I didn't tell him anything about polygamy until we had been dating for a few months, and he was blown away. He'd never met anyone from that kind of community. He couldn't believe I was so "normal." Fortunately, he had already gotten to know me pretty well, and he could tell that I had let go of so much from my childhood and was no longer connected to that way of life. I was thirty-four years old and hadn't been back to the colony in several years.

9. *On the last page of the book, you include a photograph of your siblings. Are you still close to them? Are you still in touch with anyone else from your childhood? Have you been back to visit Colonia LeBaron?*

I have been back to LeBaron three times in the twenty-eight years since I left, and each time I've been back, I've loved seeing my family, but it is also a little traumatic. The first time I went back, I saw Lane driving around town in his pickup truck with little girls in his front seat. I was so angry and upset by that. My trips back to LeBaron always felt hostile, and I would return home exhausted.

My brother Matt still lives in LeBaron with his most recent wife and children, and he is openly disappointed that my younger siblings and I don't visit him there. But I remind him that his family is always welcome in my home. We meet up in the States anytime we can. My younger siblings and I all live in the Pacific Northwest, and we are a very close and supportive family.

0. *Your brother Matt practices polygamy. What is that like for you?*

After I left LeBaron, I didn't have a lot of contact with my family there. My younger siblings and I stayed away to keep my sisters protected from Lane. But Matt was a newlywed and he was busy working in construction in Southern California. He was working with many of our relatives from Mexico. He wasn't separated from the church and LeBaron the way we were. About five years after we left, Matt started to talk about our dad. Matt became interested in our father's teachings and expressed a desire to live polygamy and date other women. I was shocked and heartbroken.

I was nineteen or twenty years old at the time and was trying to put our lives in LeBaron behind us. It was hard for me to understand that Matt—because he had always been working with so many people from our community—never really moved on from that way of life. I began having nightmares about finding Matt drowning in the ditches on our old farm in LeBaron. I'd wake up breathless and certain that it meant my big brother was in danger. I had the dream a few times, and it terrified me.

As time passed and Matt grew more and more involved with the church, I came to understand that my dreams were not about Matt dying physically; they were about how the person he had been was transforming into someone else, someone completely different than the person I grew up with. Because he was changing, so was our relationship. Subconsciously, I was mourning the loss of who he and I had been in a family together. It was a very challenging time for me, but I imagine, a necessary part of my growing up. These days, Matt has fourteen kids and is still an avid believer. I have reached a peaceful acceptance of his choices and lifestyle, and we have agreed not to talk about religion. I see him at least once a year.

11. *So much of* The Sound of Gravel *is about your relationship with your mother and your struggle to balance your love for her with your doubts about the choices she made. When you think of her now, what thoughts come to mind? Are there ways in which the two of you are similar?*

I always remember my mom as her kind and loving self, and I like to believe that that part of her would have prevailed had she survived. I definitely inherited those qualities from her. My mother and I probably wouldn't agree on anything philosophically, but I like to think that we would have been able to agree to disagree— as I have done with most of my family from LeBaron.

Of course, I feel like I'd give anything to know my mom and to be close to her again. To have just a few moments to say good-bye and to tell her that I loved her would have provided a kind of closure for me that I haven't been able to find on my own. Had my mom lived and left my stepfather like all of his other wives eventually did, I think I would have been close to her after I grew up and benefited from therapy. As with any parent, I think there are parts of my life that she would not only approve of, but would also be very proud of.

I always imagine that my mom and I would have been friends. I think that her beliefs about herself and religion limited her in a way that I haven't let mine limit me. I am both my mother and father's daughter, and from what I knew of my father, I inherited from him a confidence and boldness that my mother never had.

FLATIRON BOOKS

12. What do you want readers to take away from The Sound of Gravel?

I'm sure each reader will have their own insights according to their own life experience. I've been surprised at the diverse comments and perceptions readers have shared with me thus far, some that I would never have thought of myself. Ultimately, I'd like my memoir to inspire readers to reflect on their own lives, to find gratitude for their blessings and the choices they've been able to make. If I could grow stronger than my circumstances, anyone can. I'd also like readers to recognize the importance and power of their own family bonds in spite of how crazy and difficult circumstances might be. To me, there is nothing more important than the profound connection between siblings.